ROBBIE DEANS

ROBBIE DEANS

RED, BLACK & GOLD

by Matt McILraith

mower

A catalogue record for this book is available from the National Library of New Zealand

ISBN 978-1-927262-12-2

A Mower Book
Published in 2014 by Upstart Press Ltd
B3, 72 Apollo Drive, Rosedale
Auckland, New Zealand

Designed by www.cvdesign.net.nz
Printed by Everbest Printing Co. Ltd., China

Jacket photographs: Getty Images (front and all except top left on back); Peter Bush (back, top left).

CONTENTS

This book is dedicated to a number of people. First and foremost to Penny, a remarkable woman and amazing mother to Sam, Annabel and Sophie, all of whom in their own ways have been a source of perspective and inspiration throughout. And to my parents Anthony and Joy, who sacrificed much in providing their children with a platform to launch from, while teaching us the value of work. To my teammates for their effort, patience and 'skin' in the game, and also to my opponents for the resistance and subsequent lessons you provided.

'To achieve success, whatever the job we have, we must pay a price for success. It's like anything worthwhile. It has a price. You have to pay the price to win and you have to pay the price to get to the point where success is possible. Most importantly, you must pay the price to stay there. Success is not a sometimes thing. In other words, you don't do what is right once in a while, but all the time. Success is a habit.'

Vince Lombardi
Head Coach Green Bay Packers, 1959–1967

ACKNOWLEDGEMENTS

The author and Robbie Deans would both like to thank the following for their time, memories and invaluable assistance in helping to tell this story: Allan Hewson, Alex Wyllie, Andrew Sullivan, Andy Ellis, Barry Corbett, Ben Alexander, Bob Stewart, Brad Thorn, Charles Deans, Dan Carter, Don Hayes, David Pocock, Fergie McCormick, Geoff Miller, Guy Reynolds, John Sturgeon, Keith Lawrence, Kieran Read, Leon MacDonald, Les McFadden, Matthew Alvarez, Penny Deans, Peter FitzSimons, Richie McCaw, Todd Blackadder, Tony Thorpe, Jim Helsel, Warren Barbarel and Wyatt Crockett.

Every effort has been made to acknowledge and credit photographs published in this book. In a few instances, though, the publishers were unable to locate the copyright holders. The publishers welcome correspondence from any persons or organisations affected.

FOREWORD
By Dan Carter

It's easier to acknowledge now — and this is the appropriate forum in which to do so — that I battled with the idea of Robbie Deans becoming Australian coach. He had coached me for so long, was someone whom I respected enormously and considered a good mate, and now he was going to be coaching our arch-rivals?

It was tough to take. The Wallabies were a good enough team as it was, without having someone of his calibre coaching them.

Robbie had put so much work into my game, he knew me better than any other coach in the world. In my mind, I kept questioning: why is he doing this? With time, I did come to appreciate his reasons.

In professional sport, teammates and coaches can, and do, sometimes later become opponents. The industry is like business: you have to go where the opportunity presents itself.

The difficulty I had in accepting the change in Robbie's situation at the time simply reflected the enormous respect I have for him, after everything he had done for me.

Until he became Wallabies coach, he'd always been there for me as a player, someone I could turn to, when needed, to critique any aspect of my game. He had helped to make me believe I could reach the highest level of the game.

I can still remember clearly our first meeting. It was in 2002. I was 20, had just finished my first year in the Canterbury Academy, and had played a handful of games in the NPC while the All Blacks were away. Walking into his office, I had a few nerves, but Robbie is generally pretty laid-back with young players, and makes you feel at ease quickly.

As is his way, he got to the point straight away.

'Do you want to be a Crusader next year?'

I was blown away. I'd barely played any age-group rep rugby for Canterbury, and here he was asking me — or more accurately, basically telling me — that I was going to be getting a professional contract for the following year.

Once I'd recovered from the shock and offered a rather nervous yes in reply, he said that's great; he wanted me to be a part of the team.

Before I could relax, he got me again.

'Could I see myself starting?'

Hang on a second. The Crusaders had Aaron Mauger and Andrew Mehrtens, guys I had looked up to and, in Mehrts' case especially, idolised as a kid. And he was asking whether I thought I could be starting ahead of one of them?

Realistically, I was going to be very happy to be in the squad. I didn't say as much to him at that moment but did say that I didn't see myself starting.

Robbie then told me that I could be a starter for the Crusaders the following year, if I really wanted it and was prepared to work hard enough for it.

If anyone else had suggested that to me at the time, I'd have been embarrassed by the thought of it. But Robbie has a way, not only of encouraging young players and letting them know he believes in them, but also of convincing them to believe in themselves too. It was quite humbling.

As I left his office, I mulled over what had just taken place. It gave me a sense of drive and purpose to train harder than I ever had before. Robbie Deans is an absolute legend of the game and he was going to give me an opportunity to be a Crusader. I was determined that I wasn't going to let him down.

Our relationship became a constant one from there. Not only did we work closely together at the Crusaders, Robbie was the backs coach when I came into the All Blacks a year later.

Inevitably, in any squad, you spend the most time with your positional coach, backs or forwards. Robbie wasn't the head coach in this instance but, as he had with the Crusaders, he helped to manage my transition to the next level.

It is a big step. Having Robbie coaching the All Blacks backs provided me with continuity. We were able to continue working the way we had at the Crusaders.

One aspect of the game that Robbie really helped me with was around leadership. He didn't push me into a leadership position, instead letting me grow at my own pace, developing the sense of my place in the team. I'm naturally a fairly quiet guy. With the massive amount of experience that was around me, the last thing I wanted to do was to be piping up with my views. I had to learn, I had to earn the others' respect by playing well.

Robbie understood and allowed me to do that. He didn't impose any wider responsibilities on me until he judged that I was ready. That's one aspect of what makes Robbie such an outstanding coach. He always sees the bigger picture, but also has command of the finer detail, both around the playing strategy but also the personnel. If he'd pushed me too soon, I'm not so sure that I would have coped.

There's no doubt that Robbie's time in Australia did make some of his existing relationships back in New Zealand more awkward, and I'm sure it was the same for him as it was for some of the All Blacks guys who had previously played under him. There's always an edge when you are competing; there has to be, and the higher the level, the more intense the competition is.

Competition aside, it's just a reality that — with Robbie in Sydney — we didn't see that much of him any more.

Still, that doesn't change the fact that he has done so much for all of his former players. We are all in his debt for that: the experiences we had, the balance he made sure that we maintained in our lives, and the belief he inspired in us that helped our teams to achieve.

Robbie loves the game; he loves the team environment. His enthusiasm is infectious. So, too, is his commitment to the team, which always comes first. I have never had a coach who will go beyond the call of duty to the extent Robbie does, in order to make sure that his players are happy.

During my time playing for him, he must have returned thousands of kicks during field and goal-kicking practice, standing behind the posts fielding the ball and kicking it back to me so that I could go again.

It must be the most tedious of jobs but there he was, at the end of every training session, behind the posts, booting the ball back, providing pointers when they were needed, but also having a laugh.

For the head coach, someone who was such a busy guy, to be so generous with his time, is something I will always be thankful to him for.

Cheers Robbie.

FOREWORD
By David Pocock

The world might be full of sporting memoirs — some hugely informative, others positively inane — but if ever a biography was required to lift the lid and present the real picture of an identity, then this is it.

I'm glad my task has simply been to provide an opening to his story, because Robbie Deans is a difficult man to write about. This is not because there aren't plenty of amusing and important things to say about him, but because there is an impulse to correct the mainstream perception.

Because of the way he is. Because he is all about the team.

There is so much of his make-up, so much of his story if you like, that has never been projected in the public domain. The task of doing that has fallen to author Matt McILraith, Robbie himself and all of the other contributing identities who have been part of his life, and part of the story.

This platform provides me with an opportunity to speak of a very good man who I have come to respect deeply.

When Robbie started as Australian coach in 2008, I was coming off a good season with the Western Force but had few expectations about taking the next step at that stage of my career. The Wallabies started the Tri-Nations with a game against South Africa in Perth. While the team was in the west, Robbie asked me to come and see him at their hotel.

I was extremely nervous and excited, so much so that I mixed up the time of the meeting. Once I got there, Robbie told me to focus on the upcoming world Under-20s tournament and to continue improving my game.

I left the meeting feeling positive, but also with the distinct impression that this was a man who didn't give much away. This notion was furthered later in the year, when the Wallabies squad for the European tour was named and I was in it. As one of the youngest in the team, I was nervously hoping for even a spot on the bench when we started out. I watched a lot and tried to absorb everything I could.

The thing I was most struck by was the pressure Robbie was under from the outside. This only escalated over the following years. There was a constant tension between what he wanted to do, and what he was able to do with the team. The world of professional sport is full of injuries, politics, funding shortfalls and limitations. Those who are not directly involved rarely understand these things.

It is to Robbie's credit that he never made excuses. Nor did he ever take these pressures out on the playing group. He seemed acutely aware that shouting at the team after a loss was probably going to be unproductive. I always found his quiet disappointment more compelling anyway.

Robbie is a man I wanted to win for.

On that same tour, I'd been told I was going to start against the Barbarians. Then Stirling Mortlock got injured against Wales, and Robbie needed George Smith to start in my position so he could lead the team. I was bitterly disappointed. On the Monday at training, Robbie came to me and said that I'd play off the bench because they wanted me to get some game time. Then, with that classic Robbie Deans side smile, he added: 'I don't think you're quite ready to captain the Wallabies yet, but maybe one day.'

One of the things Robbie used to often say to me was 'Drive what's best for the team'. This, perhaps more than anything else, has influenced me as a player.

It was a particularly important focus during times of injury. The knee reconstruction that I required midway through 2013 and had to repeat again this year was especially frustrating. Both injuries could have left me sitting on the sidelines for 12 months feeling totally useless.

Robbie's mantra, that we shouldn't seek personal glory but instead be focused on the good of the team, was an invaluable pointer. You can always make a useful contribution — injured or not — because there are a multitude of ways that you can help the team.

Everyone who knows Robbie comments on his composure. You never really know what he is thinking. The one time I saw him lose it was before our game against South Africa at Cape Town in 2009. Robbie had joined the team late, having had to return to New Zealand for his father's funeral. It was obviously a very difficult time.

While he was away, the team had been playing a game called 'Killer', as a way to get everyone involved and get guys out of their comfort zones. The game sees one person within the team assigned as the 'killer'. His role is to inform people how they were to publicly exit the game while everybody else has to work out who the assassin is. The departures usually involve some sort of embarrassing public spectacle: our halfback Luke Burgess did the most impressive rendition of 'You've Lost that Loving Feeling' to the waiting staff at a team dinner!

In a rather unfortunate timing, a mass exodus of players was organised for the first team meeting after Robbie had arrived. Everyone was called together 10 minutes early to accommodate this. There was a talent show, songs on guitar and some of the shyer guys in the team had to tell jokes. It was very entertaining.

Once all this had taken place, the meeting started. Robbie stood up to speak and let rip in a way I had never seen before and haven't seen since. He castigated us, shouting about our lack of professionalism. It was one of the most impressive rants I've ever seen from a coach.

We all hung our heads.

Then, at the end of the tirade, he collapsed and feigned his death. He had also been nabbed by the killer!

It was the highlight of the game.

That he immersed himself in team affairs so quickly, despite a time of personal difficulty, summed Robbie up. There's never any self-pity. He is always there for his friends and players, on and off the field.

Robbie is an immensely good man.

I am greatly indebted to him for believing in me, not only as a player, but also as a person. While my coach, he encouraged me to be the best rugby player and teammate that I could be, he was also genuinely interested in the kind of man I was becoming away from the world of rugby.

No one could ask for anything more.

INTRODUCTION

Competitive. Direct. Loyal. Strategic. Easy going. Team-focused.

All are themes that pop up repeatedly when discussing the playing and coaching career of Robbie Maxwell Deans with those who know him best.

Robbie is, by nature, guarded with those with whom he is unfamiliar. Trust has to be deserved. Respect gained by deed rather than words. Once it is earned, the loyalty and backing Robbie offers is absolute. This is clear from the contributions some of the finest players of the modern era have made to this text. The level of their respect, gratitude and even admiration, both for his skills as a mentor, but also his principles as a man, is unmistakeable.

I experienced this first-hand during my maiden team release as media manager for the All Blacks at the start of 2002. A miscommunication with then head coach John Mitchell saw a player named in error. This discovery, during that week's captain's run, was horrifying for one so new to the role.

Returning to the bus after training and sitting down, Robbie turned to me. As I shrunk into my seat waiting for what was surely going to be a decent bollocking, he said quietly: 'Don't worry about it mate, you didn't cost us any points!'

That was my introduction to the real Robbie Deans. Positive and always looking ahead.

It has been a privilege to be able to watch much of his career — with the All Blacks, the Crusaders and the Wallabies — unfold from a front-row seat, in the time since.

Even the greatest of us have times where we can't meet all of the expectations that are placed on us, realistic or otherwise. Life provides dips for everyone, but sport is one of the few human activities where accountability can be defined. Results tell all, over time. The titles, but more particularly the winning percentages, Robbie has consistently achieved throughout his career, across four different high-profile teams, inarguably state that he is up there with the best of his profession, across any sporting code. Even his Wallaby career, where the critics were ruthless and loud, concluded with a winning ratio well in excess of Australia's historical average.

This was despite the side being exposed to the two Rugby World Cup winners of that era, and therefore the best teams in the world — South Africa (2007) and New Zealand (2011) — for a percentage of his career (in terms of the overall number of games his team played) that was much higher than was the case for any of his predecessors.

Not that Robbie would have had it any other way. He sought consistent success for the players and the Australian public, not the 'one-off glories' that have dominated much of the Wallabies' professional rugby history.

If being exposed to the best on an unprecedented scale, at the risk of damaging his overall winning percentage, gave the Wallabies their best chance of rising to the top as a consistent power, that was what had to be done.

The central platform of Robbie's success is his coaching method. Although it has been refined over time, with subtle changes as a result of new experiences, the confidence in his process has not been misplaced: the results prove that.

Those who perform have generally been rewarded, both by the success they've achieved, but also through the enjoyment they've experienced. He has always been prepared to back his judgement on when to introduce players into his team, but also around the difficult decisions on when to phase them out.

As much as he has made his players feel at ease, Robbie has repeatedly made the hard calls when he has felt they have been needed, even if this has resulted in both public and personal condemnation. Always, his motivation has been for the good of the team.

An unprecedented five Super Rugby titles, Australia's first Tri-Nations title in a decade, two Tri-Nations and the Bledisloe Cup with the All Blacks, Canterbury's first NPC title in 13 years, and a Ranfurly Shield success are all indicative of a method that works.

Depending on whose information is correct, Robbie was either miles away from the All Blacks coaching position at the end of 2007, or one small step from a role his supporters remain convinced is his destiny.

A highly placed member of the All Blacks hierarchy, well in a position to know, insisted to me that the NZRU board decision to stick with Graham Henry ahead of Robbie was a close one. Even if this wasn't so, Robbie's will still be a strong case whenever applications are called for the next All Blacks head coach.

For all that he had already achieved in a Super Rugby coaching career without parallel, and during a stint on an All Blacks coaching staff whose legacy is unarguable, Robbie has moved on from his time in Australia an infinitely better coach.

The fact that he 'survived' for long enough to end as the Wallabies' most capped coach is evidence enough, given that he was exposed to a level of challenge with complexities that have no equal in his homeland.

The lack of alignment between the national body and the state organs within the Australian game is quite simply ruinous. For an outsider, the task of changing the culture of individualism that is deep-rooted within the professional levels of rugby union was never going to be an easy assignment. It is witness to his skill that Robbie was able to raise the Wallabies' standing from fifth on the IRB rankings through to second only to the best All Blacks side of the modern era, and arguably of all time.

Australia occupied that ranking for a few weeks short of three years, before being pushed back to third narrowly by South Africa, at the end of a 2012 year of unprecedented injuries.

Even then, the Wallabies were still able to thwart the All Blacks' bid for a record-breaking winning sequence, defying the game's most free-scoring unit during a try-less draw in Brisbane, despite being forced to field a grossly under-strength team.

From the end of 2010 until the final test of 2013, England and South Africa were the only other sides to beat New Zealand. Each won once. The Wallabies beat the All Blacks twice, taking the final Tri-Nations off them, while also denying New Zealand a shot at the record for consecutive wins by forcing that draw.

While the extraordinary injury carnage of 2012 undoubtedly impacted on the Wallabies' capacity to take the next step in the year following the Rugby World Cup, the gap between them and the All Blacks was closing.

History may record Robbie's departure to have been the tipping point where the chance to press further was lost.

The distance to the All Blacks, in terms of ranking points on the IRB ratings, more than doubled in the first year after his departure from the Wallabies. South Africa, who had previously been level pegging, has also now established a significant break on Australia.

Tony Thorpe, a former teammate of Robbie's who later managed his Crusaders teams, told me on the eve of our departure for Australia of his belief that the book on Robbie Deans' career would not be completed without a chapter devoted to his time as head coach of the All Blacks.

Should that turn out to be the case — and the story on these pages provides a compelling argument as to why it should be so — consider what you are about to read a precursor to his career's main event.

It is a fascinating story of a truly great era in both New Zealand and global rugby that deserves an appropriate end.

Matt McILraith
July, 2014

1

THE DEANS OF CANTERBURY

It is entirely appropriate that, in Robert Maxwell, the Deans family provided one of Canterbury's foremost modern sporting sons. For it is impossible to divorce the Deans name from the fabric of the province's history: the name embroidered so boldly into human development on the quilt-like Canterbury Plains that its reference is inescapable, even for casual visitors to the city of Christchurch.

Commuters will drive along Deans Avenue as they circumnavigate the picturesque Hagley Park en route to the city centre. They will enter Deans Bush and drive past the cottage of the same name as they visit the Riccarton homestead. Both buildings were part of the first European settlement on the plains, the structures so solid that they came through the 2011 earthquakes largely intact.

Visitors prior to the earthquakes which rocked the city's foundations could even — albeit only for a brief time — have sat in the newly built Deans stand (2010) at the old Lancaster Park, the temple where generations of Cantabrians gathered to worship their sporting heroes.

Most descendants of the 'first' Cantabrians trace their ancestral roots to the four ships that were dispatched to Port Lyttelton from the United Kingdom bearing the original colonists in 1850; the Deans clan, however, were in what is now known as Christchurch eight years earlier — and have played a prominent role in Canterbury society ever since.

Robbie, his All Black brother Bruce, and sisters Joanne, Nicky and Sarah, represent the fifth generation of the Deans family in Canterbury. They, along with their extended family, continue an association with the province begun with the arrival of William Deans, a lowland Scot from

Riccarton in Ayrshire.

William arrived in the colony of New Zealand in 1840 — the year in which the Treaty of Waitangi was signed between representatives of the British Crown and the local Maori population, thereby legitimising the Crown's claims on the territory.

Given that one is speaking of a Canterbury institution when referring to the family it might be almost heresy to suggest it, but the Deans story could easily have been one embossed in the black and gold of Wellington.

When William arrived in New Zealand as a 23-year-old, it was into Port Nicholson that he sailed, to take up two allotments of unsurveyed land purchased in the area. The land was unsuitable for farming. Adjacent territories in the neighbouring Taranaki and Wairarapa provinces were not any better so it was eventually to the south that he turned, settling instead on the Canterbury Plains at a place he named Riccarton after the family parish in south-west Scotland.

By the time the Riccarton farm had been established and the first house on the plains built, William had been joined by John Deans, three years his junior, who, like his elder brother, essentially wound up on the banks of what became known as the Avon River by accident.

John had arrived in New Zealand the year before only to find, as his brother had, that his original land allotments, this time in Nelson and Wellington, were also unsuited to farming.

The loss for those districts was most definitely Canterbury's gain in a sporting sense: the five generations of John's lineage that followed left three All Blacks and one other Canterbury men's representative as well as a captain of the Canterbury women's team.

There's also Robbie's nephew Michael (Hobbs, son of Jock) who was a New Zealand age-group representative and also played Super Rugby, albeit for the Blues and Highlanders.

The original homestead at Deans Bush, Riccarton was completed in May 1843, after formal blessing had been given to the Deans brothers to settle the land. With the appropriate papers signed, farming could begin in earnest, and did so in June of that year when John returned from Australia with a collection of livestock, which included the first sheep to graze the plains. These were ironically sourced from Homebush near Sydney. This is an area whose linkage to the Deans family story resurfaced more than a century later once the completion of the Olympic Stadium saw it become the venue for test rugby in the city.

The family operation was well established by the time the first four ships of settlers disembarked at Lyttelton in 1850, seven years after the construction of the Deans homestead. Although the brothers helped provision the incoming population, nationalist and religious tensions from the old country accompanied the arriving populace. So much so that it required the intervention of the Governor, Sir George Grey, to thwart a bid by John Robert Godley, the resident chief agent of the newly formed Canterbury Association, to rid the plains settlement of its Presbyterian Scottish residents.

Canterbury society might have been founded on, and celebrate, its Church of England heritage, but had Grey not closed down Godley's 'Anglicans only' plan it would have cost the province's future plenty, including a more than useful goal-kicking fullback.

The attempt to kick out the Scots was a mild inconvenience, however, compared to the hurdles for the Deans clan that were to come.

William drowned in 1851 off the Wellington coast while sailing to Australia to purchase more sheep. This left John to grow the dynasty alone. He went back to Scotland the following year to marry his sweetheart, Jane McIlraith, before he returned, accompanied by his wife, to Canterbury.

John outlived William by just three years. He died after contracting a lung infection in 1854. Both brothers were aged 33 at their passing.

By the time of John's death, Jane had borne him a son, John Deans the Second. Jane, the family matriarch, whose resilience and general doggedness clearly has been passed down the generations, outlived her only son, as well as her husband. She eventually passed away in 1911 at the age of 88, nine years after the death of her son.

By the time of his death at the age of 48, John and his wife Catherine were the parents of 12 offspring, eight of them boys, and the Deans' hold on Canterbury was well and truly under way.

Stuart Maxwell Deans, Robbie's grandfather, was the youngest of the dozen children who made up the family's third generation.

Bob Deans, the fourth-born of that family, was 13 when his youngest brother was born, with Maxwell just eight when Robbie's great-uncle became the family's first All Black. A midfield back, Bob was 19 and in his first year out of Christchurch Boys' High School after four years in the college's First XV when he made his senior debut for Canterbury.

His legacy at the school remains with the Bob Deans award one of the most coveted at the institution.

Bob went on to play 25 times for his province between 1903 and 1908 and was the youngest All Black selected for the 1905 'Originals' Tour of the British Isles, France and North America.

While Bob's place in history has been entrenched forever by the try the Welsh still claim he *didn't* score, in the 0–3 loss to Wales at Cardiff Arms Park, he was awarded 20 tries from 21 appearances on the tour. This included two during the win over Ireland.

Bob played four tests on that expedition, later playing a fifth against the Anglo-Welsh at Auckland in 1908 where he finally got that try against the Welsh. Tragically the 24-year-old went to his grave later that year, dying as a result of complications from a burst appendix. He will be remembered forever for his part in the only loss from 35 games that the Originals suffered.

The sense of injustice that New Zealanders feel was only added to by the emphatic tone of the telegram Bob later sent to a British newspaper. In it, he swore that he had in fact scored the try prior to being hauled back into the field of play, before the referee arrived on the scene.

It might have come 100 years too late, but the try was finally awarded to a Deans, when Robbie re-enacted the saga with All Blacks teammates on a visit to the Arms Park during the 1983 tour. This time the referee, though being one of Robbie's teammates, arrived at the tryline on time!

Although Bob is the one who is remembered, he was not the only one of John and Catherine's sons to play representative rugby. The third youngest of the boys, Colin, also played for Canterbury, scoring a try for the province against South Africa at Lancaster Park in 1921.

While Colin's place in the catalogue of Deans sporting achievements has sat firmly in the shade of his elder brother, Robbie admits to having only a basic knowledge of Bob's exploits, prior to the inevitable comparison once he made the All Blacks himself.

'My grandfather didn't recollect much about Bob, given the age difference between them,' Robbie says.

'As a family, while there was an awareness, we didn't really speak much about it. It was not until I made the All Blacks, and then Bruce made it too, that we came to learn a bit more about Bob, primarily from the historical material produced by the media.'

Which is not to say that the family was ignorant of Bob's career. Robbie was given his great-uncle's All Blacks cufflinks upon his own national selection, with the keepsake remaining in the family as a reminder of what had gone before.

The first decade of the twentieth century might have marked the opening steps of the All Blacks, and the beginnings of a legacy that would stamp the mark of New Zealand nationalism more than any other, but unhappier times were to follow.

The Deans family was not immune to the turbulence that engulfed the world in the years between 1914 and 1918.

The Dominions were quick to answer the call of Empire when the Great War broke out in Europe in 1914, and Robbie's grandfather was called to arms, representing his country as a cavalryman in Egypt as the conflict played out.

On return, Maxwell settled at Kilmarnock, an hour and a half's drive north of Christchurch, establishing a property that remains in the family to this day, run by Bruce.

Maxwell and his wife Hilda had three children, daughters Patricia and Audrey and son Anthony. Anthony followed in his father's footsteps, both in tending the family property, but also in service of his country abroad. While the Second World War raged in an unsettled Europe and Asia, Anthony joined the navy, with the teenager serving on a minesweeper that was, for a time, based at Woolloomooloo, not too far from the Sydney suburb where his son, the future Australian Rugby Union coach, was to settle.

Anthony's war service came at a cost. A knee injury that was sustained while on active duty curtailed his rugby career.

A keen sportsman, Robbie's father had already shown his prowess as an all-rounder in the Christ's College First XI. His passion for the summer whites passed down to his two sons, with the young boys regular attendees as he played his cricket for the local Scargill club well into his forties.

The competitive drive that has served Robbie so well over the years was not limited to his father. Mother Joy skated competitively prior to her marriage and entry into motherhood, although the birth of five children in six years meant that she was to spend more of her life as a referee than as a competitor.

Although a competitive streak flows through the breed, there is no doubt that the proximity in the ages of Robbie and Bruce served both well on their sporting adventures. It ensured that they were provided with a level of competition at an early age that it could be argued was unsurpassed for either man during their senior sporting careers.

'Rugby on the back lawn was a mainstay of our late afternoons after school,' Robbie recalls. 'The farm was at the end of the bus route from Cheviot Area School, which meant we had a travel time of 60 minutes each way. By the time we were home, the banter was well and truly under way, and on the games would go!'

Not that the Deans boys would reserve their bursts of energy solely for each other. City kids, staying at a nearby cottage on the farm during the school holidays, were easy prey, with many a visiting youngster having returned to that dwelling battered and coated in mud after an invitation for a 'match' on the Deans boys' strategically watered lawn.

Robbie's first school match with Bruce was actually against him in an inter-class standard three and four game that was refereed by the boys' future Canterbury senior coach, Alastair Hopkinson.

Hopkinson's wife Marlene was Robbie's teacher at the time, but while her husband might have played nine tests for the All Blacks between 1967 and 1970, Robbie still disputes his ability as an adjudicator, after the game diplomatically ended as a draw, with both brothers scoring tries.

'The game was a draw, but that was a loss as far as I was concerned because Bruce gave it to me all the way home from school on the bus,' Robbie says.

Fortunately for the harmony of the household, the boys were seldom pitted against each other again, combining instead within a Glenmark

Under-11 side still talked about to this day.

The Under-11s, which was the first 15-aside team that Robbie played for, fielded a playing cast, the names of which still intimidate today, with the Deans boys, Richard Loe, and Andy and Chris Earl all featuring.

Nor was selection guaranteed amid the competition for places, to the extent that Joy took the proactive measure of 'feeding up' on scones the local grader driver, Roly Kirdy, who coached the team, just to make sure that her boys 'got a run'.

The ploy worked: Kirdy included the Deans boys in the team for the start of the season. They quickly turned heads to make sure that they stayed there!

With Bruce and Robbie at halfback and first five-eighths respectively, combination was never an issue, although, even then, the diligence to preparation and attention to detail that is such a key part of Robbie's make-up was in evidence.

'Bruce and I used to practise a scissors move all of the time on the lawn at home,' Robbie recalls. 'The first time we tried it in a game, it worked perfectly and we scored. Everyone watching was amazed!'

If the boys were good in year one, their second year in the Under-11s was something else again. Such was the dominance of the team, it won all but two of its matches, which were both drawn, scoring 200 points, with only six against — and three of those were scored by Andy Earl during a game in which he had been loaned to the opposition to make up the numbers!

'It was great fun, and a great grounding,' Robbie says.

'The game provides a great sense of identity, especially in country areas where families can be widely spread. The rugby club is the backbone of the community. Certainly that is the case with Glenmark: the club doesn't just create rugby players, it creates men.'

It also provided an education Robbie has shared with all he has played alongside and coached, based on loyalty, hard work and respect — life skills that were to serve him well as he embarked on the road to manhood.

The first stop was at Waihi, an intermediate boarding school for boys.

2

THE MAKING OF THE COMPETITOR

Rugby union came to dominate Robbie's life, but it might just as easily have been cricket.

From shortly after he arrived at the boarders-only Waihi School for intermediate boys, it became apparent that the young Glenmark lad had the aptitude to be successful in sport. It was just a matter of which game it would be in.

At Waihi, which sits 40 minutes to the north of Timaru and can boast New Zealand's double Victoria Cross winner Charles Upham among its old boys, Robbie threw himself into organised sport with the confidence of the competitor he is.

'Attending Waihi was a great leg up both from an educational but also a personal development standpoint, prior to entering secondary school,' Robbie says.

'It was quite traumatic as an 11-year-old to be dropped off by my parents, who then headed off back up the road to the farm. I guess anyone who has experienced boarding school has felt that initial sense of isolation, which was added to by Waihi's rural location, but the loneliness passed quickly. Once I got under way, it was fantastic.'

The experience undoubtedly furnished Robbie with a love of team environments. Overcoming the isolation of his arrival might also have instilled his sense of togetherness, and the importance of welcoming new members into any group. This is an action on which his players say he always placed a major emphasis.

While the results of his studies were promising, the two years at Waihi saw Robbie's sporting pursuits thrive. He arrived in 1971 already with a reputation, having been picked out of his all-conquering Glenmark Under-11s to play for the Country Under-11s against Town as a curtain-raiser to the previous year's Town–Country senior match on Lancaster Park.

Selection for the Waihi First XV duly followed in both of his years at the school, being joined in the team by Bruce when he arrived in South Canterbury during Robbie's second year.

At Waihi, the brothers were introduced to one of the benefits of attending an isolated institution: touring.

Although the Waihi First XV lost just once during Robbie's time, his father's love of cricket was also becoming ingrained, presenting a serious rival to rugby for the young lad's sporting affections. As a leader in the school's first XI, Robbie made the South Canterbury side for the 1972 South Island primary schools' tournament at Rangiora.

Rapidly gaining in confidence as a batsman, Robbie was nothing if not consistent at that tournament, getting out for 33 four times. His other turn at the crease saw him dismissed for 35. The performance won him selection in the South Island side at the conclusion of the competition.

Another memory that has stayed with him was a dropped catch at second slip when the batsman, the Canterbury number eight, had made just eight. The player concerned went on to tally 121 and turned out to be a more than useful bat later in life: the prolific Canterbury and New Zealand batsman Vaughan Brown.

Later a teammate, Robbie has never been slow in reminding the elegant left-hander that 'by shelling that catch, I got you started'.

The pair got to know each other well from Robbie's arrival at Christ's College in 1973, spending three years playing together in the First XI while also representing Canterbury and New Zealand Schools.

Robbie first appeared for Canterbury in the under-14 age-group. In his fifth form, he was then part of the Canterbury side that won its national tournament in Hamilton, where a lasting memory was an outfield catch that led to the end of his final innings.

'I really got onto it. It cleared mid-off and I set off for what I thought would be a three [runs]. While the fielder had to turn and chase, I thought there was no way he'd get near it,' Robbie says.

'Then I heard the applause. Not only did he get to it, he made the catch.'

The fielder's name was Gary Henley-Smith. He went on to become senior national sprint champion for the 100 and 200 metres in 1982 and 1983.

'With pace like he showed to take that catch, you could see why.'

As his school cricket career progressed, Robbie played alongside or against a number of players who would go on to make their mark with the Black Caps. This included the awkward but effective top-order batsman Andrew Jones, who Robbie encountered during his debut game for the Christ's First XI, in the annual match against Nelson College. The Jones style was unique but even then it worked, Robbie recalls, with the future test player scoring a half-century.

Nelson College was one of a number of 'traditional' fixtures that Christ's College played, in both rugby and cricket.

The annual clash against Christchurch Boys' High was another that was highlighted on the calendar, bringing with it additional pre-match nerves.

Robbie's first experience of this contest in the First XI was as a fifth former, with the pressure added to by the presence of his parents beyond the boundary rope at Hagley Park.

'Tony and Joy got to the games when they could but, with three girls and a farm at home to look after, it wasn't easy,' Robbie acknowledges. 'Bruce and I always appreciated it when they managed to get along, but it's really only when you have children yourselves, and have to find the time to get along to support their sport, that you really appreciate how big the effort was that your parents made.'

On this day at Hagley Park, Tony and Joy arrived literally just in the *nick* of time!

'I was batting when they drove in. I'd been looking about for them and saw them arrive,' Robbie says. 'They'd just got there and I edged one off Gerald Cummins, who I later played rep cricket with. It was caught by the wicketkeeper in front of second slip. I couldn't believe it and just froze. I didn't walk. I was thinking "I can't go now, my parents have just arrived." And then I was given not out!'

The incident, and the fact that he later betrayed his guilt, provided an early insight both into the competitive streak that has been a hallmark of Robbie's sporting career as well as his sense of fair play.

It also later demonstrated how well Joy knew her eldest son.

'The damage wasn't great to Boys' High, in terms of the scoreboard,' Robbie recalls, 'as I got out shortly after. But their wicketkeeper, Graham Gordon, who was to become a good friend of mine, wasn't impressed.

'He was quite openly remonstrating in front of the pavilion at lunchtime about the bloke who hadn't walked. My mother turned to me and asked me point blank: "Was that you?"'

The story had a postscript years later during senior club cricket, when the wronged Boys' High bowler took his revenge.

Cummins was batting against an Old Collegians side that included Robbie and Gordon, when he edged to the wicketkeeper where the catch was taken. Once again, the umpire called not out, at which time Cummins turned to Robbie and the wicketkeeper Gordon and, remembering the incident from their school days, said: 'You know I'm going nowhere, don't you?'

Although rugby continued to dominate his winters, by 1977 and his last summer at Christ's, cricket was placing a strong claim to be Robbie's main sporting priority.

His final school year saw him selected for the New Zealand Secondary Schools side to play the Australasian tournament in Christchurch. Brown was among his teammates again as was a future Canterbury captain in Richard Leggat, and a talented fourth form batsman from Auckland by the name of Martin Crowe.

Opening the batting, Robbie finished as New Zealand's leading run scorer, his tally bolstered by the 158 he scored against Tasmania, despite copping a fair bit of sledging from the diminutive figure at slip for the Australians: the future test opener David Boon.

Fast bowler Mike Whitney, who later defied Sir Richard Hadlee as a number 11 batsman to save a test match for Australia at the Melbourne Cricket Ground, opened the bowling for New South Wales, while Queensland's future Australian test paceman Carl Rackemann made the biggest impression.

'Even at that age, he was quick, scarily quick,' Robbie says. 'Certainly the fastest bowler I ever faced, and he was mean too. I saw the first ball I faced off him until it pitched, but didn't pick it up again until it had whistled past my nose. I was opening with [future Canterbury batsman] Anup Nathu.

'The second nut hit me on the pads. I was quite keen to get down the other end. There was definitely a run in it so I started off. Then I looked up and there was Anup, leaning on his bat, still in his crease with a big smile on his face.'

Robbie's departure from school, and the need to work to help subsidise his university study firstly at Lincoln College and then Canterbury University, placed restrictions on his time which saw cricket gradually slide onto the back-burner.

He joined the Old Collegians club in his first year out of school, and then attended the national under-23 tournament in Wellington where he was introduced to a batting helmet for the first time. It was needed, as Robbie found himself facing the future test paceman Martin Snedden bowling with a howling gale behind his back at Kilbirnie Park.

Even as the representative honours stacked up, it was becoming clear to Robbie that something was going to have to give, and that due to his success in the winter, it was rugby that would take priority.

By the summer of 1982, he was playing cricket in the country with Scargill, emulating his father's service to the club.

Alex Wyllie, by then his Canterbury coach, but also someone who had played rugby and cricket alongside Robbie, and had had a lot to do with the Deans family, believes that the move out into the country killed off any chance of career advancement in the summer sport.

Robbie was naturally talented with any ball sport, it didn't really matter what it was, Wyllie says. He was gifted, but also determined to succeed, very competitive and very driven in that pursuit.

The trouble was, playing in the country didn't extend him, with Wyllie believing the lower standard than in the Town senior competition didn't test Robbie enough or drive his development forward.

A senior cap for Canterbury did beckon, when he was picked to play Otago in a Shell Cup one-day match at Waimate at the end of 1982, but the game never finished because of rain, and washed away with it were his first-class representative aspirations.

Even appearing for Canterbury had created a conundrum for Robbie given the complexities of the strict amateur ethos that remained in rugby, while cricket endorsed professionalism.

'A cheque for $17 arrived later from the Canterbury Cricket Association associated with my involvement in that game, but I was too scared to cash it for fear of breaking the amateur protocols that were still rigidly enforced in rugby,' Robbie says.

While Canterbury cricket saved $17, ultimately Robbie chose to prioritise his involvement in rugby, which he felt provided a greater emphasis on the team dynamic.

'The tipping point came later in that summer when I returned from a Canterbury B tour down south. The A side was playing a one-dayer against Central Districts out at Dudley Park in Rangiora and I drove out there for a bit to watch.

'I couldn't stay until the end. It was going to be a tight finish when I left, with Canterbury getting down to its lower order chasing a small target it ultimately failed to achieve.

'I was driving back into Christchurch and just crossing the Waimakariri Bridge, when a car that was being driven by a senior player from the Canterbury team went past me.

'The game hadn't even finished and he'd already left the ground. That just blew me away, especially given the closeness and camaraderie I was experiencing with my rugby teams at the time.'

The decision ended any prospect of pushing on for a regular place in the Canterbury first-class squad, after he'd helped the province's B-side to the national final that summer.

Country cricket remained, however, both with Scargill and also the Canterbury Country representative side. Country featured both of the Deans boys in its line-up in 1983 when the team headed north to take on a powerful Northland side in Whangarei for the Hawke Cup — the Ranfurly Shield of New Zealand's minor association cricket leagues.

Bruce, a right-handed batsman and occasional leg spin bowler, had played alongside his elder brother in the Christ's First XI as well as at Scargill.

As with the Ranfurly Shield, the format of the Hawke Cup puts the onus on the challenger to 'take' the trophy from the holder over the three days. 'Victory' is determined on the first innings should an outright success not be achieved.

For a while, the brothers appeared on course for the sporting double at Cobham Oval, having won the Shield the previous winter with Canterbury.

Batting first, a Northland side captained by veteran seamer Bob Cunis, but also featuring future test wicketkeeper and opening bat Bryan Young, made 298.

But not without some help.

The then 42-year-old Northland cricketing icon Brian Dunning made 132 of that total, although Robbie remains adamant — 30 years on — that the local favourite benefited from some 'charity' during his innings, courtesy of the local umpire.

'We had him plumb lbw early on, but it was given not out,' Robbie says. 'The decision was so bad, we had to run him out in the end because we weren't going to get him out any other way.'

Even so, Canterbury Country was well in the hunt for the first innings win at 106 for the loss of two, before collapsing to miss by 68, with Robbie contributing 26 batting from number seven, while Bruce made 13.

Although falling short of their own expectations with the bat, the name Deans still featured prominently on the official scorecard. Between them, the brothers took eight catches for the game as the Northland second innings batted out the remaining play.

'It's a great format with it all on the line in the first innings,' Robbie says. 'The standard of the cricket was pretty fair too, with a number of first class players involved.'

While the summer of 1983 represented Robbie's last serious representative cricketing foray, he did return for one final season with Canterbury Country following his retirement from first-class rugby in 1990.

Enjoyment aside, his motivation for a final competitive summer was a simple one: to score a representative hundred.

'I just wanted to prove, to myself as much as anyone, that I could have achieved something if I'd stuck at it with cricket,' Robbie explains. 'I wanted that hundred, and eventually got it playing against Marlborough at Horton Park in Blenheim. It was a weight off. I'd got out for 97 playing against the West Coast at Dudley Park a few weeks earlier and thought I might have blown my chance.'

With the century in the scorebooks, Robbie says he 'retired' a happy man. His Crusaders charges beg to differ.

As one of the architects of the hugely successful annual charity fund-raiser for the Cystic Fibrosis Association, Robbie would lead an Invitation XI against the best that the Crusaders players could offer, initially over 50 overs per side, although the format has been trimmed to 20/20 in more recent times.

Kieran Read, who made a New Zealand Under-19 tournament cricket squad himself while representing Northern Districts, says there was never anything 'charitable' about Robbie's approach to the game. Citing his competitive nature, Read jokes that the Crusaders coach spent almost as much time worrying about the cricket in the lead-up as he did the pre-season rugby training. He wasn't even beyond the odd sledge, which would be lobbed in the direction of those declared for the Crusaders XI line-up, as the game approached.

On game day itself, Read says, Robbie was easy to spot. He was the only one in full whites!

There was always banter out on the field, but the players had to be careful when Robbie was involved, Read laughs. Sledging the boss wasn't a great move for one's selection prospects! Not that it was all one-way.

'Playing only once a year against a group of people that you spend a lot of time with has its challenges,' Robbie laughs, 'particularly if you fail, because you have to wait a full year before you get another opportunity, and the banter in between times is relentless.'

He recalls one instance in particular involving the Crusaders and All Blacks fullback Ben Blair, whose diminutive size brought him the nickname 'Critter', but whose talent sledging would make the average Australian test cricketer blush.

'I dropped a relatively straightforward catch off Benny which I should have taken,' Robbie confesses. 'I certainly wish I had. I have never been allowed to forget it.'

Robbie did finally get his man last year when he caught Blair out during a game the pair were involved in at the picturesque Willows Cricket Club ground outside of Christchurch.

Leon MacDonald, who played Hawke Cup cricket for Marlborough himself, concurs with Read's assessment with regards to the intensity of the competition, having taken on the task of organising the Crusaders XIs. When you combined Robbie's competitive nature, his enthusiasm, the emphasis he has always placed on community engagement, with his love of the game, the banter and the enjoyment that flowed from it was inevitable, MacDonald says.

Without it, the event, which is now one of the biggest fundraisers for Cystic Fibrosis, wouldn't have become such a success.

3

COLLEGE TO CANTERBURY

There are few, if any, secondary school sporting events in New Zealand that can equal the interest and the history of the annual Christ's College against Christchurch Boys' High School First XV rugby match.

The game inevitably draws a large crowd and has often been subject to a significant amount of space in the local newspaper, Christchurch's *The Press*. In more recent times it has been shown live on the nationwide rugby channel offered by New Zealand's pay television network.

Robbie's introduction to the contest came during his final school year in 1977, having broken into the First XV in unusual circumstances towards the end of the previous season, in time to feature in the annual quadrangular tournament Christ's played with Nelson and Wellington Colleges as well as Wanganui Collegiate.

'We were hosting the tournament that year so, naturally, there was heightened interest in it among everyone at school,' Robbie recalls.

'The coach of the first XV was Jeff Steel, who was also my geography teacher. In the lead-up to the tournament, he asked my class to help him pick the team.

'I'm still not sure to this day as to whether he was aware that I was in the room at the time, but all of my classmates picked me. Sure enough, when the squad was named, I was in it.'

Christ's won the tournament, which helped cement Robbie's place in the team from the start of his final winter at the school.

Boys' High is the game on which that year is judged as the Christ's team was chasing the school's first win over its traditional rival in 12 years.

For his final year, Robbie had Bruce alongside him in the squad, although his younger brother was only on the bench, being held up by the presence of the South Island Under-18s rep halfback Mike Brown on the Christ's school roll.

'We were playing at our ground, and we had a good team. Jock Hobbs was now playing No. 8, having gradually moved closer to the play after he started as a fullback and then played centre. He and I were two of five players we had who would go on to make that year's South Island Under-18s,' Robbie says.

'So we felt we had a good chance, but it was a big game. They had a massive forward pack and as many South Island reps as we had, including Loey [Richard Loe], Rob McIntosh, Ken Pope, Phil Gibson and Steve [Hansen].

'The crowd was the biggest I'd played in front of to that point, and they were right on the sideline, just behind the ropes. Those big inter-school games are remarkable events. The noise throughout was fantastic.'

The Christ's support was even noisier at the fulltime whistle as the 13–0 win allowed Robbie and Bruce to match the achievement of their father Tony, who'd also beaten Boys' High during his time in the First XV.

Robbie's profile rose even further after selection in the Canterbury side for the South Island Under-18 tournament held in Invercargill. This represented his first experience in a Canterbury rugby side and it went well, with the team going through unbeaten, beating Nelson Bays in the final.

The South Island team was selected at the conclusion of the week-long tournament, returning to Invercargill towards the end of the year to meet the North in the inter-island match. Featuring alongside Robbie in that side were the future Canterbury representatives Hobbs, Albert Anderson, Richard Loe and Joe Leota, his cricket mate Vaughan Brown, as well as his future Canterbury and Crusaders coaching partner, current All Blacks coach Steve Hansen.

The South lost a game played in driving rain, but the experience built on what Robbie had achieved during the Christ's College programme. This had included another success in the quadrangular, beating a Wanganui side which had featured the future All Blacks Rugby World

Cup-winning captain David Kirk in the final.

Within two years, Robbie would be playing for the Canterbury senior side, with his career taking off as the result of a punt taken by one of the great Canterbury fullbacks to precede him: Fergie McCormick.

Having started a Bachelor of Commerce at Lincoln College once he left Christ's, Robbie played first five-eighths for the students' Under-19 side. In those days, Lincoln College teams competed in the Town competition, and Robbie's side ended up winning its grade that year.

Robbie wasn't the goal-kicker. The team's fullback, Noel Heffernan, filled that role. The Lincoln fullback, who used the 'torpedo style' goal-kicking method which was still popular back then, was the younger brother of one of the Canterbury fullbacks of the time, Doug Heffernan.

'We were playing a game at Hagley Park and were awarded a penalty a long way out,' Robbie recalls.

'It was pretty muddy and the leather ball already had the weight of a brick. I'd only had one kick all season but, when it was suggested, I decided to give it a go.

'The kick went over. What I didn't know at the time was that Fergie, who was coaching the Canterbury Colts that year, was watching from a nearby field.'

Robbie hadn't made the Town Colts, being passed over as first five-eighths in favour of the future Canterbury cricketer Graham Kench, but McCormick, who was scouting a goal-kicker for his muster, liked what he saw and decided to give him a go.

The selection wasn't without its resistance, McCormick says, especially given that the Town selectors hadn't gone with Robbie for their side. But his team needed a kicker. That goal convinced the Canterbury legend that Robbie was the man to do it.

Even at 18, McCormick says Robbie's quality as a player was clear. He possessed natural skill and was a great reader of the game, with that anticipation suggesting to McCormick, even at this early stage, that Robbie would wind up as a top-level fullback as opposed to the first five-eighths he selected him as.

While Robbie was one of the youngest in his Colts (Under-21) team, he quickly made a strong impression, both through his willingness to listen and learn, and his preparedness to do whatever it took to get ahead.

Plenty of kids are blessed with talent but sometimes that can be a curse in McCormick's view. Attitude and application are everything if potential is to be fulfilled. Robbie had great manners, was very respectful, and a very humble young lad, McCormick says. Kids with attributes like that are the ones you take a special pleasure out of, when they do well, McCormick reckons.

Robbie quickly became comfortable in the company of the indomitable Fergie, who played an incredible 222 games at fullback for Canterbury, as well as 44 (including 16 tests) for the All Blacks, during his 18-year representative career.

Even so, the first steps with the Colts were not without their anxious moments.

'I missed the first training because I couldn't find Linfield Park [the training ground of McCormick's club, Linwood],' Robbie recalls.

'So it wasn't a good start. Then, when I made it for the second training session, the first thing Fergie did was throw me the ball and order me to start practising my goal-kicking.

'I'd always practised but Fergie was the first coach I'd had who'd given me that responsibility for the team.'

That season vindicated the veteran fullback's assessment of his young charge. Robbie won the Colts Player of the Year at the Canterbury Rugby Union's annual awards night for 1978, where he found himself surrounded by a host of the province's rugby legends.

'I'd been nervous from the start having all of those guys there. I think I'd have been even more nervous if I'd known before the evening began how it would end.'

To celebrate his first year out of school, and the freedom of life living at Lincoln's Orchard Hall, Robbie had shelled out $300 on a 1957 Morris Oxford. The car became a focal point for Robbie, but also for some of his mates, who once jammed it between two concrete barrier lines that had three posts at either end. Robbie only discovered it the next morning while walking to a lecture.

The car caused him further difficulty following the awards function, when the Morris wouldn't start.

'I ended up having legends like Alex Wyllie and Billy Bush out in the car park, giving the Morris a push start,' Robbie recalls. 'I couldn't believe my luck!'

The push provided Robbie with an insight into the power he'd be playing behind when he made his senior Canterbury debut the following year, having entered senior ranks at the start of 1979 when he relocated his studies across from Lincoln to Canterbury University.

'I was in a flat with Jock, just off Fendalton Park. My sister Nicky [the future Mrs Hobbs; the couple married in 1983] came around to our place all of the time. Officially, the visits were to see me, but we all knew she was really there to see Jock!

'Jock and I had both started playing for the Christchurch club. The team captain was Jerry Rowberry, who'd been a Physical Education teacher during my first year at Christ's College.

'There was a sense of irony for us playing under Jerry. Eighteen months earlier, he'd have had us suspended from school for drinking. Now he was filling up our glasses.'

Robbie's early season showing in the red and black hoops of Christchurch saw him rewarded with another red and black jersey, when selected to make his senior Canterbury debut against West Coast at Greymouth in May. Trips to the Coast were the stuff of legends in those days, and not just for the rugby.

Wyllie, who was in the last year of his lengthy Canterbury career, led the side, welcoming the entry of a young player he'd watched out at Glenmark since he was a little kid. It certainly made one feel old, Wyllie recalls, but he says Robbie had always been destined to make it.

As well as his competitiveness, Wyllie acknowledged determination as a key factor in Robbie's rise, not just in on-field matters, but also with relation to off-field team activities.

Such was Robbie's resolve not to let his teammates down, he once spent a whole summer practising a particular skill, in order to ensure that he wasn't the weakest link when the backs took on the forwards once the team reassembled.

1979 was a good time for a young player like Robbie to be entering the Canterbury team. He was always going to be a long-term servant for the province provided he kept up his disciplined approach, Wyllie says.

While the guard was changing, there were still enough grizzly senior players to keep the young guys in check, teaching them the habits that they'd need to be successful.

Canterbury beat West Coast 37–7 in the first of the 146 games that Robbie would end up playing for the province. He went on to play three more games for the full representative side that year, while also appearing twice for a Canterbury XV.

'Getting called up to play that first game was quite daunting,' Robbie says. 'I was replacing Doug Bruce, who'd retired, and he was a guy that I'd idolised. Fergie had finally retired too, and Alex went at the end of that year. Their departures left massive holes in the team that had to be filled.

'Jock and I had both made the Town team before that Canterbury game. Town was coached by Tiny Hill and Gerald Wilson, who were the Canterbury coaches, and I made the rep team even though we lost to Country.'

Robbie made his debut at first five-eighths alongside his 32-year-old club-mate Mick Powley, who was also on debut, starting at hooker.

'Sharing that moment with Mick was special because he had done a lot for me that year after I moved over from Lincoln to Christchurch and started playing seniors,' Robbie says.

'Mick had had to wait a long time to play for Canterbury, but he had persevered and finally got there. Seeing what it meant to a bloke I'd come to know well, and who had helped me, reinforced the honour that I'd been given in playing for Canterbury and the importance of not ever taking that for granted.'

Another club-mate, All Black Richard Wilson, was at fullback for Canterbury, and the trio went on to help their club to the Town final, where Christchurch lost to High School Old Boys.

In between times, Robbie was invited to attend the New Zealand Colts trials in Nelson. He missed selection, but remembers the experience more for the fate of his roommate for that trial, Canterbury centre Vic Simpson.

'Victor had a blinder. He got four tries. What else could you do? Then he didn't get selected. It was pretty rough. That was the first time I'd really got to know Victor, and we went on to become good mates, so we got something even more important out of that experience.'

By the end of 1979, Robbie had the taste for representative play and he resolved not to stand still in his quest for more.

'I worked on the rubbish trucks through that summer and got fitter than I'd ever been. It was a good eye-opener for a young kid working with the older blokes who did it every day of the year. I was exposed to their worry-free attitude, both to the job but also to life in general. It was a great help in terms of not getting too wrapped up in my rugby ambitions and holding on too tight.'

Those ambitions were beginning to be realised.

Back for a second crack at the New Zealand Colts in 1980, Robbie made the team, but from a new position. With Wilson away with the All Blacks in Australia, Robbie had been switched to fullback at Christchurch. McCormick's assessment of his long-term future was then matched by the national Under-21 selectors who took Robbie on playing the role at the back.

The 'ripple' effect of the move to fullback on a permanent basis impacted on Wilson but also on Robbie's future colleague at the Crusaders, Wayne Smith, who stepped in at first five-eighths for Canterbury while Robbie was away on national duty.

While Smith gained, establishing himself as Canterbury and then New Zealand's backline pivot, Wilson most definitely didn't. He returned from the All Blacks tour to find that he couldn't get back into the Christchurch team, with Robbie retained as the fullback once he arrived home. As a result the All Black, who'd spent the previous four years wearing the silver fern, was forced to relocate, joining the Merivale-Papanui club the following year.

'It was quite awkward because George Wilson, Richard's dad, was a real club stalwart at Christchurch and had been a big supporter of mine,' Robbie says. 'But while it was uncomfortable, I was able to rationalise it as a decision [in terms of his club selection] that was being made by someone else.'

While Wilson and the All Blacks party lost their series in Australia, Robbie enjoyed a successful tour with the Colts, who edged out their Australian counterparts 10–8 at the Sydney Cricket Ground.

The Australian side featured two of the Ella boys, Gary and Glen, although such was the level of the chaos that they caused, Robbie says it felt like they were up against all three of the Randwick Rugby Club's famous brothers.

They weren't. Mark, the oldest of the three, instead tied the senior All Blacks defence up in knots later that same afternoon. The Colts game was the curtain-raiser before the Wallabies outclassed the All Blacks 26–10 in the series-deciding third test.

Robbie and his teammates stayed for the main game as part of the crowd, gaining a first-hand insight into what the Bledisloe Cup meant to Australians as they watched the victorious Wallabies perform a victory lap around the ground with the trophy after it had been presented.

He returned to a Canterbury team that was struggling somewhat. NPC champions for the first time in 1977, the year after the competition had been introduced, an era was coming to an end, leaving a big rebuilding task for the new coaching team of Neil Cornelius and Gerald Wilson.

Robbie's close mate Don Hayes, who would lead the side in its record-equalling Ranfurly Shield run that started two years later, took over as captain under Cornelius and Wilson. He maintains that the two men haven't received the credit they deserved for their part in preparing the side for the shield era that was to come. Hayes says the coaches had a difficult job, and while the results in 1980 and 1981 didn't show it, they helped to create the backbone within the playing group that was to serve the province so well once Wyllie assumed command as coach in 1982.

One of the difficulties Hayes pinpointed was the number of younger players whom he maintains didn't really understand, at that point, the meaning of wearing the famous red and black jersey. The 'learning' Hayes says, came in the form of a few 'beatings', which ultimately provided benefit, even though he acknowledges that it didn't feel like progress at the time. The key, he believes, was that the team stuck together and grew alongside each other through the adversity, which may not have happened today, where players have far greater freedom of movement and shift around more.

'It was hard yards,' Robbie says, 'but the core of the group that we had went on to win and then retain the shield. We never forgot the hard times and never allowed ourselves to take anything for granted when things started to roll.'

If the lack of success left the younger players bewildered, those who had survived from the 1977 NPC title were simply filthy.

'Guys like John Ashworth, Vance Stewart and Graeme Higginson were frustrated because they'd put a lot into the Canterbury jersey previously when the side had been doing well. But their presence was important, probably more important than they realised, in terms of teaching the younger guys and bringing them forward. I was still new to fullback at that time and Vance [Stewart] gave me a piece of advice I never forgot.

'He told me that the way he, as a lock forward, assessed the quality of his fullback was in how far he had to go backwards to the ball. He reckoned that the best fullbacks brought the ball up to the forwards.'

It was straightforward but wise counsel. It also spelt out to Robbie exactly what he needed to do to keep onside with his forwards.

Not that Hayes believes Robbie needed too much advice, saying that, even at this early point of his career, the strategic nous that was to make him such a successful coach was beginning to make an impact. Robbie provided energy for the group and he was always organising things, according to Hayes.

Having subsequently worked with 'Robbie the coach' at the Crusaders, Hayes says his mate has never really changed. He loves to win and will do whatever he can in that pursuit.

For all that, there has always been more to Robbie than what happens on the field, Hayes explains. He cites the 'balance' Robbie brings to his life, and the 'seriously good values' he projects, as other reasons why he has earned so much respect from his teammates and players.

In the three seasons that had followed the province's maiden NPC success, Canterbury barely surpassed a 50 per cent success rate, winning 17 while losing 13 in the championship, but 1981 offered the prospect of greater achievement when the side opened with a promising performance against a Wallaby-strength Queensland side in Brisbane.

Canterbury lost 20–22 after Robbie missed the conversion that would have drawn the game, but he had a good excuse, having taken a knock earlier in the match that led to a delayed bout of concussion.

45

The incident carried a human side when the Queensland coach, the late Bob Templeton, later visited Robbie. The Australian's sincerity impressed on the future Wallaby coach that there was more to the game than the simplicity of win and loss.

'I'd taken a decent whack,' Robbie recalls, 'and when it came time to take that last conversion, I could see four goalposts in front of me! I tried to aim in the middle and wound up hitting one of them!

'But Bob's gesture in coming to check on my well-being, once he found out what had happened, meant a lot. He was an outstanding coach, but he was also an outstanding man. To him, the game was about its people, and that is something I have never forgotten.'

At the other end of the scale from Templeton's chivalry was the open anarchy that prevailed in New Zealand later that year for much of the controversial Springbok tour of the country.

While the National Party prime minister of the time, Rob Muldoon, believed that the support of 51 per cent of the populace for the South African visit represented a majority — and it got him re-elected later that year — for a time the tour that he allowed to proceed threatened to tear the game and the country apart.

Even though it didn't feature on the fixture list, Canterbury was not immune to its consequences. Not only was the grandstand at Rugby Park burnt down by arsonists, the three staff who worked fulltime at the union's inner-city office at one stage had to barricade themselves inside as a massive and disorderly protest raged outside.

Views on the tour divided families across the country, including the Deans clan, with Robbie's sister Jo joining up with the protest movement during its activity in Wellington where she was tutoring at the local polytech.

Robbie says Canterbury's omission from the tour itinerary was not something either he or his teammates dwelt on at the time, although he admits now that watching the Boks in action planted a seed inside him that would grow as far as his own rivalry with South African teams and players was concerned.

The Canterbury squad attended the third test at Eden Park during their North Island trip, with the side due at Pukekohe the following day where they were well beaten by Counties.

Robbie had witnessed the first test at Lancaster Park too, where protestors had broken the barbed wire cordon to litter a part of the ground with tacks and nails. This was an attempt to prevent the game from kicking off. While it failed, the protestors had already claimed one 'victory', by rubbing out the Waikato tour match, which was abandoned shortly after its scheduled kick-off time for safety reasons following a mass ground invasion by anti-tour protestors.

'Being in the crowd for that third test at Eden Park was something else again,' Robbie says.

'It was absolute anarchy outside of the ground. With this being the last game, the protestors were giving it everything, so just getting to the ground was like wandering through a war zone. Then there was the plane. . .'

In an attempt to prevent the series-deciding game from being played, pilot Marx Jones and his fellow protestor Grant Cole, who acted as 'bombardier', flew a light plane over Eden Park. The pair first dropped anti-Tour propaganda leaflets then flour bombs, one of which scored a direct hit on the rugged Manawatu and All Blacks prop Gary Knight.

There was nothing the authorities could do as the plane repeatedly dropped in over the stand, seemingly hovering at low altitude before lifting off again as it reached the other side of the ground.

If it was unnerving for the players, they didn't betray it during an absorbing contest that went down to the 80th minute before being won by the man Robbie would eventually displace as All Blacks fullback, Allan Hewson, who nervelessly drilled a long-range penalty goal to hand the hosts a dramatic 25–22 win.

Playing in the game might have grabbed the players' focus, but the aerial threat was of greater distraction to the spectators, powerless as they were when the plane wafted in and out of the stadium's air space time and again.

'It's not something that I think anyone who was actually there will ever forget,' Robbie says. 'Even watching the footage on television later somehow does a disservice to how unnerving the whole thing actually was. Every time the plane came in, you couldn't help but think that, if something went wrong with its engine, or if the pilot made a mistake, there was going to be a tragedy.'

47

With no Springbok game in the programme, Canterbury's big match of the year was a Ranfurly Shield challenge against Waikato in Hamilton, its first shield game for eight years.

The side looked capable of giving it a shake after opening its NPC campaign with three wins out of four, which included a 13–7 defeat of Auckland.

The problem? Most of the team hadn't ever played for the shield, which Canterbury hadn't held since it famously lost it to Marlborough in 1973.

Hayes acknowledges that the lack of experience found his team out in a game where the challengers were beaten 14–7. Waikato, Hayes says, used its greater 'feel' for the intensity of the contest to its advantage. It is something, he says, the Canterbury team learnt from when the time came to challenge again, the following year in Wellington.

'That match was a great education for us all in terms of shield rugby. It was another level of intensity, something none of us had ever encountered; the game was just so fast. Like the step from Super Rugby to test matches today,' Robbie says.

'Until you've played both, so you can make that comparison, you might think you know the difference, but you don't. The atmosphere that day in Hamilton was incredible. There were 25,000 in the crowd and very few of them were shouting for us. The cowbells were relentless.'

Adding to the discomfort of the defeat was the fact that Robbie knew he hadn't been in optimum shape for the game. The lead-up during the week had been devoted to crutching and shearing on the Deans farm. It was heavy work and it had taken its toll.

'I could barely run. My hamstrings had tightened so much that I very nearly pulled out. It didn't cost us the game or anything but it was a lesson. You can't approach a game half-cocked. It's all or nothing.'

Both Robbie and his captain believe that, had Canterbury not gained the experience from that shield challenge the year before, it would not have beaten Wellington in 1982 to begin the province's record-equalling shield era.

'While we were shocked by the speed and intensity at which the Waikato game had been played, we also recognised that we weren't that far off,' Robbie says.

'We'd missed a few opportunities that you have to take. The learning from that match was to reinforce to us all the importance of preparation, and the importance of absorbing the detail around the game plan within the preparation.

'Because you only get one chance at it and the game goes just like that [snapping his fingers]. Shield rugby, like finals and test matches, is distinct from all other rugby that you can play. The stakes are higher.

'If you wait until the week of the game to get your preparation done, it just isn't going to happen.'

It is a lesson all of those who have ever been coached by Robbie can attest that he's never forgotten.

4

SHIELD AND DREAMS

The appointment of Alex Wyllie as coach in 1982, with former All Blacks first five-eighths Doug Bruce as his assistant, was always going to shake things up within the Canterbury team.

While the provincial icon, who was almost universally known throughout the country by his nickname Grizz, had kept his distance from the representative scene since retiring in 1979 and says he returned to the arena with no preconceptions, it was clear to all that his no-nonsense approach wouldn't be to everyone's taste. There were going to be personality clashes — and casualties — along the way.

Robbie opted to play his club rugby in the country from the start of that year, returning to Glenmark for the first time since the Under-11s, after having finished up with Christchurch the year before.

He undertook the move with the knowledge that it would mean a three-hour round trip to Canterbury trainings, although the 90-minute each-way drive was made significantly easier after Wyllie promoted Robbie's younger brother into the team too. Bruce had played a leading hand from halfback as Lincoln College had taken out the previous year's Town championship while also beating Country's top club in the annual champion of champions play-off.

One of the few losses the students sustained had been when they were rolled by Robbie's Christchurch. Robbie says he realised, when he drove Bruce to the Town final, that he wanted to play alongside him. That provided a big boost for the Country game as the Deans boys returned together to their first club.

Due to their Glenmark background, as well as Robbie's experience playing as a teammate alongside Wyllie in 1979, the Deans brothers had a greater understanding than most of their peers as to what was coming with the new coach.

'Alex showed his hand right from the start, when he pulled in 64 players for trials at the start of the season, which were held out at Kaiapoi. The message was pretty clear,' Robbie says.

'He was open to any guys who were keen, and who were committed. No one could presume anything. The bottom line was that he was looking for strong characters.'

History shows he found them. Among the newcomers to emerge was second five-eighths Warwick Taylor, who was fresh to Canterbury after previously having been in Dunedin. Now the father of an All Black, in Crusaders first five-eighths Tom, Taylor became a long-time Canterbury teammate of Robbie's, while also sharing in the All Blacks' win at the inaugural Rugby World Cup in 1987.

Future All Blacks hooker John Mills was another to emerge out of the trial process as did the one-time All Blacks reserve Tony Thorpe, who was to become close to Robbie, later serving as manager for the John Mitchell and Robbie-coached All Blacks of 2002 and 2003, as well as the Crusaders between 2004 and 2011.

Another was winger Garry Hooper, who had appeared for Marist for a decade in the Christchurch club competition prior to finally getting his chance with Canterbury. The veteran made it count, scoring the opening try of Canterbury's successful Ranfurly Shield challenge in Wellington.

Wyllie's first player clash came early, once he'd assembled a wider squad at Amberley for training, having deliberately taken the team out into the country to keep them 'grounded'.

'Alex identified Victor [Simpson], not directly, but he was looking straight at him when he told the group that unless you were prepared to play anywhere in order to make the team better, then you best depart now. Although he didn't say it in quite such "nice" terms.'

The exchange began a battle of wills between the pair that continued for three years. Wyllie wanted to move Simpson to the wing, while the player insisted on parking at centre, despite warnings from the coach that the player who took the wing spot would become an All Blacks first.

Wyllie was right.

While the talented Simpson gave good service, Craig Green, who'd arrived up from Rakaia in Mid Canterbury as a second five-eighths, switched to the wing. He went on to play 39 games including 20 tests for the All Blacks, sharing in the Rugby World Cup win of 1987.

Simpson did make it to the next level, but his was a brief All Blacks career, consisting of two tests and two other matches on the tour of Argentina in 1985. It didn't reflect the value he had given Canterbury during his career.

'Victor was a point of difference player for us throughout that era,' Robbie says, 'as well as being a very good team man.'

Wyllie undoubtedly had the biggest influence of anyone on the Robbie Deans coaching career that was to follow, although Don Hayes says the fullback's leadership was already coming through with the backline. Robbie coordinated the backs like a chess player from his position on the field, providing plenty of voice and attacking options for first five-eighths Wayne Smith.

Wyllie concurs, saying Robbie was already emerging as a linchpin of what was a talented backline by the time he took over in 1982, with the new coach opting against making too many changes, which he thought would be counterproductive. They already had the best players in the province, Wyllie believed. The key to better performance was to get them fitter and playing as a team by creating a competitive environment where no one could take anything for granted. The scenario was strikingly similar to that Robbie would face when he took over coaching the Wallabies 17 years later, with a similar method being applied to achieve significant improvement.

Another Wyllie philosophy Robbie continued with great success once he moved into team management and coaching was improving and maintaining connection with the support base. Wyllie believed the Canterbury team had distanced itself from the likes of the union's supporter's club while it was struggling. Under his stewardship, the players mixed far more, attending the supporters' function following games while immersing themselves in community events once the Ranfurly Shield era got under way.

But it is for his legendary trainings that the players remember Wyllie most, with the rigours being such that Hayes says the games were regarded as preparation for training!

'We'd be at Rugby Park in the evening. Everyone would have been at work in the day. Bruce and I would have driven in from the country. And he flogged us as the smog rolled in to the extent that it cloaked the Port Hills,' Robbie recalls.

'Sometimes Bruce and I wouldn't get home until after midnight, the trainings were so long and tiring. And with the smog, which was a real problem for Christchurch in those days, by the end of it, we'd be coughing up black stuff!

'But they served their purpose. Not only did the hard trainings improve our fitness, they also helped bond the players together as a team.'

It wasn't a case of being clever, Wyllie says. The coaches simply insisted that the players practised what was instructed until they mastered it, as opposed to breaking away with their own alterations on the fly. Until the instructed move was done properly, and had come unstuck, the players couldn't say that it hadn't worked, Wyllie maintains. As such, no changes were permitted until a plan failed.

The role Doug Bruce played, as Wyllie's assistant, has often been understated, but not by the players who were involved.

'Doug was a great foil as a conduit between Alex and the team. He is an innovative thinker about the game and was prepared to take on feedback a bit more readily than Alex initially was.

'Alex was big on attitude. He got us fit and drove the team standards. At the beginning, nothing was negotiable but we got beyond that, and he let go to some extent, because it worked!'

The Wyllie era opened on a promising note with a 30–6 win over Marlborough, who had beaten the Wyllie-captained Canterbury nine years earlier to end the province's last Ranfurly Shield tenure.

This was followed by an equally commanding 38–7 success against the West Coast, with new winger Hooper contributing a remarkable six tries to an outcome that represented a huge improvement on the 9–9 draw between the two the previous year.

'The president of the West Coast Rugby Union in 1982 had actually refereed the game between the two provinces the year before,' Robbie says. 'So he started off the post-match function after we had won by suggesting that the West Coast side of the previous year should still be thanking him for the drawn scoreline from that game.'

Queensland, who'd narrowly beaten Canterbury the year before at Ballymore, provided the first big test, arriving in Christchurch once again with a Wallaby-strength side. Canterbury sent them packing, running out a convincing 21–9 winner.

'It was clear before, but even more so by the reactions after the game, that most people locally had expected us to lose. We did play pretty well. That match was a big step for the growth of the playing group, while perhaps increasing the expectations of us externally — but we got "earthed" pretty quick.'

The first wobbles set in during the team's next match.

A trip down the road to Ashburton saw Canterbury lowered 6–13 by an experienced Mid Canterbury side, which was taking great delight in embarrassing its northern neighbours through this period. The win extended Mid Canterbury's unbeaten run against Canterbury to four matches, while it continued the personal frustration for Robbie as it took seven games, playing for either Canterbury or Canterbury Country, before he finally beat the 'Mighty Mids'.

Then followed a 12–27 loss to New Zealand Maori, who were gearing up for their tour of Wales later in the year.

Five games in and the team had already reached a key point in its development.

'We got spanked,' Robbie says. 'The Maori kept skinning us on the outside, highlighting a flaw in how we were defending, which was a system Alex had been quite set on. We had our own ideas about how we could do it better, and it led to some quite animated conversations.

'In the end, he gave way, but he was none too subtle in letting us know that we would be held accountable if the changes we made didn't work.'

If the Maori deflated the Canterbury 'bubble', that year's inter-island game did its bit to pump it up. The traditional game, which was one of the mainstays of the New Zealand calendar for 70 years through the twentieth century, was played at Wanganui in 1982 and saw the South pitted against an all-star North Island line-up that was expected to win easily.

Auckland No. 8 Glenn Rich was the only non-All Black in the North Island line-up whereas the South Island, who were coached by the little-known Mid Canterbury coach Neville Goodwin, had just four players with test experience.

Five of the South Island players — Mid Canterbury winger Geoff Frew, Mid Canterbury first five-eighths Murray Roulston, Nelson Bays No. 8 Willie Dempster, South Canterbury flanker Peter Grant and Southland flanker Leicester Rutledge — were all playing for provinces that featured in the NPC second division at the time.

'It was a classic underdog tale,' Robbie recalls. 'We were a bunch of no-names but played way above our weight. Stu Wilson got an early try for them. That may have contributed to their complacency because, once we got back into it, we realised that we were more committed than they were, and kept growing as a result.

'Even so, I don't think most of our blokes could believe it by the end. To the credit of the North Island guys, they all acknowledged afterwards that our attitude had won it.'

The difference in the desire of the two teams was emphasised by the 22–12 scoreline, which featured four tries by the South to Wilson's effort for the North.

Sadly, the annual game was shelved after 1986, being replaced by a regional concept before fading out altogether as international rugby schedules expanded leading into the professional era.

Although he acknowledges that the formats currently in place are serving the game well through Super Rugby and the test windows, with the NPC following later, Robbie believes the loss of the inter-island game is a shame.

'While it is easy enough to understand why that game has gone, the North and South Islands are obvious entities that people identify with, and the match-up brings a lot of history forward with it.'

It also provided immediate benefit for Canterbury in 1982, as the province's five reps (Robbie, Victor Simpson, Garry Hooper, John Ashworth and Bill Bush) returned boasting no doubts about their ability to measure up against All Blacks-laden provincial opponents.

'Given where we had come from, with Canterbury having struggled in the years immediately prior, that injection of confidence was important,' Robbie says. 'How could we lead others if we didn't believe ourselves?'

While the back-to-back defeats had tested the team's mettle, Canterbury made an encouraging start to the NPC with consecutive wins over Waikato (27–16) and Otago (25–18) in Christchurch.

Although the campaign wound up promoting a number of new All Blacks, Robbie says it was a player who never made it, the skipper Hayes, who was the glue for the side as it gained momentum. It is a testimony to Hayes' humility, and team-orientated focus, that he had offered to voluntarily give up the captaincy at the start of the year if Wyllie had felt a change of leadership was needed.

The coach didn't, recognising in his skipper the same qualities Robbie so admired: his selflessness, total commitment to the team and unrelenting work ethic.

'The unluckiest player I played with never to be an All Black,' Robbie says of Hayes, 'and that's a big call because [Canterbury No. 8] Dale Atkins was extremely unfortunate too.

'Donny was calm and unassuming but we all had the utmost respect for him. He'd seen a lot both on and away from the field, which included playing alongside Alex in his last seasons, both for Canterbury and with Country. This meant that he was on the same wavelength with Alex, which was important. Donny took a lot of heat for the group as, I suspect, did Bruce and I, because Alex knew all three of us pretty well and knew we could cope.

'By making examples of us, he could get a response from the whole team because he knew that everyone would be watching.'

By now, the rest of the country was starting to recognise the growing force Wyllie was developing and the side embarked on a four-match tour of the North Island with its momentum building.

That was stalled briefly by a 13–21 loss to Hawke's Bay at its first stop, but the benefits of the Wyllie fitness regime showed through in the next match against John Hart's Auckland as Canterbury rallied from 6–15 down after an hour at Eden Park to win 19–15.

Bruce scored two tries in the game, and cemented his place in the starting XV as a result, which saw All Black Steve Scott relegated to the bench for the shield challenge in Wellington a few weeks later.

'By that stage of the year, we could all sense that we were building to something good on the back of some hard work. We were still a predominantly young group but all of the lads were eager, we were fit, the senior guys were stepping up and we were enjoying each other's company.'

Game three of the trip produced a 12–3 win over a North Auckland side that had tripped Canterbury up in each of the previous two seasons.

By now, eyes were starting to turn to the upcoming shield challenge, two weeks beyond. Wyllie was most definitely in planning mode, as the players were to discover on their drive back from Whangarei the morning after they beat North Auckland. Although the results were coming, Wyllie felt the players needed to be 'sat on their bums' prior to the shield challenge so they didn't fool themselves into believing they were better than they were. It was a calculated risk.

After playing North Auckland on the Saturday, Canterbury had an appointment with a strong Manawatu side in Palmerston North four days later. By flogging the team at training on the Sunday, Wyllie knew that he was basically sacrificing that game and — as it turned out — the NPC title, but the shield was the main goal.

As Robbie would do himself in the future, Wyllie made the hard call because he believed it was what he had to do to win.

'It was a flogging. When Alex stopped the bus at Warkworth, halfway back to Auckland, and told us all to grab our gear, everyone thought he was joking at first,' Robbie recalls. 'I think we all expected to find a keg of beer waiting for us when we hit the changing rooms. We couldn't have been more wrong.'

The team trained for three hours, with an agitated Wyllie standing in the middle of the ground for that whole time barking out instructions.

'He worked himself into such a lather shouting that he was sweating profusely by the time we finished, and he hadn't moved a yard. It was the toughest single workout I've ever had and we had some tough ones. Just never for that long.'

While Wyllie never specifically mentioned the shield challenge, it was clear to the players that it was on his mind. The Canterbury boss had already been on a scouting mission to see Wellington successfully defend the shield against Hawke's Bay. He came away from that convinced his side had a real chance, provided it had the mental and physical stamina to keep attacking the holders.

Although a leg-weary Canterbury lost to Manawatu (13–26) en route to Christchurch, Robbie believes the Warkworth session was a critical part of the team's subsequent shield success.

'Alex had a philosophy, which I practise myself, that nothing in the game should tax a player any more than what he encounters at training.

'Although we lost in Palmerston North, he got his response because it galvanised the team. He'd wanted to bring us back to earth, but not too close to the shield game, so that it didn't create doubt close to the match.

'He achieved it. We finished that match strongly, beat Bay of Plenty when we got back to Christchurch, and were able to approach the shield match in a confident but realistic frame of mind.'

It is a methodology that has sustained a lot of successful teams.

But Wyllie also had another trick up his sleeve that was to prove pivotal in the successful raid on the capital. Prior to the game, Christchurch 3ZB radio commentator Ken Anderson travelled north to conduct some pre-game interviews with members of the Wellington team. One who consented to be interviewed, and has wished he hadn't ever since, was Wellington's well-regarded All Blacks fullback Allan Hewson. When asked about the prospects in the game, Hewson replied that he thought Wellington had a good chance.

Anderson's colleague at 3ZB, Barry Corbett, admits that Hewson's response was subsequently doctored by the station, with Anderson then playing the altered version to Wyllie, who erupted and demanded a copy.

The Canterbury team had been scheduled to stay in the city on the eve of the game but Wyllie wanted to keep the side away from the hype. To achieve this, he arranged for the team to swap hotels with a Corbett-led supporters group. The visiting supporters subsequently enjoyed a sleepless night at the hands of rowdy local fans, who would have been disappointed later to learn that they hadn't been upsetting the Canterbury team.

The shield holders had good reason to be confident. Not only did they boast All Blacks across the park, and a forward pack that even Wyllie knew Canterbury could not match, but they had also dished out a 31–6 drubbing when the two teams had met in Christchurch the year before.

'We'd all crammed into a tiny room at the hotel for a final word before we departed for the ground,' Robbie recalls.

'Then Alex produces this tape and plays it. I couldn't believe what I was hearing. Here was Allan Hewson — who was about to play against us — being asked what Canterbury should do and essentially saying that we should get on the first boat home because we had no chance. It was an incredible thing to say and it didn't surprise me later to find out it had been doctored.'

Not only did the comments fuel the Canterbury fire, they also reinforced a policy Robbie has lived by ever since, as have players in his teams — never give ammunition to your opponents through the press. Assume always, in any interview, that you are talking directly to the guy you are going to play against.

While this philosophy undoubtedly has tested quote-reliant media personnel through the years, most notably during his stint as Wallaby coach, it has also helped Robbie's teams win games, as it helped on the windy day in Wellington.

'We'd always given the wind away when we played in those conditions,' Robbie says. 'It suited our psyche. Get into our work, role up our sleeves, and deny, deny, deny our opposition, until it was our turn to play with the breeze.'

It was risky if Wellington forged a big lead, but the 'fuel' unintentionally supplied by the home fullback stoked up the challengers. Hewson discovered this first hand when he was felled by a crude off-the-ball elbow from Canterbury prop John Ashworth, who was his All Blacks teammate.

Thirty-two years on, the victim can joke now that the elbow was '10 minutes' after the whistle had blown, but it produced a storm at the time, having broken Hewson's cheek. Hewson was out of the game. To the Athletic Park crowd, the Canterbury team were a bunch of thugs.

Such was the depth of the anti-Hewson feeling among the Canterbury team, the normally mild-mannered Jock Hobbs called out to the stricken

Wellington fullback as he was escorted from the field: 'Are you off to catch that boat now Hewie?'

The 'thugs' kept in touch at halftime thanks to a try created by Robbie for winger Hooper, but Wellington still led 12–10 entering the final 10 minutes of the contest. The challengers didn't panic.

'We were always within a kick of winning because we had the breeze,' Robbie says. 'So we were odds on to get a penalty if we weren't able to score a try. Even at that point of our development as a team, we were no longer burdened by the fear of losing as we had been in the previous few years. It was the opportunity to win that drove us on.'

The 'opportunity' presented itself with seven minutes to go when Wayne Smith dashed to the line on the short side from a ruck. Robbie drilled the conversion from wide out, and was later named player of the match, as Canterbury completed a 16–12 win to start the province's eighth Ranfurly Shield tenure.

The surreal nature of the outcome was added to afterwards when the Canterbury team fulfilled a prearranged commitment to film an advertisement for new sponsors Fresh Up fruit juice, back in the dressing room.

Robbie gained good 'brownie points' from the ad: he later worked for the fruit juice company in its distribution arm.

The side returned to Christchurch later that evening to joyous scenes, with 10,000 people packing out the city's airport to welcome the team home while 3ZB, who proved fantastic promoters throughout the four-year tenure, broadcast the team's arrival reception live.

'It was quite an incredible scene [at the airport] and totally blew us away. We had no idea just how much winning the shield would capture the public's imagination, how much it meant to them,' Robbie recalls.

Winning it is one thing. Holding onto it, quite another. The first defence seven days later was a daunting prospect: Counties, a team brimming with All Blacks and seasoned provincial performers who'd toyed with Canterbury in recent seasons, winning four straight, had won the NPC just two years previously but had never won the shield.

Complicating matters even further, Robbie had broken a bone in his wrist, which had made it difficult to tackle in the final stages against

Wellington because he couldn't grip with one hand. Unbeknown to the public, he underwent scans the morning after the team returned to Christchurch.

'The doctors wanted to put it in a plaster cast following the X-ray, but I said no way. That would have been season over and there were still two games to play. We ended up strapping it in a protective canvas brace, with the brace holding in place a spoon which my wrist rested on for support.'

Robbie acknowledges that the damaged wrist made his life difficult as he was impeded by it, most notably in his passing. He also suspects that news of the injury had reached Counties ears, as they peppered him with kicks during their challenge. This surprised Canterbury, who had expected the challengers to run it from every opportunity given the talented back division they possessed, which included arguably New Zealand's best centre of all time, Bruce Robertson.

In an attempt to protect his players from the excitement building around their first defence, Wyllie kept the team's weekly routine the same as it had been all year. This meant the players all made their own way to the ground on match day, before assembling for the pre-game team-talk.

The trouble was that seemingly half of Christchurch was heading to the same place, which was something the Canterbury team hadn't factored into its planning. It was an easily understandable error: Canterbury hadn't drawn a crowd remotely resembling the 37,000 of this day, in recent years. This resulted in the players being scattered all around Lancaster Park as they desperately tried to find car parking, then make their way through the throng of excited well-wishers to the relative calm of the dressing shed.

Robbie estimates he had to park a mile away from the ground. Smith, the try-scoring hero from Wellington, had even further to go. He finally pitched up, his back all 'patted' out, just before the team meeting started, an hour before kick-off.

'Whereas I'd been relatively calm pre-game the week before, you could feel the nerves in the dressing room this time. We'd had a dress rehearsal as a challenger against Waikato, before winning it at our second attempt.

'Being cast as the defender was different again, and we didn't really know how to go about it.'

Fortunately, Counties, who'd suffered heart-breaking results in its previous two challenges, being beaten 11–9 by Auckland in 1979 before drawing 20–20 with Waikato two years later; appeared to be playing with similar jitters.

No tries were scored. Robbie kicked two penalty goals, while Smith added two dropped goals, but Canterbury trailed 12–15 with two minutes to go when Southland referee Kerry Henderson pulled the Counties backs up for offside. It was just as well. By the time Henderson blew his whistle, Counties winger Robert Kururangi had intercepted the ball and was streaking away for what would have been the shield-winning try.

The penalty was 40 metres out. A decision had to be made but Hayes didn't utter a word. Robbie made those decisions, he says. If Robbie wanted to take the kick, he'd just walk up and take the ball. Words were never exchanged.

'I'd missed one from a handier position earlier in the game which had hit the upright,' Robbie recalls. 'It was obviously an important kick but you don't think like that in the moment. I was completely positive that I could get it and didn't think about anything else.

'Rather than being nervous, I was more thankful to have another opportunity, having missed that one earlier.'

Up in the grandstand, the man who had first let him loose as a goal-kicker was confidently telling those around him that the shield was in safe hands or, more pointedly, resting on a safe boot.

Robbie always knew what he was doing, Fergie McCormick says. He says Robbie wouldn't have stepped forward so quickly like he did if he hadn't believed absolutely that he was going to kick the goal.

The kick never looked like missing. It cleared the cross bar easily, taking Counties' shield dreams with it. The men from South Auckland had to wait another 31 years before they finally got their hands on the trophy for the first time.

Having coolly nailed the goal that mattered to secure both a 15–15 draw and retention of the shield, Robbie suffered a delayed bout of nerves back in the changing rooms.

'It was when I saw the Counties boys come into our shed, and seeing how distraught they were after another near miss, that I got the shakes.

It was only then that I began to think about the significance of that kick and what the consequences would have been, emotionally, had I missed.'

Even though the game hadn't been won, the Counties match was the foundation stone for the 24 successful shield defences across four years that followed.

'We scrambled well in that game, but we were like a team in its first defence with no previous experience. We certainly didn't know how to apply the advantage we had of knowing what shield rugby was all about, because we had the experience of already having won it,' Robbie explains. 'We never looked back from that point. We learned to use the psychological advantage that we had.

'If we held onto the shield, so it didn't move around the country, it meant that every team who challenged us did so, mostly with players who'd never challenged before.

'And they arrived knowing that they wouldn't get a shot at it for another two years if they failed. That builds its own pressure on the challenger, while we were used to the step up that comes with shield rugby because we were playing under that pressure every time we defended it.

'Certainly, the familiarity we had with the pressure played its part in the hyped-up defences of 1983 and 1984 against Auckland and Otago respectively. In each of those games, we exposed their inexperience in the arena and profited from that.'

Five days after the Counties defence, shield duty called again as Canterbury hosted that year's first division newcomers Wairarapa-Bush, who'd made a fair fist of their maiden season in the top league, winning three matches and drawing one.

Absorbing the lesson from the previous weekend, Wyllie assembled the team at Shirley Lodge the night before, beginning a routine that would continue through until the end of the shield tenure.

It might have been a midweek game with an end-of-season feel to it, but 21,000 still converged on Lancaster Park to watch the holders dish out a good old-fashioned hiding. Scoring nine tries to none, Canterbury made a mess of the outclassed North Islanders, advancing from a 31–0 halftime lead to win 51–6.

While he didn't score a try, and the 15 points he kicked weren't as significant for the team as the crucial three he'd landed in the 78th minute the Saturday before, the points haul did lift Robbie's tally for the representative season to 219. This surpassed the 213 accumulated by Wellington fullback Mick Williment for the most points scored in a New Zealand season, breaking a record that had stood for 16 years.

It also reinforced Robbie's contribution to Canterbury's success, although his teammates and the public were already well aware of that: despite playing with a broken wrist in the last two matches, he finished the year having won the man of the match award in each of the final three games.

Four years on from needing some of the big boppers of the Canterbury forward pack to push start his car after winning Colts Player of the Year, he was back at the CRFU awards night picking up the senior Player of the Year trophy. He was even able to drive away under his own steam this time!

And there was more treasure to come in 1983.

The goalposts on the family farm Kilmarnock, in North Canterbury, where Robbie honed a craft that would make him a household name. Note the height of the uprights.

Glenmark's Under-11 invincibles of 1970: Played 12, won 9, drew 3. Four of the players pictured went on to become All Blacks — Richard Loe (top left, fourth row), Andy Earl (third from right , third row), Bruce Deans (far right, third row) and Robbie, who was team captain (third from left, second row).

Deans Family Collection

Above: A big crowd watches Robbie burst down the sideline as Christ's College ends 12 years of hurt by inflicting a 13–0 defeat on Christchurch Boys' High in the traditional schools clash in 1977.

Fairfax Media

Right: A Black Cap in the making? Robbie is a study of caution for Old Collegians during the Christchurch first grade cricket final at Lancaster Park.

Bruce 'taught' Robbie all about the value of competition on the front lawn of the family farm: here the siblings meet on one of the few occasions where they played on opposite sides, for the Lincoln College and Christchurch clubs respectively.

Robbie in full cry for Canterbury against Queensland at Ballymore in Brisbane in 1980. A head knock suffered later in the match resulted in a delayed concussion, which prompted a post-match visit from Bob Templeton to check on his well-being. Robbie never forgot the legendary Queensland coach's gesture.

It was easy to see who the fan's favourite was at Athletic Park prior to Canterbury's successful Ranfurly Shield raid on Wellington in 1982.

Above: To the victors go the spoils. The 1982 Canterbury team poses in the changing room with their prize, shortly after reclaiming the Ranfurly Shield from Wellington.

Left: The Ranfurly Shield was back in Canterbury for the first time in nine years and the Deans boys played a big part in it. Here the brothers show off the trophy after the successful challenge against Wellington.

Bob Deans' All Blacks blazer appears to be a good fit as Robbie displays the original jerseys from the infamous 1905 Test between the original All Blacks and Wales.

It came 78 years too late, but a Deans is finally awarded a try at Cardiff Arms Park! Wayne Smith (right) acts as referee, confirming Robbie's 'score', during a visit by some of the 1983 All Blacks touring party to the scene of one of New Zealand rugby's greatest controversies.

Welcome to France! Robbie's familiar style is visible through the rain as he kicks for goal during his debut for Grenoble in 1983.

Robbie kicks for goal against South Australia in 1984 on a night where his 43 points set a new record for an All Black in one match. The Adelaide haul, which was also a world record at the time, has been bettered just once since. Simon Culhane scored 45 points against Japan at the 1995 Rugby World Cup.

The Deans clan at rest during the summer of 1985, with Robbie's knee in a brace following the operation on his ruptured ACL. With five children under the age of six years between them, they were a great source of support and humour. (From left) Jock Hobbs, Sarah, Robbie, Jo, Bruce and Nicky.

The Canterbury backs among the Cavaliers take time out from training in South Africa (from left: Robbie, Wayne Smith, Victor Simpson, Craig Green, Warwick Taylor). Note the adidas stripes and sponsor's logo on the Cavaliers training kit worn by Robbie.

5

'WE ARE RED AND BLACK, RED AND BLACK'S GOT THE SHIELD!'

The return of the Ranfurly Shield for the first time in nine years couldn't have come at a better juncture for Canterbury. While it would be stretching it to say that the shield rescued the game in the province, its presence certainly helped rugby recover some of the ground it had lost as a result of the previous year's controversial South African tour.

Its associated hype also helped to counter the rise of soccer. Even though the All Whites qualified for the World Cup again 28 years later, the epic 15-match journey of the John Adshead-coached and Steve Sumner-led New Zealand soccer side through to the country's maiden World Cup finals in 1982 captured the imagination of the public in a manner no sport other than rugby has ever achieved. While New Zealand was soundly beaten in all three matches at the finals in Spain, the mere appearance of the country's best at the same table as heavyweights like Brazil gave soccer a shot in the arm right at the moment when the previously unchallenged national game was at its most vulnerable.

Junior soccer numbers shot up and suddenly kids were wanting to grow up to be like Steve Sumner, strikers Steve Wooddin and Wynton Rufer, or other stars of the All Whites, as opposed to the biggest-name All Blacks of the time such as winger Stu Wilson, halfback Dave Loveridge or flanker and skipper Graham Mourie.

In the public's response to the shield, the Canterbury Rugby Union through its promotional representative Vic Thomas recognised an opportunity, as did the coach Alex Wyllie. They enlisted Radio 3ZB as a key support. With a summer to plan on the back of the two successful defences which had closed out 1982, and a support base already in place given that 58,000 had attended those two matches, both parties knew they were onto a winner.

And the individual who was to form one of the key planks of the campaign, as the focal point of the theme that was to be the flagship of the whole era was a less than flattered Robbie.

Barry Corbett, who had performed an unlikely service during the challenge by swapping hotels for the team with his supporters' party, became the hub for promotions via his high-rating breakfast programme. The station's innovations included the introduction of the 3ZB cheerleaders team, the production of Grizz Wyllie face masks, organisation and publicity around the hugely popular game day parades, and opportunities to win match tickets to sit in the specially named Corbett's corner section of the ground.

But it was the theme song, 'Give it a boot Robbie', for which both Corbett and the station's overall shield campaign is best remembered.

While aware even then that Robbie was a reluctant front man in public, Corbett says his role in both winning the shield and then saving it a week later had created a hero status within the province that the promotional bandwagon simply had to cash in on.

The tune from the popular Ottawan song of the time, 'Hands Up', was chosen, with Corbett and 3ZB programme director Chris Muirhead combining to write lyrics which, even now, make Robbie bristle. 'Give it a boot Robbie' was played on air, over the public address system at games, and at the shield parades through the city. Even allowing for the wide distribution, the man whose raucous and out-of-tune tones shrieked out the words admits its popularity exceeded all expectations. All people could remember was the chorus, 'Give it a boot Robbie', but that didn't appear to matter, Corbett says. The song took off, with the station deluged by requests for a copy.

Corbett still fields requests. There was a significant surge from Australian media outlets wanting to buy the song when Robbie was appointed as Wallabies coach in 2008. The song was never released publicly as the station didn't hold the rights to the 'Hands Up' song, although he says there would have been significant money to be made if it had. While station hierarchy knew Robbie 'loathed' the song, having heard via a media interview shortly after its first release that he wasn't a fan, Corbett says they appreciated that he understood why the promotion had been put together in the first place.

The radio announcer did promise Robbie he would never release it, even staging an on-air burning of what was supposed to be the only copy, although good hits never totally die, especially when mischievous characters like Andrew Mehrtens are on the case.

A child of the 1982–85 shield era, Mehrtens begged Corbett for a copy of the song when Robbie became manager of the Crusaders in 1997. This led to an uncomfortable surprise for the new team organiser before a pre-season game in Greymouth. Its subject was out on the field with the Crusaders team assisting with the warm-up as he always does, when some familiar lyrics started blasting out of the public address system. 'Give it a boot Robbie, give it a boot, when the heat's on, Robbie's got the boots on, boot it Robbie!'

'He wasn't happy with me,' Corbett recalls, 'but I was able to deflect the blame onto Mehrts.' In truth, it is a testament to Robbie's popularity as a player and a person, and all he has done for the province, Corbett says, that the song is still so well remembered, 32 years on.

While 3ZB did other rugby-related songs as the era unfolded, such as 'Red and Black's Got the Shield' which was taken from the popular movie of the time, *Flashdance*, none reached anything like the level that was achieved by 'Give it a Boot'.

Shield festivities and songs were the last thing on Robbie's mind as the 1983 season began. The Canterbury team was aware that it was now the hunted, rather than the hunter, as it sized up a demanding schedule of challenges that included a vengeance-filled Wellington and the new NPC champions, Auckland.

Robbie's road to the Canterbury programme started with the Canterbury Country representative side, for whom he'd been able to debut the previous year after returning to Glenmark, having played for Town in two of the three seasons before that. The Country side, which was selected out of the Ellesmere and North Canterbury club competitions, always prepared for the annual Queen's Birthday fixture with Town by conducting a southern tour for matches against its Otago and Southland counterparts. Other matches were usually organised against neighbouring unions who were preparing for the South Island second division championship such as Mid and South Canterbury, Marlborough and Nelson Bays.

It was often said in local circles that 'when Country rugby was strong, Canterbury rugby was strong'. Never was this more in evidence than in 1983 when the Country team that departed for its tour boasted most of the Ranfurly Shield holder's forward pack, allied to the scheming of the Deans brothers in behind.

Hayes, who also led the Country side, says Robbie was in his element on those tours, which the pair later experienced as coaches. The tours were uncomplicated, hard rugby, but good fun, Hayes says. With so many Canterbury representatives in the side, the players spent a lot of time together and so knew each other well, which Hayes remembers led to many a 'misadventure' off the field, although there was never any trouble involving the law.

Such was the Country dominance of the era, between 1975 and 1990, the farmers won 11 matches to Town's four, with the 1978 contest for the Craw Trophy drawn 9–9.

A notable exception proved to be 1983, which was somewhat surprising given the strength of the Country team. While the Town side of that year played with ruthless efficiency, the injury that was administered to Country pride was partly self-inflicted.

'We played five games in nine days, which included the tour. Those country versus country representative games were always tough. There was no quarter given, regardless of who you were,' Robbie says.

'This particular year, we'd played a club game before we went away, then played Otago Country, before playing Southland Country at Riversdale prior to coming home. We'd won all three so spirits were high — a little too high as it turned out.'

The Southland game was played in dreadful conditions. And Robbie admits the post-game revelry probably didn't help. The result was that most of the team returned from its southern stint with the flu.

'We had another club game, a few days after we got back, with the Saturday [club] game being followed by the game against Town on the Monday of Queen's Birthday weekend.

'That was the big one of the year, the one we all looked forward to, the "test" if you like. Some of the guys couldn't play, some shouldn't have, and it's fair to say that we were well short of our best,' Robbie says, 'and that was, on paper anyway, probably the strongest Country team that was ever assembled.'

If Town's 42–6 win (which was avenged by Country with a 39–6 reply the following year) came as a huge shock, it did highlight the level of competition for places in the Canterbury team, which Wyllie would use to keep all of the players honest.

The focal point of the New Zealand winter for 1983 was a full tour by the British & Irish Lions, and Canterbury warmed up for its crack at the tourists with wins over New Zealand Universities (37–6), Marlborough (16–10) and West Coast (23–9). The team also visited Brisbane prior to meeting the Lions, and Ballymore produced another tight game, although, as in 1981, Queensland shaded its visitors, this time winning 17–12.

Canterbury would not lose again in 1983.

While the Lions match was curiously scheduled for midweek, four days out from the opening test at Lancaster Park, a packed house watched a riveting game. It went down to the final whistle as Lions fullback Hugo MacNeill missed a sideline conversion, which would have stolen a draw for the visitors. Even the most patriotic of visitors would have conceded that any outcome other than Canterbury's 22–20 success would have been undeserved as the side led for much of the contest before the Lions made a concerted late effort to salvage the game. Incredibly for a province with such a proud record, the win was Canterbury's first against a major touring side since the 1959 defeat of the same visitor.

Robbie says the shield experience of the previous year was already paying dividends.

'It was helping. We'd developed an ability to handle the big atmosphere and the mentality required for one-off winner-take-all occasions.'

The win over Wellington, and the draw with Counties, had also taught the players to believe in their preparation and not to panic on the field.

'The Counties game in particular gave the group a deep-seated belief that if we'd done the work through our preparation, we could work our way out of anything. Being able to get out of that game with the shield taught us to live in the moment, and the moment alone.'

It's a philosophy that was a big part of Robbie the player, and is one of his key preachings as a coach.

Robbie's 18 points against the Lions, which included one of Canterbury's two tries, added further fuel to the national debate already raging over the respective merits of Deans and Allan Hewson as the country's premier fullback.

Nor was it a mere midweek combination that Robbie had starred against as nine of the same Lions players turned out again at the weekend as a late Hewson goal confirmed a 16–12 win for the All Blacks in the opening test.

Robbie warmed the bench behind the Wellingtonian for all four of the tests against the Lions, and says that although the rivalry played out in the media and public domain, it was never an issue for either Hewson or himself.

Of greater concern was the start of the NPC and shield season, with the former being kicked off by away wins over Wairarapa-Bush (36–7) and Otago (24–9), before the first of the shield challenges against North Otago.

Recent years have been kind to the men from the greater Waitaki Valley, reaping lower division titles in 2002, 2007 and 2010 along with the provision to the game of a once in a lifetime player by the name of Richie McCaw. But the state of the game was far different in Oamaru and its surrounds 31 years ago. The most minor of the minnows, there were genuine fears a total of cricket proportions could be accrued and so it proved as Canterbury humiliated the challengers to the tune of a record 88–0 scoreline. The mark was subsequently beaten a decade later when Auckland, with tries now worth five points, beat up on North Otago 139–5.

Canterbury scored 17 tries against North Otago, equalling the existing mark held by Hawke's Bay; Robbie scored three of them, alongside 10 conversions, to set a new record for an individual in a shield game with 32 points.

It fell in the Auckland massacre a decade later when All Blacks winger

John Kirwan helped himself to eight tries.

While North Otago was always going to be outclassed, Robbie says the excitement of defending the shield again meant that his teammates were never going to ease off as the score mounted.

'They had the thrill of a challenge and got an insight into what it was all about,' Robbie says of the North Otago players, 'but they were up against us at a time when we were excited about retaining the shield but also understood the tenuous nature of it.'

That mentality sustained Canterbury through a set of early challenges which saw off Southland 28–10, despite hooker John Buchan being sent off, before Mid Canterbury (28–0), North Auckland (39–9) and South Canterbury (50–12) were also dispatched.

Mid Canterbury, which had been so troublesome in recent seasons, was always going to be accorded special attention. This became even more so after Wyllie received a telegram from Ashburton in the week prior to the game requesting that he polish up the shield before the Mid Canterbury team came up to collect it.

'They, or their supporters anyway, made a lot of noise. It was similar to the Otago challenge the year after. With all of the bravado beforehand, there was simply no way that we were going to allow ourselves to get caught out,' Robbie says.

'Teams that win the shield have historically flown under the radar in the main. Because of the recent history — that was my first-ever win against them — we saw Mid Canterbury coming a long way off.'

Ironically, when Mid Canterbury slipped into Christchurch on the quiet two years later, they nearly spoilt all of the plans for the dream showdown between Canterbury and Auckland, getting to within two points before eventually succumbing 17–7.

A break from shield activity saw Canterbury back on NPC duty with a three-match tour of the North Island yielding wins over Waikato (22–14), Bay of Plenty (26–24) and Counties (37–3). The wins proved important in shoring up Canterbury's NPC bid, but as the scorelines show, only the third was convincing. This illustrated the difficulty the side was to have trying to reproduce the intensity of the shield matches away from home when the trophy wasn't on the line.

The shield show restarted with a 32–3 win over Hawke's Bay at a sodden Lancaster Park, with the game providing an entrée prior to what was unquestionably the toughest successful defence of the entire reign, the epic 20–16 win over Wellington.

Wyllie expected the capital to provide another stern test. As with the successful challenge of the year before, he provided a novel means of motivation immediately prior to the team's departure for the ground.

Team manager Les McFadden had been instructed to find a Wellington team jersey to use as a focal point for the preparation, which was not as easy to do in those days as now, where replica team apparel is readily available in stores. McFadden was told the jersey had to be returned, which helped him to secure it. What he didn't know was it would be returned in shreds, having been placed on the ground where all of the players had to trample on it before getting onto the bus to take their seats. It was, McFadden says, a great example of the Wyllie way, which he described as 'coaching by fear'. In this instance, he was demanding his players be ruthless.

'Wellington were better prepared than the year before, when they may have underestimated us, and it showed,' Robbie says. 'It was still essentially the same team as they'd had the previous year, with all the same All Blacks, and they knew all about the requirements of shield rugby, so we didn't have that same advantage that we had against everyone else.'

Ironically, though, it was the failure of the challengers to take one key scoring opportunity that ultimately cost their chance of revenge. All Blacks winger Bernie Fraser dropped the ball, diving for the goal-line in the 31st minute. The try would have taken his side out to an 18–6 advantage. Even though Canterbury still had the wind to come, and the breeze proved to be significant, Robbie believes a successful comeback would have been too big an ask against a side as experienced and seasoned in shield rugby as Wellington was.

Although Wellington dominated the game both territorially and in possession, two tries against the run of play by Robbie's future Crusaders manager Tony Thorpe kept Canterbury in it, while the Fraser no-try and two other key turning points tipped the balance their way.

The first, which aroused intense anger on the Wellington side after the injury suffered by Hewson the year before, saw visiting lock Murray Pierce rubbed out of the game after his jaw was broken by a Canterbury punch. Robbie didn't see the incident, and says it wasn't spoken about in the dressing room afterwards, but its impact was significant. With Pierce gone, Canterbury's lineout lost its major obstacle.

Wellington still led 16–13 with 14 minutes remaining when Canterbury received a penalty on its own 10-metre line. Before Hayes even had time to look around, Robbie had stepped forward, backing himself to make the distance down wind.

'Nothing was said, but it was the only time Donny ever questioned me,' Robbie says. 'He just gave me this eyebrow raise as if to say: "Are you sure?" It was just as well I got the kick.'

The goal broke Wellington, and Hayes finished them off, scoring the final try from a scrum to seal a memorable 20–16 victory.

'He used Hewie, who was defending on the blindside, as a turnstile but, to be fair, I don't think anyone would have stopped Donny then.'

The Wellington challenge was followed a week later by that of Auckland, which had beaten Wellington on the final day of the previous season to pip Canterbury for the NPC title. It was the Auckland union's centenary year, and the side, coached by the already high-profile John Hart, arrived amid huge expectations but found the momentum Canterbury had gained unstoppable.

Even though the scores were tied 6–6 after 30 minutes, the challengers were barely holding on. The game was blown open by two Canterbury tries before halftime, which gave the hosts a 14–6 advantage. Three more in the second half finished off a 31–9 win, which not only kept the shield safe but also stitched up Canterbury's second NPC title with a game to spare.

'It was a game where everything just clicked,' Robbie says. 'Everything that we tried came off, and we had a bit of luck on our side too.'

Inevitably after such highs, there is a let-down, and Canterbury experienced one in the season's final defence against Manawatu. While Manawatu was a side coming to the end of its cycle, with a number of senior servants on the verge of retirement, it had beaten Wyllie's men the year before, and looked for most of the match as if it was capable of a repeat.

With five All Blacks in its forward pack, marshalled by the experienced All Black Mark Donaldson from halfback, the visitors dominated possession to such an extent that Canterbury was hanging on, even though it led 18–15 with 25 minutes to play.

'They were old-school — hard and physical,' recalls Robbie.

'If anything, they probably cost themselves in the end by opting to try to go wide, spreading the ball at a time when they were really grinding us down in the forwards. It had been working but they lost patience and that allowed us to get ourselves out of it.'

A 15-minute siege of the Canterbury line, as intense as the side experienced throughout the entire four-season reign, was only lifted when a mess-up among the Manawatu backs saw the ball dropped, allowing Canterbury to boot it downfield. The home side scored a try a minute later, and another before the final whistle, to round out a phenomenal year with a slightly deceptive 28–15 win.

Canterbury had won 18 of its 19 matches, with Robbie extending the record he had created the previous year for the most points in a representative season, setting the new standard at 281.

As significant as the results were, one of the biggest influences Robbie believes the team had on the province was through the spread of its player roots. A large number of clubs had representation, which brought their districts along with them.

'We had players from right across Canterbury and that was an important part of the team's success through that era. Ellesmere and North Canterbury were well represented as were the Town clubs. What that did is it allowed the whole province to identify with the team and its achievements.

'Everyone knew someone who was either in the team, or was close to someone in the group. That encouraged the public to embrace both the team and its success. The depth of the support we had showed through in the turnouts at the shield parades, and at the games themselves.'

The final three matches of 1983 alone saw 127,000 people click through the turnstiles at Lancaster Park.

Being able to identify with the team, which Wyllie believed hadn't been the case prior to the shield era, brought the public on board. It was something Robbie didn't forget when he joined the Crusaders as manager, 14 years after the historic 1983 season.

'The importance of the public being able to identify with the team was the same when professional rugby started as it had been in 1983. At the start of Super Rugby when the Crusaders were created, it was taken for granted that the new brand would carry over the traditions of Canterbury rugby.

'It didn't. In many cases, the players had been shipped in from elsewhere and didn't identify with the local community, who had no reason to identify with them.'

The All Blacks selectors certainly identified with the Canterbury team's success of 1983, elevating seven of them, including Robbie, to the touring party for the end-of-season trip to England and Scotland.

Nor did Canterbury's momentum slow as 1984 started, with the side winning its first nine matches, which included shield defences against Nelson Bays (34–10), Buller (57–13) and West Coast (68–3). This allowed the team to set a new national record of 26 consecutive wins through 1983 and 1984, before the run was halted by a draw with Manawatu at Palmerston North. That result was followed by a more ominous afternoon at Eden Park where Hart's Auckland took their revenge for the previous year's shield humiliation, handing out a 32–3 spanking of their own.

The defeat, and the draw that came before it, highlighted the energy that defending the shield was taking out of the Canterbury side. The drubbing also signposted the threat Auckland would pose if the shield was still in place when it returned to Christchurch the following year.

Canterbury returned home to see off Wairarapa-Bush (24–6) for the second time in the shield era, but the year's big challenge was from Otago, who'd been enjoying a renaissance under the guidance of the former All Blacks fullback and future test coach Laurie Mains.

Emerging out of similar doldrums to those from which Wyllie had guided Canterbury, Otago would go on to win its maiden NPC title under Mains, although that breakthrough wasn't achieved until 1991.

Otago had won five of its first seven in the NPC when it arrived in Christchurch, with the excitement that was building in the south reflected by the invasion of the city that accompanied the team. The Canterbury players couldn't miss the southerners' presence. A supporters' group shared the Shirley Lodge accommodation with the team the evening before the game and made sure fellow residents knew of their presence!

'There was banging on my wall all night as well as a few prank phone calls to the room. A lot of the other guys reported the same thing the next morning. Most of us got little sleep,' Robbie recalls.

'We took it out on their team. Our mood was such that there was no way we were going to let them win the shield.'

And how. If Auckland had been dominated in one of the feature games the year before, Otago was simply outclassed, with Robbie scoring 25 points, and Canterbury five tries on their way to a 44–3 rout.

'It was a day when everything just stuck. If you play for long enough, you will be able to recall at least one time where it goes like that.

'We pulled out a move early on in the game we called a triple scissors. We'd practised it a lot in training but never tried it in a game. It worked perfectly and Andrew McMaster on the wing scored. It was that kind of day.'

After humiliating Otago, Waikato (16–10), Counties (27–19) and Bay of Plenty (18–13) were all fended off to end the year, although the last match was to have major implications for the future of Robbie's career when he ruptured the anterior cruciate ligament in his knee.

The injury was most likely sustained in the week leading up to the match when Robbie came to grief while riding a motorbike when he was working with Bruce on the family property.

'It was quite sore, but it settled down quickly so we kept on. It was only when I looked back in the time after that I realised falling off the bike was where I probably initiated the damage.

'When it happened in game, it popped when I went to step a defender, untouched. I tried to run it off, but it quickly became clear that it was ruptured. It can be misleading with an ACL rupture as the pain quickly subsides.'

The operation exposed a ruptured ACL as well as a damaged medial ligament and some torn cartilage in the knee, leaving Robbie's career in limbo as he contemplated a summer of rehabilitation.

'My big fear was that it could be terminal as I knew of others who had lost their careers to exactly that injury,' Robbie says.

One was his former flatmate Mark Romans who'd had a promising career, which included selection in the Junior All Blacks (New Zealand Under-23s), terminated by a ruptured ACL. He never played again after sustaining the injury.

Robbie remains grateful to his surgeon Dave Walton who did an expert job putting his knee back together, as he tested it while building up the strength of the joint through a programme dominated by time on his bicycle.

It was hard work but, ever determined, Robbie was not about to miss the big events that lay ahead in 1985.

6

MATCH OF THE CENTURY

The start of 1985 found Robbie racing against the clock.

Not only did Canterbury have the Ranfurly Shield to defend, there was an All Blacks tour of South Africa to consider, and Robbie didn't fancy the prospect of missing out on either as he worked to conclude the rehabilitation of his injured knee from the year before.

When he finally did make it back, Robbie found that he was a bit slower than he had been, and had lost what he estimates to have been about 10 metres in distance on his kicks, both out of hand and place kicking.

'It made me a better player,' he says emphatically, 'because I adapted and started using the players who were around me a lot better.'

Not that he enjoyed the rehabilitation process.

'There was a lot of anxiety,' he recalls. 'I spent a lot of time thinking about it. After any injury, but particularly one as serious as that, you always wonder whether you will make it back, whether it can be the same as before.

'Because of what was coming up, there was a rushed element to my rehab, which in itself created nerves.'

There were times when Robbie was unsure as to whether he would make it back. During one of these, he resolved to do something for the next generation of Canterbury players by putting together a paper to present to the CRFU board. It stated a case for the union to be financially compensating players who were required to travel in order to represent the province.

The board, albeit reluctantly, agreed, introducing an allowance which covered transport costs such as petrol, for players, primarily from the country, who previously had to wear the costs themselves of getting to and from representative team commitments.

The victory, Robbie discovered, was somewhat token. He and Bruce estimated the $125 they subsequently received as travel compensation equated to less than one cent per kilometre!

Robbie finally made his return for Glenmark during a club game at Southbrook. The outing provided a scare afterwards when his knee blew up. This saw a pint of blood drained out of it, the swelling the result of some broken scar tissue.

Canterbury captain Don Hayes remembers Robbie's anxiousness to return after the six-month rehab, but the Canterbury coach, after watching Robbie play for Glenmark, decided he needed more time.

While it was difficult to accept, Robbie concedes that Alex Wyllie was correct to hold him back. Cast into the same situation during his own coaching career, Robbie has always erred on the side of caution.

'The episode highlighted to me that coaches know best,' Robbie says. 'They see the whole picture of the team. While some players do see beyond themselves and take the lead, the majority don't. Most just see their own small part in the world. If anything, the advent of professionalism has only intensified this, with money now involved.'

Had the scheduled All Blacks tour of South Africa gone ahead, Robbie may not have played for Canterbury in 1985. With Wyllie holding him back, he still hadn't worn the Canterbury colours by the time Southland was turned over 53–0 in the third shield defence of the year following wins over King Country (33–0) and Taranaki (27–3).

The Southland match had been slated as the farewell for the province's seven All Blacks (including Robbie) who had been chosen to be part of the South African expedition.

Canterbury's next defence, against Marlborough, came 25 days later. By then, the legal challenge to the tour that had been pursued through the High Court by Auckland lawyers Patrick Finnigan and Phillip Recordon had been upheld. The All Blacks' visit to South Africa, in an official capacity at any rate, was off.

That meant Robbie did make his representative return playing for Canterbury. While back on the paddock, he says that it took a long time before he felt comfortable again.

'While over time I was better, for a start I was tentative, building up my confidence again. It took a fair while before I was able to feel that I was comfortable again and able to play fully spontaneously.'

His return came as Canterbury beat Marlborough 42–4. A month later, shield duty returned, with Canterbury having won four NPC matches away from home in the interim to gets its NPC campaign back on track following a surprise midweek loss against Wairarapa-Bush in Masterton.

The next challenge was from Mid Canterbury. The low-key affair, for which just 7500 people turned out, nearly proved to be the ultimate banana skin. Although Canterbury won 17–7, the warning signs were obvious with the much-anticipated defence against Auckland just two weeks away.

By beating Mid Canterbury, the team had defended the shield for the 24th occasion, which set a new Canterbury record, eclipsing the 23 defences made by the class of 1953–56.

A week later, in turning back North Auckland 29–3, the side equalled the 25 defences of the Fred Allen-coached Auckland side of 1960–63, which had previously held sole ownership of the record for the most successful games in one shield tenure.

So all was in readiness for the 'Match of the Century': the two best sides in the land, playing for both the shield and in all probability the NPC title, as well as history — sole possession of the shield record for Canterbury, or preservation of a share of the mark for Auckland.

Aware of the upcoming record, Wyllie had seen to it that the Auckland match had been scheduled to decide the record, saying it would have been inappropriate for Canterbury to have been playing anyone else.

Thanks to the cancellation of the All Blacks tour, both teams had full musters for a match that drew 52,000 to Lancaster Park. Had the tour gone ahead, the All Blacks would have been playing a test in South Africa on the same day. As it was, the ground was bulging to the extent that the crowd spilled onto the sidelines, and the day made a big impression on the next generation.

When Bruce Deans scored a try in the corner to begin Canterbury's valiant second half fight-back, a blond-headed youngster decked out in a red and black jersey was to be seen jumping up and down for joy near the corner flag next to where Bruce had scored. The youngster would go on to become arguably the most influential player in Canterbury rugby since Robbie: it was Andrew Mehrtens.

On the day the shield was finally lost, Canterbury went down fighting. Against an all-star Auckland outfit that would go on to hold the shield for 10 days short of eight years through a remarkable 61 defences, the home side was stunned by an opening onslaught that saw the challengers romp to a 24–0 halftime advantage.

'It was an incredibly frustrating game,' Robbie recalls, 'we just never got started. You always hope that you will play well on the day when something like that [the shield era] ends, but we didn't.

'It was a huge disappointment, even if we lost it to a side that is probably measured, quite correctly, as the best in New Zealand provincial history.'

Hayes remembers expecting a full blast from Wyllie at halftime. What he didn't know was that the Canterbury coach had been involved in an altercation with a disgruntled punter en route to address his shell-shocked team from the grandstand. As it was, the now grumpy coach didn't speak for long, Hayes says. The response required was obvious. The Canterbury team just had to get out there and do it.

Although Bruce put the home side on the scoreboard with his try, Auckland scored again straight away. It didn't seem to matter at the time as surely the cause was lost, but Canterbury crept back into the contest, with Robbie playing a hand in the revival.

Two of the three additional tries Canterbury scored came from kicks put in by Robbie. The third, which saw prop Chris Earl cross the goal-line, closed the score to 28–23.

From the restart, Canterbury attacked, Wayne Smith put up a high kick which bounced behind the Auckland line, and John Kirwan knocked it dead just in front of the arriving Craig Green.

Game over.

The finish was marred by post-game claims that referee Bob Francis had blown fulltime early. The claim is supported by timings taken from the television replay of the game, which suggest nearly four of the 80 minutes were not played. The high drama was probably an appropriate way to close the Canterbury shield era even if neither side could confess to having played well throughout its finale.

Wyllie, who would go on to coach the All Blacks between 1988 and 1991, reckons his side were 'poor' in the first half and Auckland 'not much better' in the second.

Still, something was missing when the Canterbury team assembled the following morning for a post-game get-together. The gatherings had been a key part of the shield era, with Wyllie saying that if the group hadn't spent as much time together off the field, and got on so well, then it wouldn't have performed as well on the field as it did.

'The shield had been such a big part of our lives, there was a lot of emotion the morning after the game where we lost it,' Robbie remembers.

'We were such a tight group and the thing that had been the focal point in bringing us together had gone.'

For Wyllie, the disappointment of the shield loss was placed in perspective the following day when news arrived of the death of a young cancer sufferer that members of the team had been due to visit.

Eight-year-old Nathan Doublett, who was suffering from leukaemia, had been scheduled to be visited by Wyllie and members of the team on the eve of the Auckland match. Sadly, with time such a precious commodity before major matches, the team was unable to fulfil the commitment prior to the game, although Wyllie hadn't forgotten, ordering team manager Les McFadden to make contact with the family on the Sunday morning to see if the visit could be rearranged.

The unfortunate McFadden had to relay the news that young Nathan had died the night before — a discovery Wyllie says was 'a kick in the guts'.

While the shield moved on, as it was always going to one day, memories of the experiences it allowed, along with the friendships it created, remain.

'The experience we had with the shield enriched all of our lives so much. It taught us so much. That's where rugby is such a great educator,' Robbie says, 'in that there is so much that you experience.

'You go through a life cycle pretty much every week with each game that you play. So long as you heed the lessons, and are open to the learning, it equips you for life.'

Robbie has endeavoured to pass some of his learning from that era down the generations through his coaching, saying one of his underlying aspirations as a coach has always been to provide the playing group with a similar experience as to that he had himself.

Certainly many of the same pillars which supported the Canterbury team through that era have been brought forward, both through the coaching approach, but also off the field where the family atmosphere, which was inclusive of wives, partners and children, has since helped to sustain the Crusaders in the professional era.

'Those team gatherings were always a lot of fun. While the beer flowed a bit more than it might now in the professional era, the mateship and the importance of placing the priority on team is just the same now as it was then.

'Having the partners and wives involved assisted with that. It gave them an understanding as to all that their men were going through, while adding to their own sense of ownership in the outcome.'

7

THE MAN IN BLACK:
BETTER LATE THAN NEVER

Imagine waiting nearly the whole season to make a test debut, then promptly missing the team bus to the ground.

Sound unlikely?

Welcome to the first day in the All Blacks test starting XV for Robbie Deans.

The drama unfolded as the All Blacks prepared to play the first test of the 1983 tour of England and Scotland. Robbie had headed away on the trip as the first-choice fullback, following the withdrawal of Allan Hewson due to the recuperation that was required for a torn Achilles.

The team talk had just concluded and Robbie shot upstairs to his room to grab a sprig tightener. As he walked out the front door of the hotel, the last of his teammates was just getting onboard the bus. To his surprise — and horror — the door closed and the bus drove off.

'I couldn't believe it,' Robbie says.

'For a second, I just stood there feeling numb. Then I began to think about a solution. I saw some cabs nearby so hailed one of them.

'It all actually relaxed me as it turned out by giving me something to think about other than the game itself.'

By the time All Blacks management realised the mistake, and turned the bus around to retrieve the player they were missing, Robbie was already moving in the other direction, comically passing the bus in his taxi as it headed back to the hotel.

But the hurdles weren't all cleared yet. Even though he was wearing his All Blacks blazer and had his full kit with him, stewards at Murrayfield weren't convinced as to his authenticity. They weren't going to allow the All Black debutant entry into the ground, until North Auckland lock and non-playing squad member Alastair Robinson came to fetch him.

'I was standing there in my number ones and showed them my boots and my jersey, but the guy on the gate still wasn't wearing it until Alastair arrived.

'It all made for a rather unusual lead-in to a test match. Everyone tells you that your first test match will be unforgettable. Mine certainly was. How could you forget all of that?'

The test itself was notable for Scottish fullback Peter Dods missing a late conversion that would have given Scotland its first-ever win over the All Blacks. Thirty-one years on, Scotland is still to achieve that.

Robbie's maiden test finished in a 25–25 draw, with the All Blacks fullback contributing two conversions and three penalty goals to his side's cause, in front of 50,000 people.

The Edinburgh test was the first of two on the trip, with the All Blacks losing the second 9–15 to England at Twickenham in London, on a tour that also saw New Zealand beaten by a Midland Division XV at Leicester.

To be fair, this was one of the least experienced All Blacks sides in history. A large number of senior players had opted not to tour after the busy workload from earlier in the year during the four-test series against the Lions, which was followed by a one-off Bledisloe Cup test in Sydney. What seems alien now was entirely understandable then. This was still the amateur era where the players weren't compensated for their time away from work.

It meant that the All Blacks required a remarkable 13 uncapped players — which was half of the tour squad — and were led by the most unlikely of captains, winger and part-time comedian Stu Wilson.

'As a group, we got on very well, but we were very green,' Robbie recalls. 'We were all learning the ropes together. The test outcomes probably reflected that.'

The disappointment in the tests failed to dampen a trip Robbie still describes as a 'fantastic' experience, which is understandable given that he finally got to play, having warmed the bench as the back-up to Hewson during the domestic season.

'The nature of the All Blacks sometimes, and it was probably the case back then, is that it can be harder to get out of the team than it is to get in it,' Robbie says.

'With the short preparation times they had back then, which could be as little as a week together before playing for the first time, the selectors tended to go with established combinations. If they were winning, who could blame them?'

Hewson had certainly performed well for the All Blacks after gaining selection in 1981. He kicked the winning goal in that year's Springbok series before leading the way against Australia as New Zealand defended the Bledisloe Cup in 1982. His 26-point haul in the series-clinching third test was a world record for the most points by an individual in a test.

'Then, as now, being selected for your country was the ultimate endorsement. It has to be earned.

'To that end, while it was a big issue in the public and media, I had no issues having to bide my time behind Hewie [Hewson]. He'd earned his place because he'd done the job for the All Blacks in both 1981 and 1982.

'As a reserve, you still went through the same mental processes as the starting XV, but replacements could only come on through injury in those times, there were no tactical substitutions, so you had to wait your turn and be ready to go — if the opportunity came.'

Selection in the 1983 All Blacks provided Robbie with the opportunity to rub shoulders with one of the most experienced New Zealand combinations ever assembled. The front row — aptly named 'The Geriatrics' — featured three of the most capped All Blacks of all time in props John Ashworth and Gary Knight, and the hooker and captain Andy Dalton. Lock Andy Haden, and loose forwards Mark 'Cowboy' Shaw and No. 8 Murray Mexted, were also permanent fixtures; while a number of the backs had served since the late 1970s.

Robbie recalls before one test seeing Knight, the long-serving Manawatu prop, asleep in the dressing room just 10 minutes or so before the team was due to run out onto the field.

'I couldn't believe it. I tapped Cowboy [Knight's provincial teammate at Manawatu] on the shoulder. He said relax, he's always like that. The pre-match practices are very different nowadays!'

Although the Canterbury representation within the squad for the Lions series had yet to reach the numbers it would at the height of the province's shield run, Robbie says familiarity with All Blacks teammates who weren't from Canterbury wasn't an issue.

'I'd met most of those guys previously, but being part of a squad with them, getting to know them better, and being able to learn from them was invaluable,' he says.

'Playing in the starting XV was the ultimate goal, but that required an injury and I had no control over that! At least, by being in the squad, I was able to gain the experience of involvement in the Lions series and then the Bledisloe Cup test, with all of the learning that provided.'

Robbie did briefly hold hope that he might get a chance in the third Lions test, which was played in atrocious conditions at Carisbrook in Dunedin. He roomed with an under-the-weather Hewson that week, and the Wellingtonian was less than 100 per cent as he continued to suffer the after-effects of the glandular fever he had endured earlier in the year.

'On the night before the test, he was coughing and spluttering endlessly. Neither of us got much sleep and I thought my chance might have arrived. But he got up the next morning and played with gloves and stockings on. It wouldn't have helped his health much playing in those conditions!'

He wasn't anywhere near peak condition, but Hewson says he was never going to withdraw, having experienced himself the danger of giving a rival the chance. His first test appearance had been gained against Scotland in similar circumstances at Dunedin two years earlier, when Otago fullback David Halligan was named to make his debut, but then withdrew after injury, which allowed Hewson to start. Halligan cruelly never received another chance to play for the All Blacks.

Although New Zealand convincingly beat the Lions, taking out all four tests, the contest stayed on the field. Away from it, the two teams got on well, receiving the opportunity to mix on a far greater scale than is allowed in the modern era, due to the tighter travel and heavier playing schedules.

Robbie made a number of friendships that remain to this day.

He also remembers his fellow Cantabrian, Ashworth, settling in at the bar after one of the matches with his giant Scottish counterpart, Iain Milne. The pair got so comfortable that they stayed put for the night and skipped the official dinner for the two teams!

Following the Lions' departure, the All Blacks headed to Sydney to defend the Bledisloe Cup in a one-off test following an agreement between the New Zealand and Australian Rugby Unions to play an annual match in years where no three-match series was scheduled.

New Zealand won 18–8, although much of the discussion around the game centred on a proposed breakaway rugby competition touted by the colourful Sydney journalist David Lord. The proposal would have seen the players quit the governance of the still amateur International Rugby Board to join an organisation that would pay them for their efforts.

The rebel circus, as it became known, was not dissimilar in concept to the proposed World Rugby Corporation, which surfaced in Australia 12 years later, and ultimately ushered in the professional era.

'There was a lot of talk and it came to a head on the flight back to New Zealand where we were all invited down the back of the plane individually for conversations,' Robbie says.

Then, as in 1995, the push to join was being led by senior players from within the team, although Robbie says their situation was understandable, having offered considerable service to the game at their own expense for so long. The financial incentive was significant too, with a suggested $100,000 sign-on fee on offer.

'Where the money was coming from, and who was providing the guarantee was a little bit hazy, but everyone was being kept in the loop in terms of what the opportunity was. But while I understood the reasoning, and certainly had no issues with the motivation of the players who were acting as Lord's advocates, my situation was different to theirs.

'I hadn't played for the All Blacks yet and didn't want to do anything that would jeopardise that. So I listened to the proposal but quickly declined.'

The rebel breakaway didn't come off, and the All Blacks were back in Australia the following year, this time defending the Bledisloe Cup in a three-test series.

After winning a two-test series against France at home, for which Robbie was again a reserve, the All Blacks built nicely into the first test. The tourists completely dominated the state opposition they faced, running up 310 points in the five lead-up games before the opening of the test series.

This included a 99–0 win over South Australia at Adelaide, where Robbie scored an All Blacks' record 43 points, which included three tries. The tally has still only been bettered once in an All Blacks jersey — Southland first five-eighths Simon Culhane bagged 45 in the 145–17 win over Japan at the 1995 Rugby World Cup, but his score came after the value of a try had been increased to five points. Applying that standard, Robbie would have finished with 46 points.

The haul came after Robbie had earlier scored his maiden All Blacks try during the 37–10 win over New South Wales in Sydney where he had taken the field on the wing as a replacement for the injured Waikato flyer Bruce Smith.

Robbie again replaced the luckless Smith during the first test, with Hewson at fullback as the All Blacks lost 9–16. Missed goal-kicks proved costly in the series opener, which Hewson believes counted against him as he, Wellington teammate, winger Bernie Fraser and Shaw 'carried the can' for the defeat by being dropped for the second test in Brisbane.

Although he was disappointed to go, Hewson says he had 'heard' Robbie's 'footsteps' closing in on his test position, and acknowledges that his rival was playing well at the time. Neither Hewson nor Fraser, who collectively boasted 42 caps between them, played another test.

Not that Robbie was to receive an easy introduction.

Within 10 minutes of kick-off in the second test at Ballymore, the All Blacks were 0–12 down and their hold on the Bledisloe Cup was in peril.

'We showed the benefit of the tour from the year before, because a lot of the guys had come on from that, gained valuable experience and were able to hold their nerve as a result. Once we got a foothold at Ballymore, we were able to work our way back into the game, put the pressure on them and finish over the top,' Robbie says.

With Robbie kicking five penalty goals, including one from his own side of halfway, on top of a try by Southland centre Steven Pokere, the

All Blacks emerged with a 19–15 success to take the series back to Sydney for the decider.

The third test basically became a penalty shoot-out, pitting Robbie against the Australian first five-eighths Mark Ella. While the All Blacks scored two tries to one, the conversion and five penalty goals he kicked were crucial factors in the 25–24 win at the Sydney Cricket Ground.

The significance of the result became apparent later in the year when the Alan Jones-coached Wallabies became the first Australian side to complete a Grand Slam of the four home unions in the British Isles. This was an achievement that the All Blacks themselves had only achieved once (in 1978) to that point in history.

The Wallabies, under Jones, would then go on to become the first Australian side to win a series in New Zealand for 37 years, when they reclaimed the Bledisloe Cup with a two–one series victory in 1986.

'They were a good side that was building to better things,' Robbie says, 'and it meant a lot to beat them, especially at the SCG where I'd watched them do the victory lap with the Cup after they won the series in 1980.

'There's no better trophy in the world than the Bledisloe Cup. It has so much history. The Rugby World Cup is special in its own way but it is still relatively new. You can't really compare them.'

Sitting in the dressing room in the old members' grandstand at the Sydney Cricket Ground, which reeks of history, drinking from the Bledisloe Cup was as good as it gets. It was, Robbie says, everything that a young player could dream of.

He didn't know it at the time, but that afternoon at the SCG was his last test. And he hadn't yet had his 25th birthday!

His ruptured ACL, later that year, was partly responsible. So too was the cancellation of the following year's South African expedition, which Robbie had used as a target during his rehabilitation, while watching the Taranaki fullback Kieran Crowley fill his position during the home test wins against England that were supposed to help prepare the All Blacks for the tour.

Given the history of division from 1981, emotions ran high about the prospect of the first All Blacks visit to the Republic since 1976, with Robbie's sister Joanne, who had participated in protests when the

Springboks visited, again voicing her disapproval.

Robbie consulted his father Tony who simply said that Robbie needed to 'own' the decision and not allow anyone else to make up his mind for him. In the end, Robbie decided that if the New Zealand Rugby Football Union thought it was right for the All Blacks to tour, he couldn't turn down the opportunity.

'All of those considerations [in terms of whether it was the right thing to do] had been done by people [at the national union] who had far greater background, as to the pros and cons of a tour, than I did,' Robbie says.

All Blacks tours of South Africa form a big part of the history of the game, with the rivalry negotiating the politics of the apartheid era through the visits of 1928, 1949, 1960, 1970 and 1976. New Zealand's inability to win a series in the Republic, with the drawn series of 1928 its best return prior to the advent of professionalism, only furthered the incentive for the players to visit.

Robbie remembers listening to matches from the 1970 tour deep into the New Zealand night on his transistor radio.

When mulling over the decision to make himself available for the official All Blacks tour, he had spoken to Fergie McCormick, who'd toured South Africa with the 1970 side, along with the 1976 tourists Alex Wyllie, Bill Bush and Doug Bruce.

'I'd talked to all of them about whether they thought it was the right or wrong thing to do. They were all supportive, which reinforced my own feelings about it. I've always been a big believer that your actions speak louder than your words. Anyone can talk.

'So the example of how you live is important. I saw then, and still believe now, that sport is a great lever for change. I've seen that in South Africa through all of the years I've been fortunate enough to go there.'

While the NZRFU believed the tour should proceed, Auckland lawyers Patrick Finnigan and Phillip Recordon challenged the decision. The pair took the union to the High Court, arguing for an injunction against the venture, on the basis that the national body was not acting according to its charter, which was to pursue the best interests of the game. The Court agreed and the Labour Government stayed out of it (National had been in charge during the 1981 tour).

The tour was off.

For now.

With South Africa now off the table, the national union moved quickly to secure a replacement, organising an end-of-season trip to Argentina. It was just the second visit by an All Blacks side to South America, following on from the pioneering tourists of 1979.

Crowley played both test matches, with Robbie watching on from the bench. That he'd even made the trip itself had been touch and go due to illness.

'The long rehab from the ACL, and then rushing straight back into the shield games, had taken its toll,' Robbie says.

'I wasn't feeling great and had lost condition. I told [All Blacks coach] Brian Lochore that I wasn't at my best and probably shouldn't go, but he said, "Come anyway".'

The tour delivered a fantastic cultural experience.

'The populace of Argentina embraced us. The games were hard but the atmosphere in the grounds was unbelievable given the excitement and fervour — and that was just with the crowd. The Argentines are, without doubt, the most passionate rugby supporters I've ever experienced!'

It was an experience he would revisit, both as coaching coordinator of the All Blacks in 2001, and then as Wallabies coach during the inaugural Rugby Championship in 2012.

While he played only three of the tour matches on his maiden visit, the 24 points Robbie gathered during the 72–9 win over Cordoba still rates as the most points scored by an All Black in a game in Argentina.

He also was able to watch up close one of the most remarkable individual performances ever encountered by the All Blacks as the Argentine superstar Hugo Porta kicked all 21 of his team's points to earn Los Pumas a draw in the second test at Buenos Aires.

'That was an amazing day, one of the great performances by a remarkable player, one of the true legends of the game. It was a privilege to be there to see it.'

8

THE CAVALIERS

The look on Jock Hobbs' face betrayed the message almost before he spoke.

'It's on again!'

With that, Robbie resumed his pre-Christmas duties with the Scargill cricket club having guessed, almost as soon as he saw his brother-in-law on the sidelines, what his unusual appearance at the cricket match had meant.

'We were both sort of over it by then,' Robbie says of the various South African tour schemes that had played out since the initial visit had been cancelled earlier in the year.

'There had been a few false dawns, but this proved to be the start of the dialogue that actually led to the Cavaliers tour the following year.'

The well-connected Auckland and All Blacks lock Andy Haden was the key organiser, with Hobbs, the future chairman of the NZRU, performing the role of chief conduit for the Canterbury players involved.

'I was still pretty disbelieving,' Robbie says. 'I thought yeah, yeah, we've been through all of this before. Penny and I got married over that Christmas break, and we basically got on with life. Right up until the time we actually departed, and even while we were in transit in Hong Kong, I still expected the whole thing to fall over.'

The assembly that became the Cavaliers tour was not the first time the players had gathered in anticipation of a privately organised expedition. Shortly after the official All Blacks tour had been blocked by the High Court in 1985, an unofficial trip had surfaced, with the arrangements developing far enough that the Canterbury contingent made its way to a rendezvous point in Wellington to await further instructions.

'It was very clandestine, and is quite hilarious when you look back now. We all piled into a van and drove up to Picton to get the ferry across to Wellington. It was all done undercover so as not to arouse the suspicion of the media, but the tension got to one of the lads.

'He saw lights off in the distance behind us for some time on the drive up the [Marlborough] coast and got quite agitated, insisting they [the media] were onto us, and we were being followed!'

The covert nature of the operation continued once the van reached Picton to embark for the capital, across Cook Strait. The seven players in on the scheme, who had all been original selections for the official tour, had decked themselves out in hats or hoodies and various other attempts at disguise. They also all boarded the ferry separately, and at intervals, in the hope they wouldn't be recognised.

Rugby players they might have been, but secret agents they most definitely were not.

'Smithy [Wayne Smith] was the last one of our party to get on,' Robbie says, 'and while he was boarding, he overheard one of the seamen say: "It looks like we've got half of the Canterbury team on board tonight!"'

The would-be tourists got no further than Wellington. After a frantic night of phone calls once they reached the appointed safe house in the capital, the attempt was aborted. Instead, they moved on to Masterton where all of their number apart from centre Victor Simpson, who played, watched from the sidelines as Canterbury lost an NPC match to Wairarapa-Bush a few days later.

Now the tour was back on for late autumn 1986, and while he remained dubious as to whether it would go ahead, Robbie didn't bother revisiting his original decision over whether to take part or not.

'I'd already done the agonising and been through the philosophical debates both for the official tour and then the first unofficial one,' he explains. 'I'd decided to be a part of it then. Nothing had changed in the time since.'

Although rugby was most definitely a white man's sport when the Cavaliers visited, Robbie has witnessed an extensive transformation take place, both on and away from the field, during his time coaching in

South Africa at both Super Rugby and test level.

Crowds are now multicultural. Coloured and black players and coaches are being developed. Robbie competed head to head with Springbok coach Pieter de Villiers, whom he holds in high regard.

'The country has changed enormously, which is great,' Robbie says. 'When we were there in 1986, and apartheid was still in force, we were staying at hotels that black and coloured people could work in but weren't able to stay in.

'While they were very friendly towards us, it was still an uncomfortable fact. Fortunately, that is an era that has long since passed. South African society has moved on, and you have to say they have done extraordinarily well as a nation.'

It is a testament to how far the game has come in South Africa that many of the younger generation of professional players today visit the country with little or no knowledge of its racial history, both in general, but particularly with regards to segregation in rugby.

Given that the Cavaliers tour came a decade after the most recent All Blacks visit, the bulk of the touring squad had a limited awareness of both the environment that they were entering and the challenges they were to face.

All Blacks legend Colin Meads, then a national selector, and Ian Kirkpatrick — who had both toured South Africa with the All Blacks — were co-opted as coach and manager. Neither had great experience in their roles — Kirkpatrick had never managed a team before — but their status added credibility to the touring party, especially in the eyes of South Africans.

The excursion was sold to the New Zealand public as a private tour by individuals who were exercising their rights of freedom to travel, and to play where they pleased.

'We tried to do the whole thing as closely along the lines of an All Blacks tour as we could, although — with the benefit of hindsight — it was always going to be difficult to achieve.

'Just the nature of how it was pulled together, the dynamics of the group and the way we prepared. It wasn't conducive to a good end in terms of outcome.'

The Cavaliers departed on the evening after the first round of the newly instituted South Pacific Championship — the forerunner to today's Super Rugby — which had begun with Canterbury avenging its Ranfurly Shield defeat to Auckland of the previous year by beating the shield's new owners at Lancaster Park.

Alex Wyllie, who was into his last year as Canterbury coach, gained an awareness as to what was going on 'about 10 days' before the Cavaliers left, but says he deliberately asked no questions of his players for fear of arousing suspicion as to his motives. It was, he says, an awkward time, as he understood why the players were going, but had his own programme, and the South Pacific Championship, to think about.

Wyllie did a good job; Canterbury won the inaugural competition, although such was the emotion surrounding the Cavaliers, he found himself offside with Meads after commenting in the media that it was a shame the players had been forced to head to South Africa in such circumstances.

Far from criticising the tour, Wyllie says he was purely lamenting the fact that the players' hand had been forced by the previous year's High Court injunction, although this left some smoothing over to do with Meads once the Cavaliers had returned. The legendary 'Pinetree' had initially taken Wyllie's comments as a criticism of the tour.

The surreal nature of the whole episode was highlighted by its start, which saw a leading NZRFU official go around both changing rooms following the South Pacific match wishing the Cavaliers players from each team the best of luck in South Africa. The same official then pursued a hard line in public once the team had departed, declaring that there would be consequences for the players on their return, which there was. All of the players were stood down from the first two All Blacks tests of the year. Some, including Robbie, never played for their country again.

If the players' departure, officially anyway, was less than friendly, they arrived to a rapturous welcome in Johannesburg. As far as South Africa was concerned, the touring team was the All Blacks, even though their black jersey featured the gold sponsor's logos for the tour.

The South African news media referred to the side almost exclusively as 'the All Blacks', while the South African Rugby Union awarded test caps to the Springboks who played against them in the four tests, and still includes the games among its official test records.

'It was the right thing for us not to be called, or considered, the All Blacks,' Robbie suggests. 'Not only were we not officially representing the New Zealand Rugby Union, it was also not a merit-based selection for the time. It was the team that had been selected for the year before. A lot can change in a year as far as player form and rankings go!'

If the South African public's enthusiasm for the tour was evident from the start, so too was the desperation of the South African players to win.

The demanding itinerary featured 12 games in six weeks. The four tests were played on successive Saturdays, with midweek matches thrown in between, allowing the visitors little in the way of respite. Just for good measure, four of the matches were played at South Africa's high veldt Johannesburg fortress, Ellis Park. This included the opening game against the Junior Springboks, which quickly provided the Cavaliers with an insight into what they were up against.

'Big men and great depth,' Robbie says.

'Each team was full of big and powerful men and it quickly became obvious that South Africa had an enormous player pool. And both of those factors are just as relevant in South African rugby today as they were in 1986.

'To their enormous credit, the game has evolved. It was a white man's game then and is multiracial now, with the African and coloured communities providing some of their highest profile and most able modern players.

'But the core strengths are still the same. Even when the game went professional and teams from New Zealand and Australia started touring the Republic routinely, it still took a long time to break down the fears about playing their big men, because they used their physical prowess to such effect, and also playing at altitude.

'When we won [with the Wallabies] at Bloemfontein in 2010, it was the first time an Australian side had beaten the Springboks on the high veldt for 47 years. How ridiculous was that? But it does offer an insight into how well the South Africans used the psychological advantage that playing at altitude provided.'

South Africans love their physicality but sometimes it can get ugly. This was the case during the second match of the tour, when Cavaliers captain Andy Dalton was felled by a punch from behind by the Northern Transvaal flanker Burger Geldenhuys. The assault broke Dalton's jaw, cruelly ruling the test hooker out of the remainder of the tour after just 37 minutes of playing time.

The lack of remorse expressed by the hosts after the incident told the Cavaliers all they needed to know about how desperate the Springboks were to win.

'The punch that took out Andy [Dalton] was disgraceful,' Robbie says. 'It just showed how hell bent the South Africans were on proving themselves. It was about winning and nothing else.

'We saw a similar mentality, albeit without the violence, during the 1995 Rugby World Cup which they were desperate to win after having missed out on playing in the first two tournaments.'

The unprovoked assault on Dalton wasn't to be the end of the violence. Robbie was on the field during the tour match against Natal at Durban where an all-in brawl broke out that involved every player on the field.

'I still don't know what started that, but it was remarkable, I never experienced anything like it at any other time in my career. By then, the frustration was growing on our part, so when you added that to the ambition of the South Africans and their determination to intimidate, I guess a blow-up of that proportion was always a possibility.'

Another hurdle the visitors would encounter was the refereeing. There were many inexplicable on-field decisions.

Despite the provocations, the Cavaliers made a winning start to the tour, beating the Junior Springboks, Northern Transvaal and then Orange Free State. The only loss of the tour, outside of the tests, was sustained in the tour's fourth match at Ellis Park when the Cavaliers went down to Transvaal.

Although the Cavaliers won eight of the 12 matches, the test series was lost three matches to one, with the sole success coming in the second game at Durban where the visitors prevailed 19–18.

'There was a sense of relief among the group after Durban,' Robbie says. 'It didn't really feel like a test win, it was more a release of the tension — for all that we had risked to make the trip, the win over the Boks had given us some credibility.'

A number of players went to novel lengths to try to create the edge that playing for the All Blacks gave them. Robbie's Canterbury teammate Warwick Taylor, one of the 11 Cavaliers who featured in the following year's Rugby World Cup-winning All Blacks team, tried wearing his All Blacks tracksuit prior to one of the tests to assist with motivation.

Robbie recalls catching a glimpse of himself in the mirror in the changing rooms prior to the final test at Ellis Park, which the Cavaliers lost 10–26.

'I saw myself in the Cavaliers jersey and thought it just wasn't the same [as wearing the All Blacks jersey].'

The players' feelings towards the jersey they wore summed up their inability to replicate the genuine nature of representing their country, as much as they had tried.

'With hindsight, we were trying to achieve something that was never going to be possible. The Cavaliers were not a merit-based selection as the All Blacks would have been. In Colin and Ian we had a coach and manager who, although they were great men, had very limited experience in their roles.

'We also didn't wear the All Blacks jersey. While many of the players had their partners on tour the whole time, which created other distractions, or pressures if you like, and wouldn't have happened on an All Blacks tour. Then there was the situation around the adjudication.'

Most crucially, Robbie says, the Cavaliers knew they did not have the full support of the populace back home.

'When you run out as a player, there is no better feeling than knowing that your whole country is behind you. We knew that was not the case in this instance and it didn't matter what we did, nothing was going to change that fact!'

To have risked so much, and finished unfulfilled, was inevitably going to create frustration. This reflected in Dalton's post-tour swipe at the refereeing and the general sense of injustice the touring players were left with.

'Andy is a very measured man, but his words mirrored how we all felt, in terms of having gone through so much but come up short. He didn't hold back and for him to have done that, anyone who knows him personally would know that something was seriously amiss.'

The players returned unsure as to the nature of their public reception, but Robbie says life resumed as normal, with few instances of disapproval experienced.

'I was operating a fruit juice distribution business by then, and so was all over Christchurch,' he says. 'There was only one person who made any sort of negative comment to me, with regards to the tour, which made me think the public attitude towards the tour was similar to our own. It was over and done with now, it was time to move on.'

So, knowing what they do now, does Robbie think the players would have chosen to tour South Africa if they had their time again?

'While it's not something I think we will ever celebrate in terms of a reunion or anything, the Cavaliers was an experience none of us who were involved will ever forget. The trip into the unknown that we had, and the learning that was taken from it, contributed to New Zealand rugby, both the following year when a number of Cavaliers featured in the World Cup win, but also in the longer term.

'A significant number of guys [Smith, Hobbs, Taylor, Kieran Crowley, Grant Fox, Craig Green, Wayne Shelford, Mark Shaw, Steve McDowell, Dalton and Robbie himself] who went on that tour have gone on to either coach or be involved administratively at the highest levels of the game in New Zealand.

'It also contributed positively to South African decisions. There's no doubt that the tour helped to accelerate change in the game within South Africa, where rugby had previously been the bastion of white society.

'So the answer is yes, I think most of us, even knowing where it was going to end, probably still would have gone. It wasn't the wrong thing to do, although we now know that it was realistically a no-win situation.

'But you make those decisions in real time and then you live with them!'

9

A GAME WITHOUT SCRUMS

As a final game, it couldn't have been more bizarre.

Canterbury's challenge for the Ranfurly Shield in Auckland at the end of 1990 will forever be remembered simply as the 'no scrums' game.

In a remarkable turn, the player whose name became most synonymous with events as they unfolded on the day didn't even start the game for Canterbury. Robbie did, as he played the 146th and last game in his 12-year provincial career. Long-serving All Blacks second five-eighths Warwick Taylor also said farewell, while John Buchan raised his 100th appearance in red and black.

It was through the sending off of Buchan, who lashed out with the boot at Gary Whetton after the Auckland skipper had himself stamped on one of Buchan's teammates, that the fuse was lit on one of the more unusual episodes in New Zealand rugby.

Under the rules of the day, front-rowers who were dismissed could be replaced without teams having to shed a man. Canterbury coach Frank Jack sent out Phil Cropper, who had been listed in the hooking position among the team's substitutes, although the converted hooker had been playing loose forward all year. When he arrived on the field, Cropper conveyed the message both to Robbie and Canterbury forwards leader Rob Penney, as well as to referee Keith Lawrence, that he wasn't on as a hooker and therefore would be unable to scrum.

A bemused Lawrence recalls the news not going down well with the Auckland team when he informed them that there would be no further scrums for safety reasons. Auckland hooker and All Blacks captain Sean Fitzpatrick, who had shared the front-row duties with Cropper years back in a New Zealand age-group side, was vociferous in his objections, Lawrence recalls, although the referee stood firm telling the Auckland side that there was nothing he could do.

Robbie, who'd had no advanced warning as to what was coming, remembers thinking that the call was a big one, although he remains adamant that it wasn't premeditated.

'Who plans to get sent off in a game, especially playing your 100th?' Robbie says of Buchan's dismissal.

'For it to have been a premeditated move, our hooker had to get sent off, and there was no way that we planned for that being the case. As it was, the first bit of foul play was committed by Gary [Whetton] who — using the same ruling that applied to John — should have been sent off too.'

Robbie presumed the call on Cropper had been made by the coaches, but this was emphatically denied by Jack at the post-game media conference, with the Canterbury coach insisting he sent the player on to hook. Given that Buchan was playing his 100th game for the province, Jack probably had no intention of replacing his hooker at any stage, which would have meant he could have afforded to carry Cropper as an extra loose forward on his bench. The best laid plans . . .

'Feelings ran pretty high, both out on the field at the time, but especially afterwards,' Robbie says. 'I remember being confronted by an emotional [Auckland assistant coach] Bryan Williams, whom I knew well, who insisted that it had been a premeditated plan.

'There is no doubt, had we won the shield in those circumstances, that it would have got ugly, both on the day but also in the wash-up afterwards where I'm sure it would have ended up with some type of legal challenge.'

As it was, Canterbury got close, with Auckland eventually running out the victors 33–30 in a fast and expansive game where free kicks replaced scrums, which led to dropped goal attempts flying in all direction, with first five-eighths Greg Coffey succeeding with three for Canterbury.

'If anything, Auckland probably reacted better to the changed circumstance than we did,' Robbie says. 'They quickly made changes once the scrums were gone, bringing off their front-rowers to get faster guys out there. We were a bit slower on the uptake.'

Adding to the irony of the circumstances surrounding his final game is that Robbie had never intended to still be playing first-class rugby. He had advised Jack of his unavailability at the start of the previous year, only to be named anyway.

'I'd taken a year out from playing anything other than club and the Country programme in 1988 because I was running the farm. At the start of the following year in the pre-season, they played a few matches involving Canterbury XVs against Invitation XVs in what were basically trials to pick the representative team from. The final squad was named after one of the games I'd played in out at Ashley, but it was a hell of a shock, having told them I wasn't available, to hear my name called out anyway. What could I do? I'd loved playing for Canterbury.

'After giving it some thought and having a quick conversation with Penny at the back of the hall where the announcement took place, I decided that I might as well line up again.'

It was good for the team that he did, as 1989 saw Robbie extend his provincial record for points in a season, setting a new mark of 279, which still stands as the Canterbury record.

For all of the points he had scored, Robbie had never kicked a dropped goal. So he challenged his fellow long-serving All Black Warwick Taylor as to which of them would be the first to kick a dropped goal in their first-class career. The deal between the pair was that only once one of them had registered the achievement could either of them contemplate retirement.

Inevitably, given his competitive nature, Robbie got there first, succeeding with the first attempt at dropped goal he had taken since his days as a first five-eighth a decade earlier.

Taylor, who would later coach the New Zealand women's sevens team and then become president of the Canterbury Rugby Football Union, decided to go out at the end of 1990 too, and wound up scoring one of Canterbury's tries in his last appearance. He, Robbie and Bruce had stayed on as mainstays of the Canterbury team after the core of the side that had served during the shield era broke up at the end of 1986. This included coach Alex Wyllie, who bowed out after a 1986 season that saw Canterbury win the newly inaugurated early season South Pacific

Championship while also inflicting a 30–10 thumping on the Bledisloe Cup-winning Wallaby tourists.

Both Robbie and Wyllie rate Canterbury's performance that day as one of the finest achieved by the team during their time. It was one of only two losses that the Wallabies suffered on the highly successful tour, with the other being a one-point defeat in the second test at Dunedin.

The Wallaby demolition proved to be the second victory of three Robbie had over the controversial Australian coach Alan Jones. Robbie kicked the All Blacks to a series victory over the Jones-coached Wallabies in 1984, and was then preferred to the high-profile Sydney talkshow radio host for the Australian coaching position in 2008.

Needless to say, during his five years coaching the Wallabies, the ex-Australian coach was one of Robbie's biggest, and most vocal, critics.

Wyllie recalls telling a glum Jones after Canterbury's victory that it had done the Wallabies a favour, suggesting that the kick up the backside would help lift the Australian players to beat the 'Baby' Blacks (as the All Blacks were known while the Cavaliers players were suspended) in the first test at Wellington the following week. The dejected Jones wasn't interested in positives at the time, Wyllie recalls, although the New Zealander's prophecy was proven correct. The Wallabies won the first test 13–12 and the third 22–9 to annex the Bledisloe Cup on New Zealand soil for the first time since 1949.

Canterbury failed in its bid to wrest the Ranfurly Shield back from Auckland later that year and while it defended its South Pacific title the following year, the final seasons of Robbie's provincial career proved to be hard slog.

The side slipped back in relation to Auckland, while struggling to stay ahead of Wellington and the improving Otago and Waikato.

So why did Robbie keep going?

'For the love of the game, basically,' he says. 'I still felt that I had something to offer and we were at a time where any experience we had in the province was vital.

'There were a lot of similarities in the last couple of years of my time playing for Canterbury to when I had started: a team in rebuild mode after a period of success, with the younger guys needing to have experienced heads they could look to as they tried to adapt to the ever increasing demands playing provincial rugby.'

Even once his Canterbury days were over, the competitor in Robbie couldn't totally give it up. He continued to turn out for Glenmark, finally retiring from club rugby at the age of 35, by which time he was already assisting Bob Kerr coaching the Canterbury Country senior side.

'Throughout my playing career, I was lucky enough to generally get most of the critical kicks that I attempted. But in the 1994 North Canterbury final, I missed one I'd really wanted to get. I told myself afterwards that there was a message in that. It was time to finish.'

Robbie began coaching the Country Colts, with Wayne Love, the year after his retirement as a representative player in 1991. The experience gave him an introduction to the city–country politics of rep selection when the Country Colts beat their Town counterparts but only had one player selected in the Canterbury team.

Robbie moved on to assist Kerr with the senior side in 1992, before roping in Don Hayes as his assistant when he took on the responsibility as Country head coach three years later.

He was still an amateur coach for now, but not for much longer.

10

A COACH IS BORN

Bermuda might have provided an unlikely backdrop for a first foray into professional coaching, but it was from the Caribbean playground that Robbie allowed his name to go forward as a contender for the vacant Canterbury coaching position at the end of 1996.

Already juggling the role as coach of the Country representative side around his increasing commitments in the business of fruit juice distribution, Robbie was away with the Classic All Blacks, at their world tournament, when applications to take over from the outgoing Vance Stewart closed.

'Don [Hayes] caught me at a weak moment,' Robbie says, with a hint of seriousness in his voice, as he recalls what proved to be a life-changing decision. 'Coaching at that level wasn't something I was seeking, so it took a bit of arm twisting from Donny for me to agree. While I was enjoying what we were doing with the Country rep side, that was a brief programme.'

'It was a totally different contemplation to taking on coaching full time. It wasn't just the time commitment; it was also the financial implications. Being involved at that level required a conscious decision to allow my livelihood to rest on coaching — if I was successful in getting the job.'

Hayes had seen a coach inside a player's body during the time the pair spent together as part of the Canterbury's Ranfurly Shield era of the 1980s. He had then coached alongside him with Country and knew that Robbie was the man to revive the province's flagging fortunes.

Although Canterbury had regained the shield off Waikato in 1994, and successfully defended it in an epic challenge from Otago two games later, the reign had been terminated emphatically by Auckland via a 35–0 humiliation the following season. The province had fallen on hard times since.

When he accepted the appointment to take over for 1997, Canterbury had gone 13 years without success in the NPC. It had not been national champion since Robbie and his teammates had gone through unbeaten in 1983. Adding to the misery, the Crusaders had been a spectacular flop in Super Rugby, which had opened the year before, tailing the field in the inaugural Super 12. The franchise's maiden journey was blighted by injury to the extent that the Crusaders were forced to pull in eight reinforcements through the season while winning just two of their 11 games.

Hayes was part of the appointments panel that chose Robbie ahead of Steve Hansen, who had taken a Canterbury development side to Argentina at the end of the previous year.

Bob Stewart, the NPC team's manager and also a Canterbury Rugby Football Union board member, was another involved in the process. He remembers the decision to opt for Robbie over Hansen as a 'tight' call.

Stewart and Hayes recall the union's chief executive officer of the time, the future NZRU chief executive Steve Tew, pushing firmly for Hansen, leading both to suspect that Tew had promised Hansen the job prior to the appointment process being conducted.

Robbie says Tew approached him on the night of his appointment requesting that he take Hansen as part of his coaching team.

'I didn't have a problem with it. We'd played together in the past and he had background with some of the players which was going to be helpful. The only real issue was that we needed a forward coach. For Steve to be involved, he was going to have to take that role.

'He was keen so we made the appointment and he got on with learning those skills.'

Stewart believes the appointment of Robbie, and his subsequent rise to the Crusaders head coaching position three years later, again ahead of Hansen, undoubtedly led to 'friction' between the pair. Both are innovative but driven coaches, Stewart says, so it was inevitable that there was going to be some resentment, although he commends the way

107

Robbie handled it, both in agreeing to take on Hansen, but also in the way he managed the entire situation.

Robbie was assertive from the start. The new coach quickly pulled together his management team, some of whom he had no role in appointing. He impressed on them the history of the jersey and the size of the challenge they faced in revitalising Canterbury's fortunes. Robbie made it clear at the management group's maiden gathering, Stewart says, that he would back them to the hilt.

It was also communicated, in what Stewart recalls as a firm message to both he (as team manager) and Hansen, that Robbie was the leader. He would make the big decisions.

It wasn't an issue, Stewart says. As the person who was ultimately accountable, Robbie had to have the final say, and Stewart, who went on to become both the CRFU and then Crusaders chairman, adds that it quickly became obvious that the new man in charge was extremely capable.

Not only is he an astute coach, Robbie is decisive, organised and thorough in all he does.

An experienced businessman himself, Stewart believes Robbie could easily have been very successful in the business world. He boasts the skills to run an organisation or company, allied with a range of management and commercial skills that he only ever used when he needed to.

Robbie subsequently coached with Hansen at both the Crusaders and the New Zealand A side. He maintains that the pair had a sound working relationship.

'We were together from 1997 and put a lot of time and effort into how we functioned,' Robbie says.

'It was never just about myself and Steve, though, or even the wider management group. It was always about the team in terms of the parameters that we put in place.

'By setting out the protocols, which everyone in the team agreed to and had to live by, in advance of the stresses and strains of the campaign, we catered for any hiccups that might occur along the way.'

Todd Blackadder, who led Canterbury during Robbie's stint as NPC coach, and also captained his first title-winning Crusaders side in 2000, maintains the Deans–Hansen coaching combination was the most 'powerful' under which he ever served. It was apparent from the outset that the pair complemented each other, the future All Blacks captain says, with any disagreements hidden from the players' view.

The assessment is reinforced by the success the coaching combination enjoyed both in the NPC and later in Super Rugby. The titles won in each competition illustrated the strength of their alignment, Blackadder says.

Robbie's appointment as Canterbury coach was quickly followed by his addition to the Crusaders as team manager. He was approached by his former Canterbury teammate Wayne Smith, himself new to the head coaching position, to take on the role. Accepting allowed Robbie to commit to the game fulltime.

'It was a good fit, catering for my need [by providing year-round work], as well as the needs of both the Canterbury rep team and the Crusaders. Being involved in the Crusaders campaign fast-tracked my knowledge of the playing group in terms of their practice habits, attitudes and personalities as well as their skills. This gave us a head start, in terms of the NPC campaign, given that we had largely the same playing group at our disposal.'

One player who was not going to be part of either campaign was the foundation Crusaders skipper Richard Loe, who was released by Smith to join the Chiefs, but was also not required for the NPC.

'We had that conversation prior to Christmas in a paddock outside Rangiora near his property, well away from the public domain,' Robbie recalls. 'The rationale was that we needed to move on as a group and start developing the next generation.

'I felt it was important that we were transparent in our decision making, that he knew where he stood, and that he found out directly from me as opposed to learning through other "channels" — most notably the media, which is something I've always found irritating.

'Richard and I went back a long way. He's a fiercely competitive bloke. I'm sure he wouldn't have enjoyed getting that news, but I'm also sure he would have respected the fact that I was upfront about it and had spoken to him directly.'

Smith's first year as Crusaders coach started the ball rolling. The team climbed from last to sixth in the second Super 12, giving the players confidence and momentum as they assembled under Robbie for the first time.

Leon MacDonald, whose career would be closely intertwined with the coaching of both Smith and Robbie, says the different areas the pair emphasised complemented each other. The blend fast-tracked the development of both the players individually, but also the two teams.

Smith placed a big focus on technical skills while Robbie, aware of that emphasis given his work as the Crusaders manager, placed importance on mental strength. He had perceived that to be a weakness of recent Canterbury teams, MacDonald says, and was quite open about the need to be tough, keep at it in games, and never back down. Robbie was looking for the competitive attributes on which he had based his own career.

Largely due to his own experience, and his belief that club rugby plays an important part in shaping players and connecting them to the community, Robbie steered the players back into Canterbury's club competitions once Super Rugby concluded in May.

He then assembled his squad at the conclusion of the club season. The first assembly consisted of a camp at Hanmer Springs, the resort town two hours north of Christchurch, where Robbie would return 14 years later with his World Cup Wallabies.

Following a process that would serve Robbie well throughout his provincial coaching career, the camp laid down a foundation for the campaign. This included the team's goals and how they would be achieved, the theme or rallying call the players would use during the tough times, and also how they would live and operate through agreed team standards.

The protocols were critical, Robbie says, as the players set them, which encouraged their 'buy-in'.

'You can rant and rave, make big statements, both in private and in public, and try to lead using the big stick, but that won't work if the players haven't bought into what is acceptable, and what isn't,' Robbie says.

'Peer pressure is the most powerful driving force, both in terms of setting the boundaries — on and off the field — as well as ensuring that they are adhered to by the whole group.

'This is where the leaders within the playing group are so important.

110

They are the ones who provide the glue, who take the responsibility to ensure that what has been agreed to is being lived up to. They drive the habits.'

Tabai Matson was the first to discover that once the protocols were agreed, Robbie would make sure the players stuck to them. The experienced centre, who went on to coach Canterbury to the national title himself, was late to training in the week leading up to the first game of the NPC and subsequently found himself stood down from the side for the week.

The preparatory work that had been done prior to the campaign immediately showed signs of reward. Canterbury opened by claiming back-to-back wins in Christchurch, with a 42–22 success against Bay of Plenty in a non-championship match being followed by a startling 73–7 walloping of Wellington. As a statement of intent, it couldn't have been more emphatic, with Canterbury running in 11 tries in its competition opener against an opponent it had lost to the previous year.

A comfortable win against Southland (42–20) at Invercargill followed before the side received a reality check during an 18–24 home loss to Waikato.

'They were a good side,' Robbie recalls. 'Highly experienced, with quality performers in all of the key decision-making positions and a forward pack as good as any in the country. We knew after we played them that they would be one of the top teams.

'They proved it by going on to take the Ranfurly Shield off Auckland before finishing at the top of the table heading into the semi-finals.'

After that setback, Robbie demanded a response from his players and he got it as Canterbury bounced back by compiling away wins against Counties Manukau (33–18) and North Harbour (20–3).

The strong start told Robbie that the moves they had made to freshen up the environment after Super Rugby, by bringing in some new aspects to keep the players mentally stimulated, had worked.

'It wasn't a case of trying to do everything new from Super Rugby. We realised that we could bring forward everything of value out of the Crusaders campaign from earlier in the year, but it was also critical that we evolved.

'The players were having to adapt to a much longer season and a heavier workload with Super Rugby only into its second year. We couldn't just repeat what they had been doing with the Crusaders. It was important we came up with new material. They helped to drive it with ideas that came out during the camp. These helped to keep them feeling fresh, enthused and, most importantly, hungry.'

One of the new innovations was the internal theme 'Honk 97', taken from the innovative Saatchi & Saatchi television advertisement of the time, which focused on geese flying in formation to protect and support each other. The players brought this to life in the opening game when prop Con Barrell, an asthmatic, was struggling to catch his breath at scrum time in the early stages. When the front-rower advised his fellow tight forwards that he was battling, they all replied with 'Honk, honk, honk'. It must have sounded strange to any of the Wellington players within earshot, but was their way of telling him that they would support him through it.

They did, and the Canterbury scrum held firm throughout the match.

The 'Honk' theme was coupled with a team ethos of attack, attack, attack, Stewart says. The idea was that Canterbury would attack when it had the ball, but also without it while defending.

If the evolution was providing value, so too was the focus on individual player habits. This helped to allay one of the concerns that Robbie had had prior to taking on the role.

'Some of the dynamics around dollars as the incentive, after professionalism had started, had created behaviours that clearly hadn't worked towards team success — with the first Crusaders season the most obvious example of that,' Robbie says.

'Going into that second year, working with Smithy and Peter Sloane in the Crusaders, but then during the NPC, we resolved to bring some of the amateur ethos forward into the professional domain. This centred around training habits and attitudes, but also other aspects of the culture in terms of meeting off-field team responsibilities, liaising with the public and the like.

'We largely achieved that change in the first year, to the extent that it became embedded. It was probably the defining factor in terms of all of the success that was subsequently achieved.'

Robbie laughs as he recalls one such example of the level of sacrifice players were now prepared to make for the cause.

'It was before a morning training and Con Barrell, who was a great team man and never short on humour, announced to us all that he had made a big sacrifice for the team the night before. We all waited expectantly for his earth-shattering pronouncement. He then declared that he had only had one pie on the way home from training, instead of two! Everyone just cracked up laughing.'

Blackadder, who worked closely with the new boss, says one of Robbie's strengths was that he kept it simple, using a 'values-based language' that was to the point. Every question had a choice in terms of how it was answered, which required the player concerned to make a judgment. It was, Blackadder says, Robbie's way of making his players believe they could achieve great things, just by keeping it simple.

'We had a code, which we'd agreed on at Hanmer, that we all had to live to,' Robbie says.

'If it is good for the team, think it, say it or do it. Thoughts are precursors to your words and subsequent actions. The earlier you "intervened" or "redirected", the better.'

And it was working.

The litmus test of the progression came in the sixth championship outing. This pitted the resurgent Cantabs against the opponent they were out to dethrone, the four-time defending champion Auckland side, coached by Graham Henry.

Lancaster Park was close to full for an epic Friday night encounter which saw the title aspirants upset their All Blacks-laden opponents 20–9, with Matson bagging the only try.

With every campaign, there is always a key moment, later to be looked back on as the time when things went right, or wrong. Robbie likes to call them 'tipping points'.

For his maiden campaign, the moment arrived the week after the side had beaten Auckland, a result that had fuelled title talk both around Christchurch, but also further afield. It came during a trip to Dunedin.

While the southerners were on the cusp of a resurgence themselves, which would see Otago sweep to the 1998 NPC title and the Highlanders host the 1999 Super Rugby final, that was still to come. When the Canterbury team arrived at Carisbrook, Otago had won just three times previously in the competition. With the Highlanders having replaced the Crusaders as Super Rugby's wooden-spooners earlier in the season, it had been a glum year.

In such circumstances, it would have been understandable if the Otago players couldn't have gotten what was their final game of the year over with soon enough. Instead, they went out with a bang.

Otago's comprehensive 35–13 win was a major shock, but one that Robbie, at least initially, appeared to take well.

MacDonald, who scored Canterbury's only try, admits the performance was poor. He attributed the lapse to the side getting ahead of itself on the back of its big win over Auckland.

It provided a lesson that the future title-winning assistant coach at the Tasman Makos has never forgotten, since embarking on his own coaching career. There was no panic, MacDonald recalls, just a quiet evening consisting of a few beers together and some reflection, before the players all assembled the following morning in anticipation of the scheduled recovery pool session.

Robbie had another plan in store. Taking a leaf out of the Alex Wyllie playbook, remembering the three-hour 'hell' session at Warkworth before they won the Ranfurly Shield, Robbie staged his own version.

As the bus parked up outside Moana Pool, the players were surprised to hear Robbie telling them to grab their boots and head in the direction of the adjacent Littlebourne training paddock within the Otago Boys' High School grounds.

As Wyllie had 15 years earlier, Robbie felt that more than words were needed to get the message across.

'It was a bit old school, but I'd committed to myself that I was going to keep them training until they complained, by which time they'd be ready for a few home truths. The session was nowhere near as long as the one we'd had before the shield game, but the meaning was just as pointed. I think they got the message.'

The results suggest that they did. Canterbury did not lose again, finishing off the round robin with a win over Taranaki (40–21) before beating Auckland (21–15) and Counties Manukau (44–13) in the semi-final and final respectively.

Robbie believes that season's back-to-back wins over Auckland were crucial deposits towards the success that was to come in the following 12 years. Those wins broke down the psychological grip the northerners had held over Canterbury ever since the Ranfurly Shield success of 1985.

'Those two games, but especially the semi-final where it was winner take all, were key to our progression because they [Auckland and the Blues] were the benchmark. They'd won four NPC titles in a row, both of the Super 12 competitions that had been played to that point, and essentially had the All Blacks team. To beat them took us through a massive mental barrier.'

Undoubtedly, the belief the players gained from the wins contributed to the following year's maiden Super Rugby success, where the Crusaders came from behind to beat the Blues at Eden Park.

'It was a coming of age, especially in the semi-final. It was satisfying for us, as a coaching and management group, to watch,' Robbie says.

He cites two standout moments from the semi-final in Christchurch that showcased the shift in the balance of power.

'Body language is a massive and often underestimated part of any sporting contest. Bad body language or reactions betray weakness to an opponent. During that semi-final, [Auckland captain] Zinzan Brooke lost it with the referee, Paddy O'Brien. He was arguing decisions, got penalised for backchat at one point and generally failed to conceal his displeasure as things started to go wrong for them. His stress encouraged our players by providing an indicator that we were on top.

'In another instance, Mark Hammett drew a penalty out of his opposite [All Blacks captain] Sean Fitzpatrick by saying something provocative, which Fitzpatrick responded to and got penalised for. It was a classic case of the young bull staring down the old bull.

'I remember smiling when I saw that because it was a complete role reversal from where we'd been. We were now the ones who were composed while they were getting distracted and focusing on the referee and his decisions. They were huffing about what had been, rather than what they needed to focus on, which was what came next.'

Beating Auckland earned Canterbury home advantage for the final after Counties Manukau had launched a remarkable second half fightback to beat Waikato 43–40 in the earlier semi-final at Hamilton, overtaking the shield holders in the last minute when winger Joeli Vidiri scored the third of his hat-trick of tries.

Beaten finalists the season before, Counties boasted a side of seasoned NPC performers with a solid core of Super Rugby experience. The visitors also had arguably the two most potent backline finishers in the world, wingers Vidiri and Jonah Lomu.

For the first time since the shield had departed three seasons earlier, the house full sign was erected at Lancaster Park and Robbie's troops produced a devastating performance, which outclassed their visitors. The six-try-to-one demolition was every bit as convincing as it sounds, although it was neither the tries nor the final score which provided Robbie's greatest satisfaction.

'The hunger to do the little things was the difference.

'The atmosphere that day was up with anything I ever experienced in my playing days at Lancaster Park, and the excitement among the players was palpable. But they were also hungry and presumed nothing.

'After beating Auckland in the semi-final, there was always the potential for them to relax and underrate Counties. That would have been fatal as they were an experienced side who had been there [to the final] before, whereas Canterbury never had.'

If Robbie had needed any confirmation that the 'message' conveyed three weeks before had gotten through, he got it early in the game. Counties and future Crusaders midfielder Tony Marsh made a break from a turnover, but was rounded up by Canterbury flanker Angus Gardiner, who turned about quickly and raced back to shut the attack down.

'He [Gardiner] presumed nothing. He didn't leave it for anyone else, or assume that someone else would be back, but took the responsibility on himself to chase Tony and shut down the attack.

'Once he'd made the tackle, he then got to his feet quickly and stole the ball, and we scored shortly after,' Robbie says.

'When I saw that mentality being shown, I knew that we would be awfully hard to beat.'

That Canterbury won the NPC in Robbie's first year came as no surprise to two mentors from his playing career, Fergie McCormick and Alex Wyllie. McCormick highlighted Robbie's solution-focused outlook as a major factor, saying his preparedness to work away until he had solved any problem that had arisen was always going to stand him in good stead as a coach. It had showed that year in how Canterbury had bounced back so strongly from its two defeats.

While Robbie is rarely uncertain, he was always prepared to take onboard advice from those he respects, McCormick says, which his former Canterbury Colts coach also believes has served him well.

Wyllie, who always thought Robbie would make the grade as a coach, cited the tradition of each generation passing its knowledge down to the next, which he believes is something that has always been a feature of the game in Canterbury. A number of the team from the 1982–85 shield era went on to coach successfully, with Wyllie observing that the trend has flourished to an even greater extent in the professional age.

A significant number of those tutored by Smith with the Crusaders, and by Robbie in both NPC and Super Rugby, have since gone on to coach at provincial level.

Perhaps the man entitled to the most satisfaction at the end of that campaign, having lobbied Robbie to take on the job in the first place, was Hayes. He was perhaps the least surprised about the season's outcome. Such was the zeal with which Robbie had approached the role, Hayes reckons that by the time that first season ended, his mate was no longer reading books about the fundamentals required for sporting excellence; he was literally writing them.

Robbie's search for peak performance involved hours doing preparatory work using images, videos or any other aids that he believed would help with either the initial delivery or to reinforce his message to the playing group.

Robbie was relentless in the way he prepared for team meetings, Hayes remembers. He was always looking for new ways to add a competitive edge to the environment and to challenge players. The presentations had to be perfect.

The team's quest for perfection continued into the next Super Rugby season, beginning a dynasty that reaped seven titles in 11 years.

It did not, however, kickstart a similar dominance in the NPC.

While the following year saw Canterbury rout Auckland 50–17, becoming the first visiting provincial side to post a half-century on Eden Park in the host union's 115-year history, this result did not lead to another title. Canterbury finished with six wins and four defeats for the year, losing to Waikato in Hamilton twice in three weeks, firstly 23–29 in a Ranfurly Shield challenge before falling 13–32 in a semi-final.

The following season was always going to be challenging with the Rugby World Cup occurring in the middle of the campaign, and so it proved. Canterbury supplied eight players to the All Blacks 1999 World Cup squad, as well as winger Afato So'oalo to Samoa, and suffered as a consequence.

Although they did edge the eventual champions Auckland 12–10 in Christchurch, and massacred Counties Manukau 80–22 in a 12-try romp immediately prior to the All Blacks' departure, the impact of the disjointed nature of the campaign was too great an obstacle to overcome.

Stripped of most of its senior personnel for much of the competition, Canterbury only scored tries in the first of its four home games, while losing to Northland and North Harbour on the road as it missed the semi-finals in finishing fifth.

In 2000, Wellington — so often the opponent on the wrong end of results in big matches during Robbie's time — proved to be the stumbling block.

Canterbury won nine of its 11 matches, but lost the championship opener 20–27 in the capital, and was then beaten 29–34 at home in the final by the same opponent.

A second title might have eluded him, but Robbie still managed an appropriate sign-off from his role as an NPC coach, given his part in the 1982–85 side, when he masterminded the 10th successful Ranfurly Shield challenge by a Canterbury side. The successful raid boasted a striking similarity to the assault on Wellington 18 years previously as well, with the Canterbury side banking the lessons of their failed visit to Hamilton in 1998 to get the job done two years later.

The Waikato side that Canterbury beat 26–18 had turned aside 21 previous challengers during a three-year period, which established that province's longest run with the shield.

When Canterbury failed in their first bid, Robbie felt his side had missed some chances. Seven of the same players returned two years later. They didn't make the same mistakes again.

Having won the shield, Robbie's men had two defences to see through before the regular season closed, with the first one against Otago providing a thriller as Canterbury came from behind to shade the luckless southerners 29–26.

Before that match, Robbie had urged his men to respect the shield, saying it hadn't been won, and wouldn't be successfully defended easily. Like a fine lady, the shield would only keep the company of those who showed her the appropriate respect.

The players took up the theme with one of their number, who had swooped to score what proved to be the winning try, piping up in the changing rooms afterwards to suggest that the team hadn't shown the lady enough admiration until he had got himself involved to save the day. Needless to say, the player concerned had long had a reputation for his relations with the fairer sex.

With Robbie having already decided to give up the representative role after 2000, so that he could concentrate on his new role as head coach of the Crusaders, the lost final to Wellington was his last match as Canterbury coach.

He finished with a strikingly similar success rate to that he was to return from his nine years running the Crusaders: 29 wins and 12 defeats from 41 games for a 71 per cent winning ratio.

Eleven new All Blacks were selected from the team during Robbie's term as coach.

By the time he stood down, Robbie had already replicated his achievement with Canterbury by winning a maiden Super Rugby title as head coach of the Crusaders earlier in 2000. That was the Crusaders' third championship in as many years, but given that they had kept winning the title through this period, why hadn't Canterbury?

Robbie cites the cumulative effect of the increased player workload:

10 of the 2000 squad also featured in every Crusaders game as well as the full All Blacks season.

'Our guys were playing close to three months more high-intensity rugby than just about any of our opponents,' Robbie explains. 'They were getting a full Super Rugby season, including play-offs, then the All Blacks, then they were coming back into the NPC, which featured at least one play-off game in three of those four years.

'There's no doubt that excitement levels dropped at the back end of the year given all of the rugby they had played. That was understandable.'

It is now commonplace that top All Blacks don't feature in the NPC — Richie McCaw and Dan Carter both last appeared in the Canterbury jersey in 2009. This was not the way 14 years ago. That part of the game's evolution was still to take shape. Robbie, and the Crusaders, led the way in the transition.

'It was actually a great point of growth for us as a coaching and management group,' Robbie contends. 'We had to recognise that we were part of the problem. We hadn't adapted by changing our methods, and the team routines, to cater for the individual needs of the players.'

That meant tailoring approaches to each player in order to get the best out of them.

'Instead of appreciating that every player had a different circumstance, and some needed greater management in terms of their physical workloads, and their mental well-being, we were reverting to the old 'go to' in times of underperformance: we were driving them harder — quantity on the training field rather than quality.'

The advantage they had, Robbie says, was their familiarity with the players, having retained the core of the group through this period.

'We knew both the players, and their history, so we were in the best position to evolve the group, both in terms of personnel, but also individual player management.'

It is a skill Robbie believes is now gaining more traction in the professional game, with a greater emphasis placed on coaching experience now than was the case a decade ago.

'If you look at the coaching ranks of New Zealand in particular, you are seeing a lot of experienced men coming back into the NPC with provinces. These are men who have previously coached at Super Rugby or in the international arena — sometimes both.'

'At the turn of the century, the game was only in its infancy as a professional sport. Even now, in relative terms, professionalism is still new and we are still, as a game, learning as we go.

'One of the areas of growth is coming from the lessons of other codes with a far greater history in professionalism, such as Australian Rules Football, rugby league, soccer [football] and even American football [NFL]. If you look at these sports, a much greater emphasis is placed on age and experience in their coaches than perhaps has been the case previously in rugby.

'Many of the coaches at the top end in those sports are not just guiding the players, they are also coaching and developing the other coaches on their staff, bringing the next generation forward so to speak.'

Certainly, coaching development has been a part of Robbie's progression. All of his provincial assistants, barring Hayes, have gone on to head coaching positions in their own right.

Hansen took over as Canterbury NPC coach for 2001, winning the title before beginning a journey that took him to the All Blacks, via a character-testing stint with Wales. His successor Colin Cooper, who assisted Robbie in 2002, had been with Taranaki but subsequently left the Crusaders for a nine-year stint leading the Hurricanes before going back to Taranaki, while also taking over as New Zealand Maori coach.

Hayes was on board for the 2003 and 2004 seasons before opting to concentrate on his Rakaia farm.

Next came Vern Cotter. He had successful head coaching experience with Bay of Plenty before he arrived in Christchurch at the end of 2004, having presided over that province's first Ranfurly Shield success in its 93-year history shortly before his appointment. The Crusaders won the title in each of Cotter's two seasons with the team before he moved on to France, subsequently taking glamour club Clermont Auvergne to the Top 14 title as well as the final of the European Cup.

It was something of an irony that Cotter made his move into the test arena, signing on to guide Scotland, at the same time as Robbie finished his five-year stint with the Wallabies.

Cotter's departure from Christchurch after the 2006 campaign saw the ex-players Hammett and Blackadder establish themselves on the coaching staff. Both have since been Super Rugby head coaches in their own right: Hammett with the Hurricanes, while Blackadder succeeded Robbie in presiding over the Crusaders.

Rob Penney, who subsequently coached Canterbury to four NPC titles, was also involved. Penney acted as a forward's assistant to Cotter before he gained the head coaching role with the NPC side. The Burnside loose forward, who was a Canterbury teammate of Robbie's through the latter stages of his playing career, subsequently coached Irish province Munster before moving on to Japan.

As Wyllie noted, the flow of knowledge from one generation to the next is a consistent strand in the success of Canterbury and Crusaders rugby.

11

BIRTH OF THE CRUSADERS AND THE MAKING OF THE MEN

The start of the second Super Rugby season found the Crusaders with a lot of work to do.

Not only had the wooden-spooners of the first year failed on the field, the competition's arrival had made a limited impression off it, with the Lancaster Park crowd numbers dwindling as the Crusaders' losses, and injuries, mounted.

'There had been a fair few presumptions made around the Crusaders, that the traditions and history of Canterbury rugby would come forward with them,' Robbie says. 'The first year showed that they hadn't. As an entity, the Crusaders were something new. As such, they needed to build up their own identity.

'We were all conscious of that as we began planning for that second season.'

In Robbie, and the new coach Wayne Smith, the Crusaders had two front men whose history was indelibly etched in Canterbury rugby folklore.

Smith was joined on the coaching staff by the former North Auckland (now Northland) skipper Peter Sloane, with Robbie forming the third part of the leadership triangle as team manager.

'It worked well,' Robbie suggests, 'because we all had the same end in mind. We were all striving to firstly see the Crusaders do well and then have Canterbury succeed later in the year. Given that it was largely the same player group for both campaigns, the synergy was there.'

Which is not to say there weren't disagreements.

'There was robust discussion at times but that was fine. We wouldn't have got there any other way.'

Todd Blackadder admits there was a danger having a coach on board as team manager, especially one who would be coaching most of the players through a different campaign later in the year. Blackadder says Robbie was careful not to cross the boundary between managing and coaching during his initial years with the Crusaders. He provided the required level of support to the coaches while ensuring there could be no perception that he was undermining them.

If any advice was needed, Leon MacDonald says, Robbie would do it via a quiet word as opposed to really pushing forward his views. He was a particularly useful conduit for the Crusaders fullback, who says it felt like having his own personal mentor on the team staff.

Both Blackadder and MacDonald agree that Robbie was a great choice as manager, with MacDonald noting that he was the first team manager he had experienced who brought his boots with him to training and ran around with the players as if he was one of their number, offering individual pointers and analysis when asked.

Robbie understood what the players needed on and away from the field, Blackadder says, and they certainly didn't lack for anything during his time in that role. He was also very good, the skipper says, at maintaining a suitable balance in his approach to the team. He liked to have a laugh and make the players feel at ease, but was also very clear in making them understand what he expected of them.

'It was deep end stuff, in terms of my entry as a team manager, but I had good support around me,' Robbie says. 'For sure, it was a tough arena, but that was exciting. No one had enjoyed coming last the year before, but in many ways that was the best thing that could have happened for the Crusaders.

'It was the foundation for what followed. It highlighted that nothing could be presumed.'

This included the support of the public. The task of reconnecting with the people of the region was one of the new coaching and management regime's immediate priorities.

The Crusaders are the people's team. Robbie understood that, and drove that mentality within the environment, Blackadder says. He placed great importance on educating new arrivals about the status the team carried within the local community, and the privilege they all had in representing the people of the region.

Embracing the support base is something that is now ingrained in the Crusaders DNA, Blackadder says, with Robbie having had a big part to play in that.

'There was always the potential for professional players to function within a bubble of their own making,' Robbie says. 'Getting them out and about, connecting with the wider community at large and becoming part of the community, was an important way of guarding against the team becoming insular.

'And it was a win-win. It's often suggested that professionalism changed the game. It actually didn't. The ethos and the values are still the same, but there is always the potential for professionalism to become a distraction, and for the players to get away from what the game is really all about.'

This is something Robbie viewed first hand later, coaching the Wallabies, where the peripheral distractions and acts of individualism from within the playing group were often far greater than he had been accustomed to in Christchurch. It also reflected the pressures created by a more tabloid media in Australia, more emphasis on individualism by the players through the actions of their managers, and also the greater focus within the culture that was placed on financial reward.

'While we were never remunerated directly in the amateur era, we were indirectly. It's the old story: you give and you will get back. If you, as a sporting organisation, give to your community, they will give back by getting in behind your team and supporting you. That's what we experienced after that first year at the Crusaders.'

While the years of success undoubtedly helped, the Crusaders remained proactive in the community even once they had been firmly embraced by their public, running a number of successful community projects whose success is best judged by their longevity.

The Crusaders allied with the Christchurch City Mission to conduct the 'Can crusade', which sees the players man stalls at supermarkets around the city signing posters and merchandise for the public in return for food donations which are used to help feed the homeless. This programme has been running for over a decade.

Another hugely successful annual fundraiser has been the Cystic Fibrosis cricket match. This draws a large pre-Christmas crowd for an event featuring a charity auction where each player donates a piece of personal equipment or memorabilia to be sold. All of the funds raised go to Cystic Fibrosis.

The community connection extends well beyond Christchurch. Blackadder memorably named all seven of the contributing provinces in his acceptance speech after the Crusaders maiden title at Eden Park in 1998.

The franchise has always taken its pre-season matches to the hinterland, preparing in the local district while undertaking community work.

'We held working bees,' Robbie says. 'The idea was to achieve something that would remain after we'd left, so that we'd made a difference to the community.

'How it worked was that local representatives would identify the task we could do, and the team would then work on it around preparations for the pre-season game.'

The motivation driving all of the activities, Robbie says, was to leave a tangible mark. The players got to mix and mingle with the community and feel their support while achieving something constructive.

'There was a fair amount of apprehension at times, especially for the younger guys who were experiencing going out into the community for the first time. But from it invariably came growth. The players would return with stories to share from their experience, usually with plenty of humour involved!'

One programme, which took the players out of their comfort zone, was run in conjunction with the Salvation Army in Christchurch. The idea came to Robbie after he met Bob Miller, who ran the Salvation Army's nightly operation feeding the homeless throughout the city.

'Bob invited me to go out with him one night to observe some of their work, and the idea grew from there.'

'What impressed me most was Bob's ability to relate to all and sundry that we met, and we came across a wide range of people that night with many different backgrounds. He had a great ability to connect with people. I learnt an awful lot from him just through observation.'

Robbie was generally stunned by the experience, but also saw it as an opportunity.

'I had no real idea how many people in need Christchurch had,' Robbie confesses. 'It's quite scary because if you aren't specifically looking, you won't see them. That's where it became evident to me that there is such a fine line in life.

'It also struck me that it was too good an educational opportunity to turn down.'

Thus began a successful programme where the players take their turn accompanying the Salvation Army on the nightly operation.

The experience has served the Crusaders well in terms of keeping the players 'earthed'.

'It gave our players the opportunity to understand how tenuous life can be, reinforcing that they shouldn't take for granted the privilege they had,' says Robbie. 'But it also showed them, as did a number of the other community engagement programmes we ran, that they had the capacity to give back.'

If the drive to connect with the community laid a key pillar for the dynasty that was to follow, the Crusaders' on-field efforts in 1997 also contributed to the foundation.

Although the Crusaders finished four competition points out of the semi-finals places, the side returned five wins and a draw from the 11 matches, and matched the number of wins achieved by the fourth-placed Sharks.

They also gained their maiden win on South African soil, at their sixth attempt, when beating the Free State Cheetahs 16–11 at Bloemfontein. The visit, which opened with a 22–23 loss to the Bulls at Loftus a week earlier, represented Robbie's first time back in the Republic since the Cavaliers, 11 years earlier.

'It was nice to be there on an officially sanctioned tour,' Robbie notes wryly. 'But it was good to go back. While South Africa as a nation had changed significantly in that 11-year gap, the passion and fervour for the game hadn't, nor had the size and approach of the South African players!'

The Crusaders had played four matches in South Africa the year before, losing two in the pre-season and two during the competition proper.

The breakthrough win at Free State Stadium was a significant moment for the franchise as it dismantled the barrier that winning on South African soil represented. The game also provided the manager's first experience of the judicial process, defending halfback Aaron Flynn the next morning after he was cited for a late charge.

Such is the level of Robbie's competitive nature, the players came to believe that he thrived on the cut and thrust nature of the judicial process, where the thoroughness of his preparation, allied to an in-depth knowledge of every aspect of the game, made him hard to beat.

He is so into winning, Robbie takes almost as much satisfaction out of successfully defending a judicial case as he does a game, MacDonald says, even in cases where he knows that the player concerned is probably guilty of the charge that has been laid. Unsurprisingly, Robbie's record at the judiciary through the years has been very good.

Robbie remembers the Flynn case well.

'I pulled a clause out of the IRB handbook that flummoxed them,' he grins. 'It threw the panel into a panic and we were successful in getting the charge thrown out.'

The campaign closed on a positive note when the Crusaders hosted the previous year's top qualifiers, the Queensland Reds. The Reds of that year were a shadow of the previous edition, but they were led by Australian skipper John Eales, and still boasted a largely Wallaby playing roster. Not that you would have known it when they were carved up 48–3, six tries to none.

It was a sign of what was to come.

12

TITLE YEARS (PART 1): THE DYNASTY BEGINS

The Crusaders had good reason to feel confident when they got together ahead of the 1998 campaign.

Twenty-two of the squad had featured for Canterbury six months earlier, and the NPC had already proved to be a very good form guide for Super Rugby, with both of the Blues' titles having come after Auckland had won New Zealand's national title the year before.

That optimism was fuelled further when the Crusaders beat the Blues at the pre-season four-way Southern Cross tournament at Coolum in Queensland. Despite the low-key conditions in which the win was achieved, with the players cycling to the ground from their accommodation before kick-off, the Crusaders first-ever win over the Blues was still an important step.

'They [the Blues] were the same players we would encounter later on in the regular season,' Robbie says, 'so beating them, regardless of the circumstances, was still significant for us.

'It built on the achievements of the year before while giving the playing group another deposit of belief.'

It was needed.

Four games into the regular season, the picture was very different. The expectation that had been raised by the province's first NPC title in 14 years, which had come on the back of a much improved second edition of the Crusade, appeared to have been based on false premises. Unthinkably, the class of '98 was only marginally better off than the eventual wooden-spooners of two years earlier had been at the same point.

The '96 version had only a draw to their credit after four matches before finally cracking the franchise's maiden win in week five. Two seasons on, the Crusaders had lost three of their first four, and that had plenty questioning whether the Crusaders were the real deal.

Time to panic?

Well, no actually.

'While the public expectation had grown off the back of the NPC, it wasn't such a big factor for the playing group. What the early performances did highlight was that the element of surprise had gone. The teams we played were clearly expecting more of us than had been the case in the past.'

An eight-day turnaround following the third of those defeats, against the Blues in Christchurch, provided a pause, and with it time for reflection.

As a result, a more focused Crusaders outfit reappeared the following week, blasting out to a 25–0 halftime advantage against the visiting Bulls, before a less impressive second half saw the South Africans close the gap to 31–20 at the finish.

Even though the Bulls of that year were not the imposing beasts they were to become, and won just three games, the Crusaders' performance against them was still significant.

'It got a bit ugly at times, but that game was a real turning point, not just because of the result, but because of the way the playing group responded. They took more ownership, both individually and collectively. It reflected recognition from the players that we'd meandered.

'By reasserting the habits that had served us in the past, we knew we were capable of beating anyone in the competition, and that was exciting.'

Sixty-four days after the win over the Bulls, the Crusaders would be crowned champions for the first time, having won nine straight.

Through that time, there were learnings — both on and away from the field — that would serve the franchise well, not only in the 1998 campaign, but also through the years, and the titles, which followed.

The South Island derby against an improving Highlanders side, coming off the back of four straight wins, was one of them. The match proved to be the beginning of a rivalry that would become familiar around the pointy end of the competition. The two sides subsequently met in three play-off games between 1999 and 2002.

On this occasion, the Crusaders showed resilience to overhaul a 16–21 halftime deficit as they powered to a 40–24 win. Of nearly equal significance was that the match, played on a Friday night in Christchurch, drew a crowd of 32,000. This provided recognition of the work that the Crusaders were doing off the field, connecting with a fan base that was now taking ownership of the team.

By the time the Crusaders hit Durban for the second match of their South African tour, they'd won six in a row and had already secured a maiden semi-final berth. All that remained was the decision on where the following week's match was to be played. Regardless of the result at King's Park, the Crusaders would be playing the Sharks again.

This meant Robbie had to make arrangements for the two scenarios, with bookings in place both to travel home but also to be accommodated, with training facilities secured, for the extra South African week.

'That was a big, big game,' Robbie recalls, 'both for that campaign, and for the franchise as a whole.

'While winning it didn't guarantee success the following week in the semi-final, it did make a powerful statement, both externally but also internally, that we could go toe to toe with the best, and prevail over adversity.'

The Sharks, coached by the ex-Springboks coach Ian McIntosh, were an experienced and capable side, which had made the inaugural final in 1996, and the semis a year later, losing to the Blues at the seemingly impregnable Eden Park in both instances.

Expectations were high in Durban, but the Crusaders shut the locals out, with the 32–20 scoreline flattering the home side.

A week later, the two sides went at it again in front of 34,000 in Christchurch. The Crusaders blitzed the South Africans in the first half, leading 20–0, but the Sharks showed their play-off pedigree, recovering to lead 32–26 before the Crusaders scored the last 10 points of the game.

Luck was with the home side as the Sharks first five-eighths Botha

Wessels was unluckily yellow-carded at a critical time, allowing the Crusaders to take advantage of their short-staffed opponents.

As he had been all season, a big factor for the Crusaders was the Northland winger 'Stormin' Norman Berryman. One of eight players from other provinces secured by the Crusaders via the draft system then in place, Berryman was simply sensational in the winning run to the final. He scored seven tries in four weeks, which included doubles in each of the back-to-back wins against the Sharks.

'Norm required a lot of management when he first arrived from Whangarei,' Robbie recalls. 'It was a very different environment to what he was accustomed to and he took a while to settle in, pushing the boundaries a bit, which saw us having some "conversations". But he offered us a lot, and played a massive role in those first two titles.'

Berryman gained as much as he gave.

'It worked both ways, he offered us a lot and we offered a lot to him,' Robbie says. 'During his time with us, Normy grew as a person, both away from the game, but certainly within it. I wouldn't say he always conformed, but it became a very vibrant and robust working relationship as he came to understand what the organisation and the team was all about.

'He was a big point of difference for us in the 1998 and 1999 campaigns, there's no doubt about that.'

Berryman was one of a number of 'individuals' who required 'handling' during their settling in period.

Another whose memory causes Robbie to smile was the Counties Manukau hooker John Akurangi, who spent a season in Christchurch in 1997 after playing for the Blues a year earlier, before then being picked up by the Chiefs for 1998.

'He arrived armed with his two cellphones and a smooth attitude, but also with certain expectations of what would be laid on for him,' Robbie says.

'As with Normy, that led to a few conversations as we set a few boundaries. He pushed them early on but gradually settled down, and ended up making a valuable contribution during his time with us.'

Akurangi only wound up playing two games for the Crusaders but his presence added to the competition for places, which Robbie says was an important part of the evolution of the team after its shaky start.

'Although he could cover prop, Axe [Akurangi] was effectively the third hooker in the group. That created a bit of testiness, but that was part of the growth we needed, with guys putting pressure on each other, which raised the bar in terms of our performance, both individually but also as a team.

'As they look back now, I think our other two hookers of the time, Mark Hammett and Matt Sexton, would both concede that Axe actually helped push them into achieving greater heights.'

Statistically, the Crusaders 20–13 win in the 1998 final, which represented the Blues' first-ever defeat on Eden Park, shouldn't have happened. The Blues dominated possession in the game, and led 10–3 after overturning a 0–3 halftime deficit, before laying siege to the Crusaders goal-line through a series of five-metre scrums.

Somehow the Crusaders held out against the Blues' All Blacks pack, clawing back to 13–13 before Andrew Mehrtens poked a chip in behind the home side's defence with just a minute left, and the former Blues winger James Kerr got the right bounce to score the match-winning try.

'That period as we built up the side, both in Super Rugby but also with the NPC team, was based on defence, on our tenacity in refusing to concede, our ability to strike from turnover and also on our kicking game,' Robbie says.

'It helped, of course, having one of the best kickers in the world at that time in Mehrts.'

All four of those ingredients were in evidence in a victory Robbie still marvels at, 17 years on.

'The seeds of belief had been planted by the wins [against Auckland] in the NPC the year before, and then [over the Blues] in the pre-season. We also had the momentum of eight straight wins going into that final.

'So there was a cumulative effect in that game. The habits were becoming ingrained and the guys just refused to submit when it looked like the tide was against them.

'The fact that we'd gone for so long that season with our backs to the wall, after the poor start, had generated the belief that we can't actually fail here, we've just got to hang on, keep going, and we'll find a way through.'

A noticeable aspect of that historic day in Auckland was the presence of a large amount of Crusaders support among the crowd. And it was evident that it wasn't just those hailing from the Crusaders region who were willing the side to win.

'Auckland, through both the NPC and then the Blues in Super Rugby, had dominated the scene for so long, that everyone not aligned to that region seemed to be in our corner,' Robbie says. 'Even a lot of the Sharks players, gutted as they must have been after the semi-final, had been quick to wish us well for the following week, offering words of encouragement and saying it was time for the Blues' run to be halted.'

In his post-match speech prior to accepting the trophy, Crusaders skipper Todd Blackadder paid tribute to all seven provinces that make up the franchise. The action highlighted the team's commitment to the whole franchise area, representing the top half of the South Island. The smaller regions were not to be forgotten now that the job was done.

With the mission successfully completed, Robbie had organised a flight back to Christchurch that evening. This allowed the celebrations to begin on home soil, but the party that began that night was a mere entrée to the main event: the first of what became a regular feature, the Crusaders street parades.

The first parade, which was held in the week following the final, saw the central city flooded with bodies as the people of Christchurch and beyond paid homage to their victorious heroes.

'The turnout blew us away,' Robbie says. 'It showed just how much our win had meant. It also reinforced to the whole group how much we had achieved off the playing field, in terms of connecting with the wider community.

'There were more people lining the streets of Colombo Street and beyond than we could ever have fitted into Lancaster Park.'

The dynasty was under way. Could the Crusaders do it again?

The start of the 1999 season certainly suggested they could.

Three matches against New Zealand opponents first up saw the Crusaders outclass the Chiefs 48–3 and beat the Jed Rowlands-coached Blues 22–16 before drawing 18–18 at home against the Hurricanes.

This game was drawn after the one-time Crusader Mal Arnold, who'd been with the team in 1997, slotted a late conversion from the sideline to win a bet with All Blacks fullback Christian Cullen.

Cullen proved a real thorn in the Crusaders' side during his Hurricanes career, scoring seven tries against them, including two in each of the 1999, 2000 and 2001 games. It was after the second of his scores in 1999 that he promised Arnold a Big Mac hamburger from McDonald's if he could kick the goal to tie the scores.

The West Coaster obliged, winning himself a feed, while unwittingly tipping his former teammates into a slump that saw them win just one of a run of five games. This included a 23–36 loss to the Queensland Reds at home along with conclusive losses to the Highlanders (6–23) in Dunedin and the Stormers (19–28) in Cape Town.

All three of those sides were to feature alongside the Crusaders at competition's end, in the play-offs, but Robbie says, of the three, the performance of the Stormers in Cape Town was the most potent.

'They were the best side we played that year. They were clinical all over the park, had experience in all of the key positions, and a lot of variety in terms of their approach. It made them hard to contain.'

Ironically, while the Crusaders were unable to inflict fatal damage on the Stormers' championship hopes, an incident in the evening after the game did.

Star Stormers loose forward Bobby Skinstad ruptured the anterior cruciate ligament of his knee in a car accident, having left the players' post-game gathering in an emotional state following an altercation with Crusaders halfback Justin Marshall.

Fortunately, Robbie was present at the time of the incident with Marshall.

'I had a policy in those days of being the last to leave to make sure that I'd rounded everyone up,' Robbie explains.

'There was still a genuine transition from amateur to professional going on at that time. Some of the amateur habits were no longer appropriate in the professional era, especially given the attention to detail that was required in player preparation, but also given the additional level of scrutiny that was now involved in the game.

'It's fair to say, back then, with professionalism only into its fourth year, blokes who'd spent most of their careers as amateurs were still struggling with some aspects of the new landscape.

'Skinstad's injury was a shame because, although he made it back [going on to be part of South Africa's Rugby World Cup-winning squad in 2007], he was never quite the player he had been prior to that injury, in terms of the impact he could have on a game.'

As is often the case, the incident found its way into the media, although it took its time to surface, Robbie receiving a phone call from a South African journalist on the eve of the final, suggesting that his paper was going to run a story blaming Marshall for the Skinstad injury.

'I told the journalist to be very careful,' Robbie says, 'because I had been there and was aware what had happened [with Marshall]. He wasn't.'

The journalist backed off, and no story ever ran.

Of more pressing concern to the Crusaders in the immediate aftermath of the Cape Town defeat was their state: they were now back where they had been after the poor start to the previous season, needing to win every game just to qualify for the semi-finals.

That task began the following week in Pretoria on an afternoon best recalled for the two-fingered 'salute' given to the local fans by an emotional Mehrtens, following the Crusaders first five-eighths' late dropped goal, which had secured a priceless 30–28 victory.

The All Black's response came after he had been roundly jeered for missing a penalty goal attempt moments earlier, with the Crusaders trailing by a point. While the footage of the extravagant reaction received a wide airing, there was no formal disciplinary process to deal with as a result, and the team moved on.

'It just reflected the position the team was at,' Robbie says. 'We were on a tipping point. We knew it, and that's when emotions tend to flow.

'The irony of what happened is that while there was a bit of tut-tutting from some people, the fans that the signal was directed at probably appreciated Mehrts, not so much for the gesture, but for the way he had kicked that dropped goal under extreme pressure.

'South Africans respected Mehrts enormously for his ability. He was always one of our most popular players when we went to South Africa and what happened that day at Loftus [Versfeld] didn't change that.'

It was presumed by most following the Loftus match that the Crusaders were back in business. Their last three matches were all against sides struggling to stay in the semi-final running. Two of those were at home.

No problem? Surely?

It only took a calamitous 30 minutes at Nelson against the Cats to determine otherwise.

Having headed to the top of the South Island with momentum, the Crusaders were given a serious rev-up by coach Wayne Smith prior to kick-off, but he might as well have been talking to the South Africans. It was they who appeared to take on board the messages, scoring four tries as they rocketed out to a 31–6 lead.

'They [the Cats] kept coming, wave after wave of attack,' Robbie recalls. 'For a while there, we simply couldn't live with them, and weren't going to be able to unless someone stood up.'

That someone was Berryman, whose actions in the face of that onslaught defined his Crusaders career, Robbie says.

'He literally said to the rest of them: "Just give me the ball and follow me!" That afternoon showed how far he had come; the transformation from free spirit to leader was complete. He had become a warrior in both his outlook and his mindset.'

Inspired by the big winger's two tries, the Crusaders swamped the Cats in a torrent of points, winning the remaining hour of the game by a 52–7 margin as they surged to an astonishing 58–38 win.

'It was a remarkable game. The comeback reflected the spirit and belief within the group. They were getting hammered but still never lost hope in their ability to turn it around.'

That was the case again a week later when another South African opponent found that a big lead was no guarantee of success.

Needing a win to keep slim hopes of a fourth straight semi-final appearance alive, the Sharks led 22–6 at halftime in Christchurch, but were eventually overrun 34–29.

Despite the heroics of the previous three weeks, the Crusaders still needed to beat the Waratahs in Sydney to make sure of a finals place, while awaiting the outcome of other matches to see where they would be playing, if they got there.

The first part of the deal was taken care of comfortably enough, with Berryman again making his presence felt by scoring two tries in a 38–22 win. The Waratahs had led at the break, but the Crusaders were only teasing, outclassing their rivals 21–0 in the second period.

Robbie now had to wait for the results in South Africa before he could finalise the team's logistical plans for the semi-final preparation.

It was just as well he waited.

A topsy-turvy final weekend of qualifying saw the top two sides, the Stormers and the Highlanders, both lose. This allowed the Queensland Reds to overtake them, which meant a trip to Brisbane for the fourth-placed Crusaders.

'We were meant to be heading to South Africa, which would have meant going straight on to there from Sydney, until the Stormers lost at home to the Cats. This dropped them down to second, and confirmed the Reds as our opponents.

'But the South African game didn't finish until 4 am. A few of the senior guys were still out and I had to track everyone down so that we could make a decision as to what we were going to do in terms of our preparation.'

The Crusaders had come away to Sydney prepared, gear-wise, for an onward trip to South Africa, as that had appeared the most likely outcome. The decision now was whether to stay in Australia, or to return home, and then head to Brisbane closer to game day.

'I was keen to stay in Sydney as I thought it would be good for morale, in terms of the chemistry of the group, by keeping us together and keeping us tight,' Robbie says.

The senior players and coaching staff agreed, with the decision playing a significant part in the subsequent 28–22 win that knocked out the Reds, as top qualifiers, a game short of the big dance for the second time in four years.

'You play how you prepare and the week [leading up to that game] was outstanding for us.'

The Crusaders even gained the benefit of some intelligence courtesy of a few Reds lineout tactics, which had been left on a whiteboard the Crusaders used, after the Queenslanders had stayed at the same hotel a few weeks earlier. Robbie had always been careful about not leaving any tactical information lying around where it could be viewed by non-team members. This episode reinforced that habit.

The fact that the Reds had comprehensively outplayed the Crusaders in Christchurch earlier in the competition may also have played a part in their semi-final demise.

'They may have underestimated our group, second time around, having won so easily earlier on. You do see that happen a fair bit in sport,' Robbie says. 'And we were a very different team eight weeks on, when we played them again, both with the momentum of four wins behind us, and because of the belief that we had gained from all that we had already been through.'

The early hours of the morning after the Brisbane win brought more good news, from a Crusaders perspective, as the Highlanders upset the Stormers 33–18 in Cape Town to set up an all South Island final.

Instead of climbing on a plane for the long trip to Africa, the Crusaders could now journey home to their beds and prepare quietly away from the spotlight. Meanwhile the Highlanders had to deal with the long return flight across 10 time zones, as well as the excitement of a home final and the pressures associated with it. As a bonus, the Crusaders also had an additional day to prepare, with the final put back to a Sunday in order to give the Highlanders extra time to recover following the trip back from Cape Town.

Logistics aside, the Crusaders had other reasons for being happy to avoid a return to Cape Town.

'It wasn't going to be easy [going to Dunedin], but it didn't hold the same burden for us that Cape Town might have,' Robbie says. 'We'd lost in Cape Town earlier in the year, and while we'd lost in Dunedin too, we could prepare for a game down there while sleeping in our own beds for much of the week. Carisbrook was also a ground we had greater familiarity with at that stage.'

The game, which became known as 'The Party at Tony Brown's' following a successful promotion centred on the Highlanders first five-eighths, brought together two sides with similar backgrounds.

Both had overcome adversity in away semi-finals to qualify.

The Highlanders were also following an identical pathway to that the Crusaders themselves had walked the year before. The 1998 NPC winning Otago team, who provided the bulk of the Highlanders playing staff, was now seeking to dethrone the defending Super Rugby champions, as the Crusaders had the Blues.

That's where the similarities ended.

While the game was played in a fantastic atmosphere at Carisbrook, with strong support for both sides, the Highlanders couldn't muster when it mattered. Despite the home side leading 14–9 at halftime, after having taken first use of a strong breeze, the Crusaders dominated the second period and came from behind for the fourth time in five weeks.

The 24–19 final score was actually a bit deceptive as the Highlanders' last try came when the game was all but over.

At least, in defeat, the southerners didn't lose their sense of humour. As with the 'Party at Tony Brown's' campaign, which ripped off a television insurance advert of the time, so too did their parting shot at the Crusaders, taking off an emphatic statement that was being peddled in a Toyota trucks commercial of the age.

'We were on the bus driving out to the airport and there it was, on a big sign, standing there for us to see,' Robbie recalls. 'It was hard not to have a chuckle.'

It was one word that summed up the collective feeling of a region.

'Bugger!'

13

TITLE YEARS (PART 2): 'THERE'S A STORM COMING!'

One of the key ingredients in the Crusaders' ongoing success was the ability to identify and recruit talent from outside the region. This initially took the form of the draft, which enabled franchises to secure fringe players who were not required among the initial selection of their home region. As professionalism developed, and the focus on talent identification sharpened, recruiting talented kids straight from school became imperative, prior to their futures being locked in elsewhere.

Initially, recruitment duties were shared between the NPC and Super Rugby programmes, with Robbie and Wayne Smith both active, at the same time ensuring that all acquisitions were going to benefit both programmes.

The effectiveness of their work was best measured by the number of gems who were picked up, either having failed previously elsewhere, or having had their potential identified by the Crusaders brains trust before anyone at their home franchise had cottoned on.

Players like the Northland pair of lock Norm Maxwell and winger Norm Berryman were prime examples of early Crusaders success on the recruitment front. Western Samoan wing Afato So'oalo, Counties Manukau midfielder Tony Marsh, Taranaki fullback Daryl Lilley, Bay of Plenty (via Auckland) winger Caleb Ralph, Hawke's Bay prop Greg Somerville and Taranaki prop Greg Feek were other notable success stories from the first seasons.

Occasionally, the prospective recruits took some convincing, with

Somerville providing Robbie with an amusing anecdote when he first made contact with the promising prop while he was boarding at a rural agricultural facility in the North Island.

'When I rang, they went to get him, and I could hear these footsteps as he walked to the phone,' Robbie recalls. 'He picked up and I introduced myself, saying it was Robbie Deans here. Yoda [Somerville] has the most distinctive laugh. I wouldn't be being unfair to say it's not entirely dissimilar to the squeals of a donkey.

'When I said who it was, he replied, "Yeah, right," and began laughing. So that was my introduction to Greg Somerville.'

Most players who came south ultimately signed for Canterbury to play in the NPC on top of their Super Rugby duties. Once they had been in Christchurch, few left for other New Zealand teams. Those who did more often than not regretted it.

Nor was it just the on-field success that kept the players in Christchurch, Crusaders fullback Leon MacDonald says. Keeping the core of the playing group together over a period of time tightened the bonds, both between the players but also between their partners; who were skilfully catered for by an off-field organisational effort coordinated by Robbie's wife Penny, with Kate Thorne (née Mehrtens), wife of Reuben, also prominent.

This would include organised 'get-togethers' for the 'girls' while their husbands or partners were touring, a specific partners and families corporate box at home games, so they could share the emotional roller-coaster of the match together, and also assistance with a number of other daily challenges that can sometimes become an issue for young women without support.

MacDonald recalls being invited around for dinner by Robbie and Penny shortly after he and his young wife Hayley had arrived in Christchurch from Blenheim. The interest made an impression, given its clearly genuine nature and intent. This was not a one-off welcome to be quickly forgotten. Penny stayed in touch regularly and was a handy point of contact for advice on schooling issues and babysitting. She was also known to pop up with meals and support at opportune times, when young mums were battling with children while their men were off defending the Crusaders honour.

The environment created, MacDonald says, a family in the truest sense of the word; hence players didn't want to leave, because they had an emotional attachment to the place.

That attachment also grew the leadership from within, as players genuinely felt like they were representing their family, as much as they were representing their team.

The fallout from the All Blacks' failure to win the 1999 Rugby World Cup saw John Hart resign as coach, with Smith elevated from the Crusaders to take his place. The flow-on from that appointment saw Robbie take over as Crusaders head coach with Steve Hansen, who had replaced Peter Sloane as Smith's assistant for 1999, remaining in that role alongside Robbie.

Although Robbie stayed on with the Canterbury team for the NPC later that year, he wound up stepping down from that role for the following season, which gave Hansen the opportunity to try himself out in the NPC as a head coach.

Robbie knew that, in replacing Smith, much would be expected, given that the Crusaders entered the 2000 season as the two-time defending champions. History has shown it is often harder to defend a title than it is to win it in the first place. Backing up is a feat achieved in Super Rugby by only four teams: the Blues, Bulls, Chiefs and the Crusaders — who have done it three times.

While he might not have been coaching them previously, Robbie knew the Crusaders inside out. He knew the players, he knew their habits, he knew their opponents and, most importantly, he knew what was going to be required to succeed. The Crusaders would have to adapt their game, and bring something new if they were to stay ahead of the chasing pack.

'Through the first three years of my involvement, which had included the titles in 1998 and 1999, our game had been structured around defence, with attacking opportunities from turnovers stemming from that,' Robbie explains.

'Looking ahead to 2000, it was clear that the same approach wouldn't cut it, because our opponents had seen what we were doing and would have put their strategies in place to counter us.

'So from 2000, we widened the base of our game by placing an added emphasis on our attack. To achieve that, we modified our approach, but we also added some grunt, bringing in some players we expected to help bring the team forward.'

Promising North Harbour No. 8 Ron Cribb was one of those players, Taranaki centre Mark Robinson another. Both became All Blacks as soon as that year's competition finished. But the real masterstroke proved to be the recruit that was the hardest to get, with the pursuit involving a trip to Fiji for a meeting Robbie was warned might not happen.

The target was Fijian winger Marika Vunibaka, who had starred for his nation as they narrowly missed out on a quarter-final berth at the previous year's Rugby World Cup.

The Fijians had been denied by a refereeing howler from New Zealand whistler and future IRB refs boss Paddy O'Brien in their crucial pool match against France. Even so, Vunibaka had returned from that tournament having added to the perception he'd previously created on the IRB Sevens circuit as a supreme talent.

Robbie had headed up to Fiji for a short break, hoping to coordinate a meeting with the potential recruit while in the country. The initial attempt at liaison failed so Robbie stayed on. It was worth it as he eventually got his man, convincing the quietly spoken flier that he would be a smash hit as a Crusader.

'I remember [Fiji national coach] Brad Johnstone telling me how surprised he was that we'd got him,' Robbie says of Vunibaka's signing. 'Brad said Marika was so shy, he hadn't expected him to even show up for the meeting.'

Not only did Vunibaka make it to Christchurch, he thrived, as Robbie had predicted he would.

The 25-year-old arrived alone but was well looked after by the Deans family, and quickly embraced by his new teammates, especially after his performance at the team's speed testing session on the day of his arrival.

'He'd only just got in and had no gear of his own, so he had to run in someone else's track pants and runners, into a southerly gale, yet he easily ran a quicker time than anybody else in the squad.'

The speed testing told Robbie he was onto a winner. Vunibaka quickly confirmed it. In his freshman season, the Fijian scored a franchise record

11 tries. By the time he had signed off, after the 2004 crusade, that tally was up to 35 tries from 50 games.

'Marika was a freak, one of the great wingers Super Rugby has seen, but it wasn't just the tries he scored that made him such a class act, it was the invisible stuff he did that people don't often look for or recount,' Robbie says.

A quiet man, with a huge smile, who enjoyed the off-field humour within the team, Robbie jokes that Vunibaka scored more tries for the Crusaders than he had spoken words. Yet one of his favourite Vunibaka memories is of a defensive play. The speedy Stormers and South African winger Breyton Paulse had snapped up a dropped ball and streaked away. With the Crusaders backs stopped in their tracks and having to turn around, a try seemed certain. Paulse was fast, but Vunibaka was faster. He turned about in an instant, which in itself is no mean feat for a 96-kilogram frame, and then tracked back, mowing Paulse down before he'd even got near the goal-line.

'That was the thing about Marika; while his speed brought us a number of tries, it also saved a few,' Robbie says.

'He was equally fast turning around and chasing back as he was when he had the ball going forward.'

Vunibaka provided the Crusaders with an edge, but it was not until fourth week that he opened his try-scoring account. It didn't matter: plenty of others were scoring tries, to the extent that the Crusaders posted in excess of 25 points in each of the first five games, as the campaign opened with five wins.

Although they eventually lost three matches during the round robin phase, their participation in the play-offs was never in any doubt, with the 31–54 loss to the Cats in Johannesburg resulting in a travel experiment being placed in the never-to-be-tried-again bin!

The enormous travel requirements of Super Rugby, and in the Rugby Championship, are a massive factor in the southern hemisphere competitions, making them unique from any other rugby that is played. Given the almost weekly schedule of matches throughout both tournaments, limiting the impact of the time spent on planes, and managing the recovery from its effects, is crucial.

With the objective of getting back to New Zealand a day early, the Crusaders took advantage of the afternoon kick-off to their match at Ellis Park by scheduling their departure later that evening on the 6 pm flight to Sydney.

Normally, the team would have had to wait until Sunday night to depart, which would have resulted in a Tuesday arrival back into Christchurch after more than 24 hours of travel. Getting back a day earlier, given that they had another game the following Saturday, was worth trying.

Unfortunately, the new arrangement, which saw the players having to be on the bus to the airport as soon as possible after the final whistle, proved a distraction. The players' minds were already on the plane. This manifested itself in a number of aspects of the performance, most notably when in possession.

'We'd been doing a lot of work as part of our attacking strategy, around identifying space and using little kicks in behind [the defensive line] to take advantage of it. We profited from it over time, as it created the try [scored by Ron Cribb] that was the point of difference for us in the final.

'But that afternoon a few of the players got kick happy, we kept turning the ball over as a result, and the Cats really punished us. We learnt from that experience. Our judgement around using those kicks improved dramatically as a result.'

The travel strategy might have backfired in Johannesburg, but it didn't sway Robbie from executing an even more audacious plan during the team's final round loss to the Brumbies in Christchurch. Only this time, even in defeat, it worked.

'The game was one versus two. We both already had home semi-finals, and in all likelihood were going to have to play each other again,' Robbie recalls. 'So we took a risk and decided to limit the goals on what we actually wanted to achieve out of the game.

'We would take the win if we could get it, but I told the players to focus on being physical, and making as much contact with the Brumbies players as was possible, while leaving anything beyond that in terms of our attacking ambitions.'

The rationale was to leave a substantial bodily mark on the Australians that they wouldn't forget if matched against the Crusaders again in the final. Not only did Robbie intend to plant the seed within the minds of the Brumbies players as to how tough his team would be physically, he also sought to illustrate to his own players how close they could get to the Brumbies while being one-dimensional. This could only give them confidence going into a rematch, knowing how much more they could bring to their game.

While the 12–17 defeat hardly gave Robbie any sleepless nights, the game did leave one problem, with All Blacks halfback Justin Marshall limping out of the rest of the competition. The injury cost Marshall his second appearance in a final, after he'd missed most of the Crusaders' maiden title two years previously due to a torn Achilles.

Aaron Flynn had deputised superbly for the All Black in 1998, but Robbie took a gamble this time, opting instead for the 21-year-old Ben Hurst.

It was a brave call. While Flynn had finals experience, Hurst had never played Super Rugby, and boasted just four appearances for Canterbury from the previous year, only one of which had been as a starter. The decision was tactical. Hurst had the better pass, and the coach was banking on that allowing his first five-eighths Andrew Mehrtens more time and space to make his decisions.

As it was, the rookie halfback, who is the son of the 1972–74 All Blacks midfield back Ian Hurst, performed with such composure under intense pressure that it was somewhat surprising that he didn't go on to make the All Blacks grade himself.

It wasn't their new halfback, but mechanical problems that provided the Crusaders' biggest hurdle before the semi-final, with the team bus refusing to start after they'd boarded following their team meeting, in order to head to the ground. A mad scramble ensued, with cars being flagged down on the road, and all manner of contingencies being put into effect. It all resulted in the last of the players finally making it to what was then known as Jade Stadium just 20 minutes before kick-off.

Robbie knew the Highlanders' well-respected manager Des Smith from his own days as team manager, and remembers seeing the southerner watching from outside the Highlanders' dressing room as their opponents straggled in.

'Des had this knowing smirk on his face, you could see he was thinking: "Ha, we've got you".'

They hadn't.

With Vunibaka supplying two tries for the fourth time in his extraordinary maiden season, the Crusaders overpowered their rivals in the final quarter, coasting into their third straight final on the back of a convincing 37–15 win.

Robbie believes the pre-game fuss probably aided their cause. As with his own test debut 17 years earlier, it helped to settle the players' nerves by giving them something other than the game to think about.

While the players hadn't appeared to be affected by the occasion, their driver obviously had been, as the players learned after the game that the reason their bus hadn't started was because the gear lever had been left out of park!

Unsurprisingly, the Brumbies came through against the Cats in the other semi-final, setting up the title showdown Robbie had expected, and had plotted for.

What he hadn't planned for was the weather.

Ever meticulous, Robbie had his pre-match sermon to the players all mapped out, and was running through his comments in the team room at their Canberra hotel when a fierce clap of thunder exploded nearby outside.

Thinking on his feet, Robbie changed his script, blurting out a memorable line off the cuff that no one who was in the room will ever forget.

'There's a storm coming to Canberra,' he snarled, 'and it isn't the weather!'

In truth, the weather was dreadful, but nothing was going to stop the Crusaders that night. They had bashed their opponents two weeks before, had studied their game intently, and were ready for anything that might come up.

'We turned their strength into a weakness,' Robbie says very matter-of-factly. The Brumbies were very deliberate and predetermined in their approach — paint by numbers rugby is what I call it. They did it well, and it was very successful for them, but we were just coming into the era of analysis and we'd done our homework.'

The Crusaders knew that after play A came play B. Critically, they'd observed that the Brumbies were very deliberate in terms of following the same script around contact.

'They'd often pre-empt the contact and concede the tackle by going to ground, with the idea of drawing opponents in, while creating quick ball and space elsewhere,' Robbie explains. 'We'd observed this so we decided to stay on our feet and not commit numbers to the tackle area as they wanted. The effect it had was to deny them a ruck situation.

'As a result, it was still general play when they went to ground, so we could walk over the tackled player, attack the ball and drive them back.'

The result was that while the Brumbies held the ball for huge periods within the game, their time and space was cut down, and they made little progress.

The numbers produced from the final are staggering: the Brumbies recycled the ball through 165 rucks to the 34 of the Crusaders, yet they scored just one try. So too did the Crusaders, with the drafted No. 8 Cribb more than earning the next day's All Blacks call-up, when he crossed for the visitor's try.

If it was ironic that defence would win the day for the Crusaders after a campaign largely spent expanding their attacking threat, that didn't surprise Robbie. Finals, like test matches, and especially like big test matches such as Rugby World Cup play-off games, are won by defence. The intensity and the physicality are both greater, players are more desperate in their actions, the contests are generally a lot tighter, and the scoring chances are few.

'Defence is critical in those sorts of games, in terms of matching up physically, but attack is not forgotten. It was still a point of difference for us that night in Canberra,' Robbie says.

'We didn't have anywhere near the amount of ball that the Brumbies did, but we did much more with it!'

Even so, it was a close-run thing.

After being in front for most of the game, the Crusaders fell behind with eight minutes to play, but they didn't panic, while their opponents did. The anxiety among the Brumbies players betrayed itself almost immediately after going in front. From the restart, they were penalised for not releasing the ball at the subsequent ruck, handing Mehrtens a kicking opportunity he was not going to miss.

His goal made it 20–19 and that's the way it stayed, securing for the Crusaders their third title.

Eleven of the victorious squad were named by their former coach Smith in his maiden All Blacks team the following day.

The transformation in the number of the team's playing staff who were now required at national level was startling. When Robbie had joined the Crusaders as team manager, there were just two All Blacks regulars: the inside back combination of Marshall and Mehrtens. By the time the side assembled for the pre-season four years later, 10 players were returning from the previous year's All Blacks tour of France and Italy. A further six had been involved on the simultaneous New Zealand A excursion which took in Wales, France and Romania.

It wasn't just the players who were feeling the effect of the workload. Robbie, Steve Hansen and two other members of the Crusaders' off-field staff had also featured on the A team tour, with the late November return from Europe condensing the planning time that was available to the team's brains trust prior to the beginning of the new crusade.

Between Canterbury, the Crusaders and then the New Zealand A programmes, Robbie had been in campaign virtually non-stop for 48 months.

He acknowledged that it was too much, taking the decision during the 2001 Super Rugby competition to give up his NPC coaching role.

'I accepted that it was taking its toll on me, as much as it was the players, in terms of compromising my ability to prepare properly for each campaign,' Robbie admits.

He wasn't to know, as he gave up both the Canterbury and New Zealand A roles, that another national job was just around the corner.

'I'd enjoyed the New Zealand A tour, getting the chance to coach a national team, and deal with different players.

'On its own, it wasn't such an issue in terms of the pre-tour planning requirements. It was only when you added in completing the Canterbury campaign, while also planning for the following year's Super Rugby season, that it became too much.'

The New Zealand A concept, which has now morphed into the Junior All Blacks, provided international rugby for the next tier of players — and coaches.

On its 2000 tour, Robbie's team beat French Universities, Wales A and Romania, while losing to a strong French Barbarians outfit, which had originally been assembled to play the All Blacks.

The most memorable performance came in the tour finale in Bucharest, where the Romanian national side was put to the sword 82–9.

Robbie believes the performance reflected the build-up.

'There wasn't much to do in Bucharest and the players largely stayed around the hotel, where they were climbing the walls,' he says.

'The city was pretty deprived, there were dogs running loose in the streets and the signs of poverty were everywhere. I think the players were just happy to get stuck into the game.'

Both the All Blacks and the As finished their tours on the last weekend in November. The turnaround, before they began preparing for the 2001 season, was brief. The strain on the playing group was best reflected by the circumstances facing the skipper Blackadder, who returned to pre-season work after what was a little over a two-week break. And this was following a year which had seen him play all 13 games for the Crusaders, seven of the 11 played by Canterbury, as well as all 10 test matches through a campaign where he had been bestowed the honour of captaining his country.

It was, Blackadder says, a recipe for disaster, with the team under pressure from the start as it sought to extend the Crusaders' reign to four consecutive titles.

Success is a moving target, MacDonald says. Because of the tight turnaround from the previous year, the Crusaders opted not to change much of the playing method from that which had worked the previous year. That mistake, the fullback maintains, not so much saw the Crusaders standing still, but saw them going backwards. Teams had adapted, which meant that the Crusaders were chasing from the start.

MacDonald's sentiments are echoed by Richie McCaw, who had debuted for Canterbury the year before, and was brought in to participate in the pre-season before going on the South African tour as injury cover.

It was obvious that everyone was pretty buggered, the future All Blacks and Crusaders captain says. The workload was just too much. The 20-year-old, who would be an All Black before the year was out, had grown up watching the Crusaders set the standard. Now they had fallen back into the pack.

It was apparent from early on that a fourth title in a row was going to be beyond them.

A grand final rematch against the Brumbies in Canberra, which opened the competition, saw the Crusaders belted 16–51. The impact of that result went beyond the coach and his players.

'Sam, who was 10 at the time, was playing cricket the next day,' Robbie recalls. 'When he arrived at the crease, his team was struggling to save the game. From behind the stumps came the voice of the wicketkeeper who said: "Your dad failed last night and you are going to fail today!"'

It was the first time in his career that Robbie's children had been exposed to public criticism aimed at their father. It wasn't to be the last, in what proved to be a tough campaign. The Crusaders won just four of their 11 matches, finishing 10th. It was the only time they finished outside of the semi-final positions during Robbie's nine-year tenure as head coach.

Yet he believes that without the hardship of that season, the Crusaders might not have been able to go on to extend their dynasty as the dominant team in Super Rugby.

'The strain of all the high intensity rugby that the guys had been playing clearly showed but that was a defining moment for us. It led us to managing workloads tailored to individual player needs. This is something the advances in technology have accelerated since, with the use of GPS units providing us with accurate data on the players' workloads.

'Over time, GPS has allowed us to build up a statistical history for each player. This has provided us with a greater awareness of their potential physical vulnerability, with the database identifying the moments, or the loads, that have contributed to previous injuries. Those numbers provide a red flag, telling us when we need to ease back.'

While not totally foolproof, the advances in physical monitoring have clearly proved an invaluable tool for injury prevention, especially in New

Zealand where the centralised system sees information on player welfare and physical well-being shared between the provinces and national union. The national and provincial coaches and medical teams then act in concert, formulating plans to cater for both the player's needs and that of his provincial and national teams.

As Robbie was to discover, the same alignment does not prevail between the state and national programmes in Australia. This contributed massively towards the horrendous injury toll Robbie had to deal with as Wallabies coach, and clearly leaves Australia at a big disadvantage when competing against the highly centralised systems of player management in South Africa and New Zealand especially.

If the 2001 crusade provided crucial learnings at an organisational level, Blackadder also believes that year helped to shape the man at its head. The pressure inevitably started at the top, he says. When under pressure, Robbie simply took more on, in order to ease the burden elsewhere. While that was an understandable response in the circumstances, the Crusaders skipper says it made the coach more introverted.

With the benefit of that experience, he says the Robbie of today would have sought help and tried to delegate more.

Inevitably, during times of stress, what is usually a strength can become the greatest weakness. In the case of Robbie, Blackadder says that while he is a great competitor and an outstanding coach, he was prone to taking on even more responsibility under pressure.

Robbie never shied away from the accountability that goes with being the boss, and never will, Blackadder says, but he has learnt over time to trust those around him more by giving them greater responsibility.

14

TITLE YEARS (PART 3): PERFECT CRUSADE

Perfection: That which is complete — which contains all the requisite parts; that which is so good that nothing of the kind could be better; that which has attained its purpose — Aristotle, 'Delta of the Metaphysics'.

For the first time in four years, the Crusaders returned to work without carrying the status as defending Super Rugby champions. Most, including their coach, expected a reaction from the group. Few could have anticipated just how emphatic the response would be: 13 wins and the only perfect Super Rugby season.

'We came out of 2001 frustrated,' Robbie recalls. 'It was clear from the first time we assembled that the guys were hungry. That was great but it's not, on its own, enough.

'We'd always had a great team ethic. Everyone had worked as hard in 2001 as they had previously — probably even more so, as there is seldom much difference, in terms of the work and effort put in, between a successful campaign and an unsuccessful one.'

The difference for 2002, Robbie says, is that the Crusaders were going to be smarter. Smarter in the way they played, evolving their game, but — even more critically — smarter in the way they prepared.

Throughout Robbie's time with the team, the side was blessed to be able to call on some of the best strength and conditioning (S & C) coaches in the business. They played a big role in the Crusaders' successful run.

Mike Anthony had refined the preparation habits after the fruitless inaugural season. His work laid the platform for three title-winning crusades.

Andrew Hore, later to work with Wales and now the General Manager at the Ospreys club, then took over in 2002 after his predecessor was recruited for the All Blacks. Hore helped to deliver an unbeaten season.

He was followed in turn by Ashley Jones, whose prowess saw him later employed by both the All Blacks and then the Wallabies, having provided the physical platform that led to three titles.

Robbie has always placed a major emphasis on physical conditioning as a critical component in preparation. He likens it to the production of a motorcar — with the S & C coaches 'building' the engines before the players 'race' them!

The change to the construction technique applied to the 2002 model ensured that it became the factory's best product yet.

'The generic approach to preparation was binned. Some of our players had played from the end of January to the start of December the previous year. Others hadn't,' Robbie says. 'That year, for the first time, we recognised the cumulative effect of the workload in our preparation. It was a big change and it made a big difference.'

It was not, however, the only change at Camp Crusader.

Robbie had a new face by his side.

Somewhat controversially, after having guided Canterbury's next generation to an emphatic NPC title the year before, Steve Hansen abruptly left for Wales, to assist his future All Blacks boss Graham Henry.

The well-performed Taranaki NPC coach Colin Cooper was his successor.

'He brought a different perspective and provided a great point of difference,' Robbie says.

'Coops is a real team man. He didn't approach his work looking at what was in it for him personally. He's totally holistic in his outlook. Because of that, he fitted into our environment perfectly.'

It was a testament to the impact Cooper made that his stay in Christchurch lasted just one year. The Crusaders would have loved to have retained him, but the Hurricanes offered him their head coaching role. Understandably, the lure of being the boss of his home franchise was too great to turn down. It was a position he held for eight seasons.

While the coaching change was significant, the biggie as far as the front office was concerned was the captain. After six seasons as the face of the Crusaders, Todd Blackadder had moved on. Canterbury's NPC final win over Otago the previous year was his last game in New Zealand before he left for a new career in Scotland.

The departed skipper had wielded a massive influence, most notably on the field in times of difficulty where he was a galvanising force for the team.

In his absence, Robbie challenged the playing staff as to who was going to step up and fill the void that Blackadder's departure represented.

Back came the response: 'We all will.'

'It was the answer that I had been seeking,' Robbie says. 'They were taking ownership and responsibility.'

This manifested itself before the season had even started, when Robbie assembled the group at Hanmer Springs to set the foundation for the campaign. Following the conclusion of the previous year's competition, Robbie had headed offshore, researching how sporting codes in other countries approached their preparation, the methods and motivations they used, and how they built up their team culture.

'In the early years of the Crusaders, we'd always looked externally for some of our inspiration because we didn't really have any performance history of our own. One of the key points that came out of my research of other sports was a belief that inspiration and innovation came from within rather than outside of a group. Once we accepted that, and started to personalise some of our methods and our motivational theming, we really took off.'

Robbie and his management group drove discussions around a team theme at the camp, coming up with a concept around 'the power of one', which was taken from the book of the same name.

The players split into five groups and discussed their views before presenting feedback. Four of the five were in favour. One wanted change, arguing that the concept didn't provide the team with the focus and vibrancy they were looking for.

'The fact they wanted to change it was not a bad thing; it was totally the opposite, as it reflected their growth as a group. They had to adhere to the meaning of whatever theme they decided on, so it was critical that they owned it, that they had driven whatever the final outcome on the theme was.'

Further discussion, with the assistance of the Christchurch-based sports psychologist Gilbert Enoka, saw the players settle on the phrase 'Labor Omnia Vincit'.

It means 'work conquers all' and was taken from the recently released hit movie *Gladiator*. Although the star of that movie, Wellington-born actor Russell Crowe, was more into his rugby league than his union, the co-owner of the South Sydney Rabbitohs would have been proud of how the Crusaders lived the motto.

Three players who especially lived the theme that year were halfback Justin Marshall, lock Norm Maxwell and first five-eighths Andrew Mehrtens. Even though he wasn't the skipper, Marshall was always going to wield a big influence. His season's work showed that he had brought under control the one aspect of his game that had sometimes been his undoing in the past.

'Justin was a big driver within the group. He was always the ultimate competitor, and still is if you run into him on the squash court,' Robbie jokes. 'Even when a cause was lost, not that any were that season, he'd still be in there competing and stirring things up as if we were in front.

'The big step he had started to take, however, and it showed through during that campaign, was getting on top of his emotions. He was learning to manage the emotional side of the game, and added more value to the people around him as a result.'

This showed when Marshall followed up the unified response from the playing group as to how they would replace Blackadder by reminding his teammates that it was all very well saying they would step up collectively in the comfort of a team camp: they had to live that commitment in the heat of the moment.

It was a comment, Robbie says, that took the team's commitment 'to the next level' by providing a reality check as to what the players were all committing to.

The Marshall belligerence wasn't always positively channelled.

One exercise during the camp, which involved a physical conditioning-based orienteering event, saw Marshall's team prevail. This won them the right to select the best equipment and site on which to pitch their tent, as the whole group was sleeping outdoors that evening as part of a team-building exercise.

Unfortunately, the weather deteriorated, as did Marshall's humour, with the combative halfback subsequently refusing to take up the right to choose a tenting site, suggesting they should bed indoors.

'I told him that the experience, in terms of taking the hard road and sticking the rain out in the tents, would mirror our reality, in terms of what was to come during the season,' Robbie says.

'Temptation — which in that instance would have been to call it off, and sleep indoors — was always going to be at our doorstep. It would be taking the easy way out.'

Marshall didn't agree, nor did he forget, subsequently recalling the incident with Robbie after the Crusaders had won the final, grumbling: 'What good did sleeping out in the rain do for the campaign?'

Robbie says: 'Staying true to ourselves was what had gotten us through, especially as even though we wound up winning every game that year, quite a few of them were close entering the latter stages, before we finally saw them out.'

Stubborn he could sometimes be, but Marshall was a fighter, and a valuable asset to the group.

So too was Maxwell, who'd graduated to the All Blacks three years before, and had one of the biggest hearts in New Zealand rugby. At 107 kilograms, he was on the light side for an international lock, but that didn't stop him consistently punching above his weight.

'Norm Maxwell. What a legend,' Robbie declares.

'Normy was always one who went against the tide, even though he didn't really have the frame to do some of the things that he did. That year, he was able to operate in a vehicle [the forward pack] that was functioning.

'It allowed him to adapt his game more. He carried the ball more that season, which he enjoyed and was good at, purely because people around him were catering for the team needs that previously he had to fix.'

A willing personality, Maxwell was also one of the leaders within the group. He helped keep the team tight. Everyone has a Norm Maxwell story. Most of them are hilarious.

Humour was a big part of the Mehrtens make-up too, but so was resilience and class. Both were on show throughout the seventh crusade.

'Mehrts typified the state of the leadership within the group,' Robbie says. 'He'd had his challenges, but he came out the other side, playing some of the best rugby of his career that year. As well as being a great player, he was also a willing teacher, both for Aaron [Mauger] but also for another youngster we had coming through who went alright.'

That lad's name was Dan Carter. Robbie was planning to unleash him on Super Rugby the following year.

One of the discussion topics that had been a part of the Crusaders' set-up from the franchise's early days was the concept of 'the ultimate Crusader'.

'We talked a lot about what he would look like, the habits he would have. The idea was to create a template, in what we all thought the ultimate Crusader would look like, that everyone in the group should aspire to,' Robbie says.

The concept helped Robbie determine Blackadder's replacement.

The job fell to the unassuming Reuben Thorne, a man similar in his approach to the game and in his understanding of team and work ethic to Robbie's former Canterbury captain, and good mate, Don Hayes.

It was, Robbie says, an easy decision to make, despite the presence of some vastly experienced men within the Crusaders ranks.

'Although he was relatively quiet, Reuben was hugely respected within the group. He was a worker in the true sense of the word, and very similar to Todd in that regard.

'He also, along with Leon MacDonald I would suggest, most closely encapsulated all of the traits we saw in the ultimate Crusader.'

Of course, Thorne had no shortage of wisdom and experience around him, with the Crusaders playing roster featuring experienced All Blacks such as MacDonald, Daryl Gibson, Mehrtens, Marshall and Mark Hammett, alongside two young guns who had already been earmarked for future leadership roles in Mauger and Richie McCaw.

'We had an experienced set of leaders, and all of these players were going to lead anyway, so we were going to get the benefit of their leadership regardless of who held the title of captain.'

'It was a maturing group who had been earthed by the disappointment of the year before so they were really in the ultimate state: still at the height of their powers as a playing force, but presuming nothing and aspiring to a lot.'

Thorne went on to captain the All Blacks later in the year, leading the national side to back-to-back Tri-Nations titles, New Zealand's first Bledisloe Cup series win in five years, and to the 2003 Rugby World Cup.

Yet his appointment and position with the national team was still the subject of consistent criticism, in much the same manner as Robbie would experience during his Wallaby career, when he opted for the polarising figure of Rocky Elsom as one of his skippers.

'I think at times the public and media misunderstand the role of the captain,' Robbie suggests. 'It's not to be everything to everyone, but it's someone who is at the hub of the team, and particularly the "spiritual" hub.

'It's not particularly about the noise [both publicly and within the team] he makes; it's about being a reference point for some of the key benchmarks — in terms of performance — that the team has set in advance.'

A lot of the strategic on-field decisions are made by other players.

'The captain is the player who keeps the group glued together and aligned,' Robbie explains, 'so it wasn't a difficult decision opting for Reuben. He was fulfilling much of the role, as far as his peers were concerned, already.'

The seamless nature of the transition became apparent once the season kicked off, with the juggernaut quickly building momentum. Although four of the first five games were won by the margin of a converted try or less, the Crusaders were always on the right side of the ledger. They also kept scoring points, with the 30 they posted on opening night against the Highlanders being the least they managed from any game through the entire competition.

The addition of Mauger as a second backline playmaker — a ploy that would become a feature of Robbie-coached teams — undoubtedly added to the Crusaders' potency.

160

Above: The triumphant trio. Robbie joins his assistant coach Steve Hansen (left), captain Todd Blackadder (centre) and the silverware after Canterbury's 1997 NPC title, its first for 13 years.

Left: Reaching for the stars! Two-year-old Sophie hitches a ride on her father's shoulders following a team gathering during the historic 1998 crusade.

Like daughter, like father. This time it's Robbie who's in the air, carried on the broad shoulders of Jonah Lomu during an All Blacks training drill at Whangamata Beach before the start of the 2002 test season.

Dan Carter (left) and Brad Thorn are all smiles as they flank Robbie in the Eden Park dressing room following the return of the Bledisloe Cup to New Zealand possession in 2003. As Crusaders coach and All Blacks coaching coordinator, Robbie had a significant influence on the careers of both players, overseeing their introductions to the test arena.

'It still holds the same amount . . .' So Robbie joked with the press as he and John Mitchell (left) showed off the Bledisloe Cup following the All Blacks' 22–16 win over Australia in the series-deciding test of 2003. The result saw Robbie join an elite group who had won the Bledisloe as both a player and a coach.

Sing when you're winning! The 2005 final not only brought the curtain down on the 12-team format in Super Rugby, it was also the closing chapter in the Crusaders' careers of Justin Marshall, Andrew Mehrtens, Greg Feek, Norm Maxwell, Dave Hewett and Sam Broomhall. Marshall, Hewett and Mehrtens are all alongside each other in the centre of the front row here, with Feek tucked in just behind as the Crusaders enjoy the moment following their 35–25 win over the NSW Waratahs.

The fog of war. Robbie watches on as Mose Tuiali'i (left), Kevin Senio and Richie McCaw warm up ahead of the inaugural Super 14 final in 2006, which saw the Crusaders overcome both the Hurricanes and the elements to claim the franchise's sixth title.

There are many ways to get a message across. Robbie offers guidance as his players enjoy the sun on a training day at Rugby Park.

The Crusaders family. Robbie joins franchise directors Gary Lund (right), Karl Smith and Philip McDonald (left) after the win over the NSW Waratahs in his last final. McDonald was one of 182 people who were tragically lost when a force 6.3 earthquake struck Christchurch on 22 February 2011.

Fairy tales do happen. Robbie shows off the prize, flanked by Crusaders stalwarts Greg Somerville (left) and Brad Thorn, following the presentations at the end of his last crusade.

Above: The night of the sword. Departing veterans Reuben Thorne (left) and Caleb Ralph help Robbie do the honours, as the team watches on, in the traditional sword planting that follows every Crusaders' title success.

Left: If all of the attributes that the players believed made up the 'ultimate' Crusader were pooled together, Leon MacDonald would be pretty close. Here the Crusaders fullback joins Robbie after the team had sent their coach out a winner in the 2008 final.

The team behind the team. The wives and partners celebrate in the changing room after the last Super 12 final in 2005 where the Crusaders beat Ewen McKenzie's NSW Waratahs 35–25 in Christchurch. Penny (second from right, back row) played a central role organising the Crusaders 'off-field' team.

Robbie joins son Sam as he gets ready for his turn at the crease for the Hawkeswood Wanderers at the Willows Cricket Club just outside Christchurch.

So too did the vast experience the side boasted across the park. By the end of the campaign, nine squad members had featured in excess of a half-century of Super Rugby games while two more were within one and two games respectively of the milestone.

'The group was coming of age, both in terms of the composure they were showing in tight situations, but also as far as their overall option taking was concerned.

'The fact that we were consistently scoring a lot of points was indicative of how we had added to our game.'

Evidence of that is provided by the fact that the regular back three — fullback MacDonald and the wingers Caleb Ralph and Marika Vunibaka — contributed 27 tries, or 44 per cent of all of the tries scored by the side, between them. Eight of those came in one game: the astonishing 96–19 humiliation of the second-ranked NSW Waratahs.

'Everything that unfolds, in terms of how the team plays, we generally see first in training,' Robbie says. 'That year, we could see the growth of the group, and how they were coming along as a team before the public did. The confidence and belief within just grew and grew as the campaign developed. Ultimately, it's all about the critical mass . . .'

That mass simply blew the unfortunate Waratahs away.

While New South Wales coach Bob Dwyer, perhaps anticipating another meeting two weeks down the track, hid six of his regular starters from the Crusaders, their presence wouldn't have made much difference.

Australian test prop Patricio Noriega, who started for the Waratahs that night and later coached Robbie's Wallaby scrum, reckons his team could have had 30 players and they'd still have struggled to contain the home side.

He was not the only one who interpreted the game that way. The match was the first one that Robbie's then five-year-old daughter Sophie had attended.

'She's a quick learner,' Robbie says proudly. 'At halftime [with the score at 63–0], she asked her mother whether the blue team had as many players as the red team!'

One of Robbie's lasting memories of the night was his, and Cooper's, entry into the dressing room in between the halves.

'It was quite amusing,' he recalls, 'because they were all sitting around, looking at us, their expectation obvious, wondering what we were going to say. It's 63–0. What can you say to us now?'

The sermon, which was delivered with a straight face, simply endorsed the performance to date, but reminded the players that they may have to face the Waratahs again [in the final]. Because of that, they needed to keep inflicting damage.

It all got a bit much for the players as they headed back out for the second period. One of their number called 'It's 0–0; just start again', McCaw recalls. At that moment, most of the players burst out laughing.

While Robbie had spoken of a possible second bout with the New South Welshmen, he didn't really believe it. The rout had to have destroyed their confidence and it had, to the extent that the Waratahs were blown away 51–10 by the Brumbies in the following week's semi-final in Sydney.

The Crusaders saw off the Highlanders 34–23, but then had to receive a Brumbies outfit who'd run them closest of all in the preliminary rounds, losing out to a late dropped goal by Mauger in a 33–32 defeat in Christchurch.

And the defending champions weren't about to concede the title without a fight.

While the Crusaders dominated much of the contest, the resilient Brumbies held on, taking the one try-scoring chance they had when winger Andrew Walker stole an intercept and raced away to score. The rugby league convert's try closed the Brumbies to 13–14 with just eight minutes remaining. The unthinkable — that the Crusaders might lose — was suddenly possible.

The mood in the coaching box remained calm.

'That game was probably closer than it needed to be but, in some ways, that maybe reflected the confidence that our group was playing with.

'The Brumbies were a good team with a finals history. They knew how to hang in under pressure and used that experience, but our leaders didn't panic. It was pretty clear what they needed to do: steer the team into the right place on the field and finish the job off.'

They did just that.

From the restart following the Walker try, the Crusaders worked their way into an attacking position, from which Mehrtens kicked a dropped goal.

That made the difference four points. A penalty goal couldn't win it. The Brumbies now had to play.

In doing so, it exposed them to the risk of turnover, and the Crusaders pounced on two Brumbies' mistakes to create tries that Ralph finished.

At 31–13, game over. The title was back with the Crusaders. The team had realised Aristotle's dream.

Inevitably, the plaudits flowed in the direction of the key players. While they were deserved, Robbie attributes the success of that season to the whole group, saying the spirit of the team-first ethic was encapsulated by the actions of the players who barely saw action.

'We had Orene Ai'i down from Auckland that year. What a man. Totally selfless. He got a try in a pre-season game that must have raised his expectations, then got injured and unfortunately didn't get to play. But he contributed at every opportunity in preparation. All that mattered to him was the team, and he played his part.'

Northland prop Nick White, who made just one appearance as a substitute off the bench, is another Robbie cites as having inspired the group by his unfailing commitment.

'What you don't want, among the players not getting regular game time, is blokes that turn sour, and just get in the way. Not everyone gets the privilege of wearing the jersey every week, and there is inevitably emotion that flows from those decisions.

'The key thing is that the team comes first, so judging the character of the players chosen is an important part of the recruitment process. This is especially so in the case of those brought in from outside of the province, as those are the blokes you generally don't know so much about.'

In choosing Ai'i and White — as with pretty much everything else in that perfect season — Robbie made the right choices.

15

A NEW ALL BLACKS JOURNEY

Robbie never expected to win the nod as All Blacks coach in 2001. Although encouraged by the New Zealand Rugby Union to apply, after Wayne Smith had dramatically questioned his own incumbency, the hesitant applicant was pretty sure that the job would go to someone else. Instinct told him that, after the two previous head coaches — Smith and John Hart — had been backs, this time the NZRU would go for a forward. The make-up of the appointment panel, who were all ex-test forwards, further suggested the scales would be tipped in favour of a forward.

Robbie was right.

The former midweek All Blacks captain, England assistant and one-season Chiefs coach, John Mitchell, got the job.

The demise of such a capable individual as Smith, who wound up questioning his own abilities after just two years in the position, spoke volumes about the intensity and scrutiny that accompanies the role of All Blacks head coach.

It was a timely reminder of the confidence, experience and maturity that would be required before taking on the head coach duties in the game's most challenging arena. Having worked closely with Smith, both as a teammate and then in tandem as part of the management staff at the Crusaders, Robbie had nothing but sympathy for his plight, and admiration for the integrity he showed.

'Smithy is a quality bloke and a quality coach, as his record shows, but he does feel the pressure. Why? Because he cares,' Robbie says.

'He cares so much that the intensity does get to him. That's what we witnessed when he took on the ultimate challenge, coaching the All Blacks. The stresses and pressures of the role are enormous.'

It was in deference to Smith that Robbie was initially reluctant to consider filing an application.

'Wayne is a mate. I'd been working with and for him, and didn't feel it was appropriate to put my name in if he was reapplying. I wasn't prepared to stand against him.'

There was also the matter of Robbie's existing commitment with the Crusaders. He had already proven that he was a man of his word three years earlier in 1998, when approached by Hart to join his All Blacks coaching team. While flattered by the request, Robbie said no, as he'd made the commitment to coach Canterbury and wasn't prepared to give that up.

His resistance to applying this time was broken down by a conversation with the man whose job he was effectively seeking to take.

'Even though I was fairly certain I wouldn't get the job, the NZRU kept encouraging me to apply. So too did Smithy. When we had a chat about it, he was emphatic that I put my name in even though he was standing again himself.

'Eventually, I did. If nothing else, I thought the experience would be a good one in terms of being exposed to and gaining an understanding of the NZRU's appointments processes.'

He didn't know it at the time of Mitchell's appointment, but Robbie was to wind up seeing a fair bit of the NZRU and its processes over the two and a half years that followed.

'I was on holiday in Australia, staying out at Manly in Sydney, when the phone rang. It was Mitch on the line, asking me if I'd come on board as his assistant.

'All of a sudden, I was back where I'd just been, wondering whether I wanted to be involved at the next level, and whether I would be allowed to take on a role while retaining my position at the Crusaders.

'Because, whatever happened, I was going to honour the commitments that I had already made.'

While the public and NZRU perception of Robbie was to become locked into that of Mitchell during their time together steering the All

Blacks, the pair actually didn't know each other especially well prior to their respective appointments. Robbie had attended one Bermuda tournament alongside Mitchell in the Classic All Blacks, while they had played against each other on a couple of occasions at the back end of his career with Canterbury.

Mitchell pitched the approach as wanting to get the best coaching support around him that he could.

With an NPC and a Super Rugby title behind him in the previous five years, and an extensive knowledge of the playing resources, which Mitchell didn't have given he'd only been back in the country for just over a year, Robbie certainly fitted the required profile.

Despite having just given up both the Canterbury NPC role and New Zealand A, the lure of being involved with the national team was too attractive to turn down, so long as Robbie could keep his Crusaders position.

'We had a group [at the Crusaders] that was maturing, and was ready to go, as they showed in 2002 and beyond. I think when people look back now, they could see pretty easily why I didn't want to give that up.'

The decision to retain the Crusaders, while taking on the All Blacks role, didn't meet with universal approval.

Crusaders chairman Bob Stewart says his board, which had expected to lose its coach, backed Robbie to do both roles, even though he personally was uncomfortable with it.

Stewart's unease centred around Robbie's workload, particularly given the experience of earlier in the year, where his Canterbury and New Zealand A commitments had impacted on the Crusaders' preparations. It was something the pair had 'strong words' about in private but, having been upfront to Robbie with his concerns, Stewart was publicly supportive.

The relationship between the Crusaders chairman and its coach proved to be an important feature of Robbie's time in charge. It provided him with a direct line to the board, which he used to the team's advantage. Having previously worked together as coach and manager in the team environment, the pair had a level of trust that was undoubtedly enhanced by their similarities.

Discussions could be 'frank', Stewart says, but both were always clear that the team came first.

As Hamish Riach, who took over from Steve Tew as Crusaders chief executive at the end of 2001, didn't have a strong rugby background 'and didn't understand a lot of the instinctive parts of the game', Stewart says the chairman–coach relationship was a lot closer than it might have otherwise been. The pair worked in tandem on recruitment and staffing, as well as any liaison with the NZRU on franchise issues, most notably around the player-reconditioning plan before the 2007 Rugby World Cup.

Robbie's retention by the Crusaders was no issue for Mitchell, who saw it as advantageous having his assistant remain involved at the coalface through the Super Rugby season.

As Mitchell had co-opted the former All Blacks Kieran Crowley and Mark Shaw for his selection panel, Robbie stayed out of that domain. He only became involved once the national side had assembled and his conflicting interests, through the Crusaders, had ended.

'It [the selection process] wasn't an issue as far as I was concerned,' Robbie says. 'As a head coach, you involve all of your people. If you are not going to use them, there is not much point having them there. The process has to be inclusive otherwise you won't be getting the best out of your people.'

'While I wasn't a selector in the first instance, once the group came together I effectively became one as I was obviously asked for my views.'

Inevitably, down the track, there were claims of selection bias towards Crusaders players, most notably when only one non-Crusader started for the All Blacks in the second test against Ireland at Eden Park in 2002.

What the critics didn't acknowledge at the time, of course, was that those same players had flattened all-comers in the just concluded Super 12. Oh, and the All Blacks smashed Ireland 40–8 that evening, after having laboured to a 15–6 win against the same opponent the previous week in Dunedin.

'People who were not directly involved did suggest then, and have in the time since, that I had a greater role in the decision making than was actually the case,' Robbie says. 'That was more perception based, largely around the number of Crusaders who were involved. The presumption was always going to be there.'

It is not backed by the facts.

Of the 23 new All Blacks who were introduced during Robbie's involvement on the coaching staff, just five were from the Crusaders.

Robbie also notes wryly that charges of provincial bias in selection are nothing new: the same was being said in the late 80s and early 90s when the All Blacks team was drawn almost entirely of players from the champion Auckland sides of the era. Ultimately, history judges the successes and failings of the selection process.

It seems almost incredible, given what we know now, but the selection of a promising young openside from Canterbury for the opening tour of the new era provoked as much criticism as any.

While Richie McCaw had been a standout figure in what had been a stellar NPC campaign by his province, his call-up was greeted with dismay by no less than the 54-test former Otago star Josh Kronfeld, who argued that the former New Zealand Colts captain had been included prematurely.

'There was a fair amount of comment about it [the McCaw selection]. That it was premature after just one full NPC season, but he'd been coming through the programmes — both nationally in the Under-19s [where Shaw had coached him] and the Under-21s, as well as his involvement with Canterbury and the Crusaders,' Robbie says.

'We see these players, and what they offer, before the public does. Richie was a good example of that.'

So too, a year later, was Dan Carter.

Robbie recalls, a few years prior to Carter's entry onto the national stage, encountering Sir Brian Lochore, who bemoaned the lack of an obvious successor as All Blacks first five-eighths for Andrew Mehrtens.

'I told him not to worry; we already had him here, in Dan, and that he may even be better than Mehrts had been,' Robbie recalls.

'It's fair to say that he was a bit taken back, but that's where we have the advantage. We see the players day in, day out, so we know what is coming.'

It took McCaw just 80 minutes, in what was a competitive test against a Warren Gatland-coached Ireland, to justify his presence, kicking off what was to become arguably the greatest All Blacks career of all time.

The Irish really put it to their visitors, leading 21–7 just after halftime, before the All Blacks took control, outscoring Ireland 33–3 during the next period, before a consolation try by the home side saw John Mitchell's first test as coach finish in a 40–29 victory.

The on-debut flanker was named man of the match and given a standing ovation at the post-test dinner.

For his part, McCaw says Robbie's presence as Mitchell's assistant, 'helped significantly' with his maiden All Blacks experience.

The future All Blacks captain remembers first meeting Robbie as a wide-eyed 10-year-old, when he accompanied his uncle Ian, who was flatting with Jock Hobbs at the time, to a Canterbury–Otago game that Robbie was playing in. It was a 'pretty big deal' he recalls, meeting a guy he'd always looked up to as 'a bit of a hero'. Little did he know how much their futures would be intertwined.

His next experience of Robbie came a decade later, after he'd just returned from the New Zealand Colts programme in 2000. Out of the blue, the phone went. It was Robbie, calling to explain why he hadn't selected McCaw for that day's Town–Country game, but advising that he would be including him in the Canterbury squad.

As he was only in his second year out of Otago Boys' High School, McCaw again admits to being taken aback, having not even considered either possibility. Adding to the awkwardness of the conversation, he notes, was that Robbie was never that easy to talk to on the phone, especially when you are a nervous kid!

Eighteen months on from that phone call, McCaw says that Robbie's presence provided reassurance for his All Blacks entry, both in terms of knowing how he coached, but also offering a trusted sounding board if he needed it. It helped also that he was not the only one on the trip doing it for the first time.

Twelve of the players selected for the five-match tour, which featured midweek matches against Ireland and Scotland A combinations, as well as three tests, were on debut.

There was also a new coaching staff, but with the changes having happened so quickly, not everyone had got the news.

'After Super Rugby had finished that year, I went on a research trip overseas, and called on USA Rugby while I was in the United States in September,' Robbie recalls. 'Jack Clark, who was basically running the place then, actually offered me a job helping them, which they thought I might be interested in around my Crusaders role.

'He was then in Dublin on IRB business [the International Rugby Board is based in Ireland] and went to the All Blacks test. I saw him afterwards and he said "What are you doing here?" It had all happened so quick, he hadn't heard the news.'

Robbie's trip to the United States coincided with the September 11 attacks on the country. He had been scheduled to fly through New York on the day the terrorists struck, but fortunately had changed his travel plans. Instead, he was in a San Francisco hotel when the hijacked airliners struck the World Trade Center buildings in New York.

'It was still the middle of the night back in New Zealand but, as soon as I heard about it, I rang Penny. She was probably one of the first people in the country to hear the news.'

The terrorist strike, which saw four hijacked airliners deliberately crashed, two into the World Trade Center buildings in New York and one into the Pentagon building in Washington, saw United States airspace closed down for a few days. That delayed Robbie's return home slightly as he got into All Blacks mode for the first time since his days as a player.

The return of midweek matches to a tour schedule saw the All Blacks beat Ireland A 43–30, and Scotland A 35–13, in games that offered a lot in terms of player development.

'Those matches were great opportunities for fringe and young players to get tested at the next level. It allows them to see the responsibility and the meaning in wearing the jersey, to see the excitement of their opponents as they get to line up against an international side, and to take the learning from that.

'We as coaches, of course, can then assess how they handle themselves looking ahead to the future.'

The plethora of meaningless test matches now cluttering the calendar as well as the lengthening of Super Rugby has seen midweek opportunities cut back again after Robbie reintroduced them during his time as Australian coach, to fast track the development of some of his players.

'They were certainly a very useful tool in the Australian environment, prior to the expansion of Super Rugby. The way the Australian calendar was structured, there were essentially no representative development opportunities for players after Super Rugby concluded, and that finished before the start of the June tests.

'Without an NPC or Currie Cup to turn to, it was a lot harder, both to search out the next tier of future test players, but also to provide anything other than club rugby for those on the fringes, so that they would be ready to step up if needed — which many were.'

Lack of rugby was never an issue for the New Zealand game, and the performance of the All Blacks on the 2001 tour showed that. All three tests were won despite the infusion of new blood into the team. After seeing off Ireland, the All Blacks outclassed Scotland 37–6, in a game that was notable for the Scottish test debut of Temuka-born Brendan Laney, three weeks after he'd appeared for Otago in the NPC final.

The comfortable nature of the win also belied what a thorn the country of his ancestors would be for Robbie during his career: he could only draw with them on his test debut, lost to them playing for Canterbury in 1990, and twice came up empty coaching against the Scots with the Wallabies.

The final test of the trip, in front of 70,000 passionate Argentines at the River Plate Stadium in Buenos Aires, was anything but comfortable, with the All Blacks needing a 77th minute try by No. 8 Scott Robertson to claim a come-from-behind 24–20 win.

The atmosphere that evening was one none of the New Zealanders will ever forget.

'The stadium, which is an old one, was moving — it was like being in an earthquake,' Robbie says.

'We got out of jail too, with Razor's [Robertson's] try coming off a counter-attack sparked by Ben Blair, but it was a great experience for everyone involved. It's a great, albeit tough, place to play.'

Still the tour had been a success.

The new coaches had made a good start at the helm, and the

expectations had been raised for the following year as the All Blacks looked to reacquire the Bledisloe Cup, and the Tri-Nations title.

Robbie and his Crusaders players returned to the All Blacks environment the following June fresh from their perfect crusade.

Player management had been a key factor in the winning run. This was something Mitchell was keen to introduce into his programme as well, looking ahead to the Rugby World Cup in Australia the following year.

The decision was made to go 'full noise' after the Bledisloe, which had not returned since it was lost in 1998, as well as the Tri-Nations, which had also sat in Wallaby possession since the All Blacks' last success, in 1999.

'Player management was becoming an important skill, as important at test level as it was in Super Rugby,' Robbie says. 'It was not only about managing the physical load; we also needed to make sure all of the players had access to a playing opportunity, that everyone in the squad received their chance to impress.'

This served to preserve the players' excitement levels at being involved, while also ensuring they all maintained their enthusiasm and work ethic at training, which guaranteed healthy competition for places on game day.

'It's the norm now, but it was a quite revolutionary approach then and provoked a lot of debate, some of it healthy, some not.'

The All Blacks swept through their June tests unbeaten, outclassing Italy (64–10) and Fiji (68–18) on either side of a competitive two-game series with Ireland.

The Tri-Nations began on a wet and miserable evening at Jade Stadium, but although no tries were scored the 12–6 win meant the All Blacks had started the competition well, while taking the Bledisloe to a decider in Sydney.

A week later, the All Blacks saw off South Africa in Wellington, completing their home season with a commanding 41–20 win, in which they outscored the Springboks five tries to two.

So far so good, but the defining game was likely to come next, in Sydney. Win and the Bledisloe–Tri-Nations double was on. Fail and the All Blacks could come away with neither.

While the Wallabies started well, to lead 8–0 shortly before halftime, the All Blacks came back strongly, taking the lead when McCaw scored his maiden test try. With a 14–8 advantage entering the final quarter, they were in touching distance of the Bledisloe before another late, late show by the Australians ripped the trophy away again.

The Wallabies had famously defended the Bledisloe with an 80th minute penalty goal by John Eales at Wellington two years earlier, and then denied an All Blacks win in Sydney when No. 8 Toutai Kefu smashed across for a 79th minute try a year later.

This time, it was a controversial 80th-minute penalty goal that did for the All Blacks again, after a second Australian try had left the visitors clinging to a one-point advantage for the last eight minutes of a pulsating contest.

All Blacks fullback Leon MacDonald was unluckily penalised for not releasing at a ruck by South African referee André Watson. Australian fullback Matthew Burke stepped up and kicked the goal, and the Bledisloe was gone again after a 14–16 defeat.

The season then went from the controversial to the surreal the following week in Durban as the All Blacks beat South Africa 30–23 in a match best remembered for the disgraceful second-half attack on Irish referee Dave McHugh by a disgruntled spectator. The Irishman was hurt in the incident, while the ground invader copped a few decent right hands for his uninvited participation, most notably from a couple of the Springbok players.

When the dust settled, the All Blacks' win put them in pole position for the Tri-Nations, with the title being confirmed the following weekend after the Boks beat Australia in the final tournament game.

On the face of it, the decision to leave behind 18 members of the Tri-Nations-winning squad from what shaped as a demanding three-test November tour, facing England, France and Wales, was a big risk. Given that the leading players were potentially looking at a record year for 2003 — with 14 tests likely — on top of a full Super Rugby programme, there was no choice.

'The demands on the top players had been huge. We'd witnessed that both in 2002, but over the preceding years,' Robbie says. 'As a result, a conscious decision was made to freshen up some elements of the playing group. To allow them to condition properly, and have a proper pre-season, building into what was always going to be a demanding year.'

Of course, the absence of so many players also created openings for others. There were 14 new players on that trip. Four of them — Ali Williams, Andrew Hore, Tony Woodcock and Keven Mealamu — would go on to feature in New Zealand's Rugby World Cup-winning side nine years later.

Inevitably, there were suspicions raised around the motives, and Robbie's part in the decision, when 12 of the rested players were Crusaders. But they'd easily had the biggest workload. McCaw was a case in point. In the 11 months between the start of the 2001 NPC, and the end of the following year's Tri-Nations, the young flanker had played 30 games, which included 12 test matches and two play-off games for each of Canterbury and the Crusaders.

'Each player was assessed on a case-by-case basis centred around the amount of high-intensity rugby they had played, with the decisions based on what was the best approach for each individual.' Robbie contends.

While the All Blacks had been advantaged by New Zealand's centralised system before, this was taking intervention a step further. As it was, the provinces gained the immediate benefit in this instance. Their rested players came back in a fresh state for the start of their campaigns, while the new All Blacks were also guaranteed to return to Super Rugby with a spring in their step.

It was indicative of the quality within the player pool in the New Zealand game that the All Blacks were still more than competitive in Europe. Although beaten 28–31 at Twickenham, the All Blacks gave their experienced hosts a fright, roaring back from 14–31 just after halftime to go down narrowly. They could even have won but for blowing a likely try-scoring opportunity near the end.

In a ghost of season's past, Jonah Lomu tormented England, scoring his last two test tries, as an All Blacks outfit featuring seven on debut gave the soon-to-be world champions a real shake. All 15 of the players who started for England 11 months later as they beat Australia in the Rugby World Cup final featured on that November afternoon, with 12 of them starting against the All Blacks.

While not satisfied with the defeat, it took just two weeks to place the performance in perspective after England then beat a full-strength Australian side 32–31, before obliterating South Africa 53–3.

The All Blacks tour concluded with a 20–20 draw with France, after the visitors had three players yellow-carded by Australian referee Scott Young, and a 43–17 win over a Steve Hansen-coached Wales.

It was not known at the time but the latter match proved to be the sixty-third and last in the stellar career of Lomu, who was hospitalised after the game as the impact of his kidney disorder began to take hold. It was a triumph of his will that Lomu did return to rugby, albeit briefly, although his ongoing health battle soon terminated any remaining playing aspirations.

'A remarkable player, and a quality man,' Robbie says of Lomu. 'His profile was unprecedented. I think some New Zealanders still underestimate the level in terms of promotion to which he has taken the game, yet he has retained a remarkable sense of humility.'

Robbie recalls the All Blacks being greeted by a massive poster of Lomu on a billboard during the visit to Argentina in 2001, which underlined the big winger's global status as a sporting icon. Even in places where rugby lacked the profile of other sports, Lomu would be mobbed in public, which forced him to spend much of his time at the team hotel.

'In many ways, he was before his time, both in terms of what he could do on the field, but also the peripheral distractions off it that surrounded him, and have now come to be associated with the professional game.

'Yet he never allowed any of those to become an excuse. For Jonah, the team always came first. That ethic, on its own, provided great inspiration and leadership, especially for the younger players around him.'

16

SILVERWARE BUT NO GOLD

John Mitchell had labelled it a 'journey'.

By year's end; not only had the word become an established part of the Kiwi vernacular, it was also being used frequently in a manner discrediting the fallen All Blacks coach. This was unfair.

Mitchell didn't help himself either publicly or privately by exhibiting some erratic behaviour, and he retreated even further into insularity as the pressure mounted, but the All Blacks of 2003 did achieve some spectacular results.

New Zealand had never before hoisted a half-century of points on either South Africa or Australia. Mitchell's men inflicted the indignity on both, inside of a week, and at their residences to boot.

The Tri-Nations title, which had only been won by New Zealand in three of its six years prior to the arrival of Mitchell and Robbie, was secured back to back during their two seasons at the helm. Most importantly, the Bledisloe Cup was reclaimed.

Given that this success started a New Zealand possession of the trophy that stretched into a second decade, it would be easy to underestimate the significance of the moment when it was regained.

Australia had won and then held the trophy through five consecutive series prior to its return across the Tasman. This was a substantial tenure in the context of the Bledisloe Cup's 83-year history, especially if you consider the fact that the Wallabies had won just eight of the 55 Bledisloe series played prior to the start of 2014.

The five-year absence between 1998 and 2003 was, for New Zealanders, almost parallel to the torment felt by the Australian rugby fraternity through the subsequent ownership of the All Blacks.

Pointedly, the core of the playing group who developed into decade-long defenders of the trophy were introduced on the 2001–2003 watch.

The nationwide euphoria that greeted the return of the Bledisloe when the deciding game of the series was won at Eden Park didn't last. As significant an accomplishment as that was, Mitchell didn't achieve the outcome on which his fate depended, by prevailing at that year's Rugby World Cup.

New Zealanders are not, and have never been, great losers when it comes to the All Blacks. This has especially become so since the advent of the Rugby World Cup, which provided a four-yearly cycle from which the world champions of the game are proclaimed. As many a young Kiwi living or travelling overseas can attest, being ranked number one between tournaments means nothing in the eyes of the world, if someone else holds the Rugby World Cup.

While, four years on, there were none of the nasty scenes to replicate those that had greeted John Hart on his return home after the failed campaign of 1999, there was also no doubt, for either Mitchell, or for Robbie, that their retention by the NZRU was not going to be an option. They were told as much in the changing room, within minutes of their exit from the tournament, when spoken to by the union's chairman Jock Hobbs and chief executive Chris Moller.

Moller, who was ultimately Mitchell's boss, then launched a scathing public attack on his coach through the media.

The timing of the criticism was inappropriate. It also made a mockery of both the NZRU's post-tournament review process as well as its procedure to appoint the next coach by making it clear that while the incumbent had been asked to reapply for his position, he had no realistic chance of being reappointed.

It took just a month — compared to the three-month lag in the reappointment process following the 2007 tournament — for Graham Henry to be installed as the new All Blacks coach. In this instance, the union had wanted to capitalise on the national disappointment, and to be seen to be acting swiftly and decisively as it installed its new man.

Four years on, the drawn out process — after the post-defeat promise of a thorough review — was undoubtedly tactical in order to allow the emotion to subside before the incumbent was reappointed.

The fact that Henry had strong support from within the NZRU hierarchy undoubtedly helped to save his position.

By not endearing himself to NZRU powerbrokers — who have to take a share of the blame for rather feebly refusing to rein in their headstrong but politically naive coach — Mitchell had been tainted goods.

Robbie was guilty by association.

Leon MacDonald who, through no fault of his own, became embroiled in one of the most discussed selection decisions of the Rugby World Cup campaign, believes the biggest mistake the NZRU made was the pecking order of the coaches. Robbie, MacDonald argues, should have been in charge of the programme. He had a level of head-coaching knowledge, and experience of all of its associated duties, which far exceeded that boasted by Mitchell.

This, MacDonald believes, would have enhanced the All Blacks' prospects, most notably in terms of insulating both individuals and the team itself from the external pressures heading into and during the tournament. Due to his previous success with both Canterbury and the Crusaders, Robbie knew what worked, and what didn't, MacDonald explains.

But while Robbie had his own ideas and wanted to have an impact, it wasn't his programme, and he had to be on the same page as Mitchell, whether he agreed with a decision that had been made or not.

The Crusaders coach would have done a lot of things differently, MacDonald says, most notably around educating the players on the importance of balance between their rugby and home life, the importance of humility and in appreciating what they had.

The man who finally led the All Blacks back to the Rugby World Cup Promised Land, 24 years after the country's maiden tournament success, backs this view. Also a member of the 2003 and 2007 tournament campaigns, Richie McCaw says a look at the differences between the All Blacks of that era, and Robbie's Crusaders group, shows why he should have been in charge over Mitchell.

While Robbie did have coaching input with the All Blacks, McCaw cites the team culture, which faces its biggest test under pressure, as the critical difference between the national team and Crusaders teams of that period. The two environments were different in terms of how they operated internally, with player participation in decision making a greater feature at the Crusaders, McCaw says.

There were also differences in how the two teams were perceived externally, with the Crusaders viewed favourably by the public and media while the All Blacks were regarded as indifferent and insular, even though a significant number of players featured in both campaigns.

Both were factors, McCaw believes, that built pressure on the players and the coaches, and ultimately contributed to the failure and subsequent personnel changes for 2004.

The experience provided a valuable lesson for Robbie, McCaw says. Not only did it see him become a better coach and develop his man-management skills, it also reinforced his insistence on the Crusaders placing a big emphasis on their external involvement, to ensure the team was viewed as being part of the community and not above it.

While he understandably won't criticise his former coaching partner, Robbie acknowledges the player's perception, saying that it was Mitchell's programme and 'he ran it'.

'He did give me my head to some extent around the coaching and the strategy, but that is part of the assistant–head coach relationship.

'Ultimately, how much input there is from the assistants depends on the preference of the head coach. He has the final say, as he does off the field and in all of the non-rugby aspects of the programme such as sponsorship liaison, media and dealing with head office.'

While 27 new players had been afforded their opportunity through the first 18 months of the Mitchell stewardship, the first squad of Rugby World Cup year was still notable for the inclusion of five new faces. All of them have left a big footprint on All Blacks rugby.

The Auckland outside backs Mils Muliaina and Joe Rokocoko, Wellington centre Ma'a Nonu, and the Canterbury pairing of first five-eighths Dan Carter and lock Brad Thorn, all entered the test arena at the start of the year.

One name that didn't feature was Andrew Mehrtens who, after a brief

All Blacks return the following year, concluded his career in Europe following the 2005 Super 12.

Even though he wasn't a selector, the exclusion of the long-time All Black was inevitably laid by some at Robbie's door, reviving speculation of a bust-up between the pair that had first surfaced during the difficult 2001 crusade.

'The speculation and innuendo is never easy to deal with, but the longer you are around the game, the more you come to realise it's just part of it,' Robbie says.

'You can't waste your time on it. Ignoring it isn't easy, particularly for those around you who have no control over what is being said, but you just have to stay tight, push on, and focus on the things that really matter.'

Robbie and Mehrtens go back a long way. Robbie recalls, during his own playing career, being asked to have a private kicking session at Christchurch Boys' High School with a bright young prospect whose father Terry was a former Canterbury representative.

'I'd taken a keen interest in Andrew's career, right from that kicking session. When John Hart became national coach, he got a few of us in to help Mehrts and other All Blacks players by acting as mentors for them, so there was a fair amount of history there, even before I began coaching him directly myself.'

Contrary to the speculation, the pair got on then, and still do now: Andrew's wife Jacqui was one of Robbie and Penny's early babysitters and a friend.

But coaching is a hard-nosed business. Decisions have to be made, players brought in, and moved on. Electric fullback Christian Cullen and ex-captain and hooker Anton Oliver were two other long-serving players who didn't make the cut for the Rugby World Cup, being shaded by the emergence of Muliaina and Keven Mealamu respectively.

Muliaina and Mealamu both went on to exceed 100 test appearances.

While Mehrtens had enjoyed a virtual mortgage on the Canterbury, Crusaders and then All Blacks first five-eighths positions for much of his career, the clock was ticking for him also. The emergence of Aaron Mauger, and Carter in particular, couldn't wait.

'As you see the next generation coming through before the public does, you also see the guys coming to the end of their time first as well,' Robbie explains. 'For a player of the profile and performance history of Mehrts, that's one of the great challenges — not only for the player, but also for the coaching staff in terms of how you manage those transitions.'

Robbie acknowledges that managing the 'transition' around Mehrtens' status provided a good point of growth for his coaching in terms of how he interacted with players heading into the back end of their careers.

'We want the players to thrive and we want the team to thrive, and it does involve a fair bit of emotion. We all want the same things. When you don't get the outcomes, everyone feels that.'

'What I learnt around Mehrts was that, because I was so intent on helping him, I became part of the problem.'

Mehrtens was doing the same things he had always done, the things that had made him the game's premier first five-eighths. What had changed was the way that opponents were responding, and how they were countering him.

'One of the toughest things for great players to address is the need to continue to adapt,' Robbie says. 'You want to avoid the situation where you do what you've always done and expect to get the same result, because you are underestimating your opposition if that is the case.'

While he has promoted some great players during his career, with his judgement on the timing of Mehrtens' exit being backed by the extraordinary heights that his successor Carter scaled, Robbie has also had to lower the boom on a number of high-profile stars. It hasn't always been easy, most notably in Australia where agents and pliant media outlets did conspire on occasions to create a fuss, but the need of the team has to come first. This is why such judgement calls are made.

'The element of public reaction, and speculation, will always be there, whether it is being manipulated by certain factions to their own end, or whether it is simply due to the emotion of the decision.

'People will jump to conclusions and they will make presumptions. It's part of the game, living in the public eye. The key to it, in the case of Mehrts, was that both of us cared about the bigger picture. We both understood that we were part of something that was bigger than both of us. It wasn't about Andrew Mehrtens or Robbie Deans in isolation, it was about what was best for Canterbury, Crusaders and then All Blacks rugby.'

The All Blacks, without Mehrtens, and with his great rival Carlos Spencer at first five-eighths, made a false start to the year when beaten 15–13 first up by England at Wellington.

Superbly marshalled by skipper Martin Johnson, who was one of 11 Englishmen involved that night who had featured at the previous World Cup, the experienced visitors used their nous to slow the game down. This prevented the All Blacks from gaining any attacking impetus.

There were an incredible 18 stoppages for injury breaks during the 80 minutes, most critically during a series of scrums, five metres out from the England line.

The defenders were without loose forwards Lawrence Dallaglio and Neil Back at the time. They had both been sin-binned for cynical professional fouls. The delays helped kill off the All Blacks' attacking momentum.

After attempts to hurl the understaffed English scrum back failed, the frustration and inexperience of the All Blacks showed, with a bad choice made. Instead of keeping the pressure on by continuing to reset scrums, which would have inevitably placed pressure on Australian referee Stuart Dickinson to consider a penalty try, the All Blacks impatiently tried to ram their way over the goal-line.

The ball was spilled and England survived the siege. The impatience cost the All Blacks the game, while showcasing the cunning that would lead England to its maiden Rugby World Cup later in the year.

They beat Australia 25–14 a week later in Melbourne on their way back to London.

While there was lingering disappointment in the All Blacks camp after the rare home loss, it dissipated to some extent a week later when Carter was unleashed on the world stage, less than a month after his maiden Super Rugby season had concluded.

The unfortunate opponents were Steve Hansen's Wales, who were on the end of a 55–3 mauling, with the 21-year-old announcing his arrival with 20 points on debut.

Even though his future was always going to rest at first five-eighths,

Carter was introduced one place further out in the backline. The rationale, which Robbie subsequently employed in Australia managing the test introductions of Quade Cooper, James O'Connor and Kurtley Beale among others, was to allow Carter to get a feel for test play without placing too much decision-making responsibility on his shoulders too soon.

His virtuoso performance against Wales fully justified the move, while also endorsing Robbie's strategy of dual playmakers in the backline, which utilised the tactical skills of Spencer, Mauger and Carter.

It was the first of seven scores in excess of 50 points that the All Blacks would post from 14 tests for the year, with Wales suffering twice.

Another new star announced his presence the following week in Christchurch during the 31–23 win over France.

Joe Rokocoko scored three tries in just his third test appearance, having skinned the Welsh for a double the week before. The remarkable 20-year-old flyer thrived under Robbie's guidance, scoring 11 tries during the seven mid-year tests of his astonishing freshman year, before running in another six at the Rugby World Cup. To put that strike rate in perspective, the haul ultimately represented 37 per cent of the 46 tries that Rokocoko wound up scoring through his eight-year, 68-test career.

One of the reasons for Rokocoko's success was the manner in which the All Blacks game was developing. The strategy was designed to produce up-tempo rugby that brought New Zealand's strengths into play, while creating accuracy and intensity at pace that opponents couldn't cope with.

'The comprehension of the method, in terms of how we were trying to play, really grew through that mid-year period,' Robbie recalls. 'Time together is important, especially for a national team, where players are coming in from other teams and assembly time is at a premium.

'That year, we had three flyers [Muliaina, Rokocoko and Doug Howlett] out wide, and our play evolved through the games before the Rugby World Cup as the wingers began to understand that they could increase their involvements.

'They were all so capable, we wanted them involved in the game as much as we could. Being on tour gives you more time to have those conversations with the players.'

The All Blacks reached their height during the away leg of the Tri-Nations. There has never been a week like it in All Blacks history.

The late Sir Fred Allen, captain of the 1949 All Blacks, who had been beaten 4–0 in South Africa amid claims of refereeing bias, presented the jerseys prior to the opening test of the competition at Pretoria. He lived up to his nickname 'The Needle' by giving the players a rousing speech that included some honest individual appraisals.

The All Blacks responded, with the performance that afternoon reducing the great New Zealander to tears of joy at the after-match function.

In a breathtaking assault, the visitors blitzed the Boks at their high veldt citadel, with the 50,000-strong crowd, who'd turned up anticipating a South African win, left in stunned silence following the seven-try-to-one, 52–16 demolition.

Seven days later, the Wallabies were on the end of a similar battering at Sydney's Olympic Stadium, with Rokocoko bagging his second hat-trick of the season, and the All Blacks eight tries in all, during a 50–21 rout.

Fifteen tries had been scored in a week: eight by Rokocoko and his fellow winger Howlett.

Perhaps the only sour note to the Sydney performance was its aftermath. Rather than celebrating what had been an extraordinary week, the players returned to the team hotel and went straight into a meeting about proposed Rugby World Cup bonuses. This was a lingering issue that hadn't been finalised earlier when it should have been.

Robbie believes the emphatic nature of the win may have contributed to the All Blacks' downfall when the two teams met again at the same venue four months later.

'Hindsight is a great thing, but you'd say now that the result that night, and the manner in which it was achieved, did contribute to our challenge at the Rugby World Cup, in terms of recognising the Wallabies as a threat and respecting them as such.'

It was not a mistake the class of '03 made on its own. In both 1999 and 2007, New Zealand posted over 50 points in mid-term wins over France, only to fail the more important examination against the same opponent in Rugby World Cup play-off matches later in the year.

An insight into the intensity and physicality that was to come in the tournament play-off matches was provided by the two home tests that concluded the Tri-Nations, with both South Africa and Australia presenting sterner challenges.

The All Blacks beat South Africa 19–11 in Dunedin, and then secured both the Bledisloe Cup and the Tri-Nations with a 21–17 win over Australia in Auckland, but the latter success was every bit as tenuous as the four-point margin indicates.

Although the home side scored two tries, both by Howlett, to Australia's one, they were unable to shake the Wallabies. This ensured a tension-filled finish to the 100th Bledisloe Cup test when Australian flanker George Smith scored with five minutes remaining to close his side to within a try of the upset.

'The contrast between the Tri-Nations tests in Sydney and Auckland was huge,' Robbie says, 'and we talked about it with the group after the game. The Wallabies were tough, they were incredibly tough, and they kept coming at us until the 80th minute.

'Whether the players underestimated them when we played again, who knows?'

The first challenge at the Rugby World Cup was provided by injury as opposed to the opposition. Experienced centre Tana Umaga lasted just 23 minutes of the opening game against Italy before getting tangled up with Spencer in a tackle, which resulted in a tear of the posterior cruciate ligament of his knee.

The loss of Umaga saw firstly Nonu then MacDonald employed in the midfield, with the latter winning the nod for the bigger matches due to his greater experience, dependability, strong defence and his goal-kicking accuracy, which was superior to the sometimes erratic Spencer.

Goal-kicking had become a key issue due to the partial posterior cruciate ligament tear that had been suffered by Carter, also in the Italy match. While able to be managed through ongoing treatment so that he could play, starting Carter became a risky proposition, which meant Spencer and Mauger had to carry the load through the playoff matches as the first and second five-eighths.

To help ease the responsibility, and its associated pressures, on Spencer, MacDonald was required to kick the goals. The decision to go with MacDonald was widely questioned both at the time and four years later — to Robbie's great surprise — during his interview for the head coaching position after the 2007 World Cup.

The irony was that the man most of the critics said should have been centre in MacDonald's place, Muliaina, wound up playing in the position during the lost quarter-final against France four years later. That wasn't subsequently used as ammunition to unseat the coach after the tournament.

In actuality, MacDonald did a much better job than he received credit for, scoring tries in his first three outings at centre, while also contributing 55 points off the boot during his five appearances as the first-string goal-kicker.

Eleven years on, Robbie remains adamant that playing MacDonald at centre was not a game-changer that proved fatal to the campaign.

'People will always find reasons — and scapegoats — when you come up short. It was the same after the 1995, 1999 and, dare I say it, 2007 Rugby World Cups. What is the saying? "Victory has many fathers, but failure is an orphan"!'

For a time at least, it appeared as if the injury to Umaga hadn't disrupted the All Blacks. Wins over Italy (70–7), Canada (68–6), Tonga (91–7) and Wales (53–37) saw the side set records for the most points (282) and tries (42) through the pool matches.

'The method was working and the players were enjoying it, playing with front foot ball. The risk in that, as it usually is in the changeover from round robin to play-offs, as soon as you encounter an opponent who denies you quick and clean ball, how do you react? If the resistance coming the other way increases, how do you cope?'

Initially, the All Blacks coped well, outmuscling a determined and desperate South African outfit during a convincing 29–9 quarter-final win in Melbourne. The same was not true of the semi-final in Sydney, which was always going to be a tougher assignment for the All Blacks than many had been predicting pre-game.

Tournament hosts have an excellent record at Rugby World Cups.

What proved to be the signature blow to New Zealand's Rugby World

Cup hopes was delivered after just eight minutes, when Robbie's future Wallaby skipper Stirling Mortlock ran almost the length of the field to score after intercepting a cut-out pass from Carlos Spencer.

Robbie had been working hard with the All Blacks first five-eighth through the tournament trying to get him to adjust his game. He was worried that opponents were working out Spencer's attacking options, in particular his desire to make the decisive play.

A cut-out pass has hang time. This allows an opponent to adjust his line or advance, where a ball through the hands keeps each defender honest in his channel of the defensive line.

Television replays of the intercept confirm that quick passing would have outflanked the advancing Australian defensive line, and may well have created an All Blacks score, alleviating the need for the gamble that the cut-out pass represented.

As it was, Mortlock was the one who scored the try, the Wallabies led 7–0 after eight minutes, the stress on the pre-game favourites increased, and the All Blacks never really recovered, finally losing 10–22.

'It is easy in hindsight to attribute a result to a specific moment or event but there were other elements just as significant,' Robbie says.

In a remarkable quirk of fate, the try triggered the turn of events that eventually led to Robbie becoming coach of a Mortlock-captained Wallabies five years later. The pair have never discussed the semi-final and Mortlock's role in it, although Robbie has no doubts as to the severity of his impact.

'That try rattled us and they stymied our momentum as a result. They'd done their homework and had identified what the key tenets of our game were, and made life difficult for us. From there, the elements of the occasion kicked in.'

The All Blacks finished third, beating France 40–13 in the bronze medal play-off, two nights before Australia fell 17–20 to England in extra time of the Rugby World Cup final. The French win was the All Blacks' 12th of the record 14 tests that the team had played for the season.

While the performance was not enough to keep either of Mitchell or Robbie in their posts, the legacy of their tenure has still been an exceedingly good one.

New Zealand possessed neither the Tri-Nations title nor the Bledisloe Cup when they assumed command. Even more importantly, the foundation of the player base was laid ahead of a period that must rate as the most dominant in All Blacks test history.

'If you look at where the All Blacks were before that tour at the end of 2001, we were a long way back, so we'd come a fair way in order to put ourselves in a position both to win the Tri-Nations and the Bledisloe — but also to challenge for the Rugby World Cup,' Robbie says.

'But it was still a young group. They still had a fair bit of learning to go through particularly from a leadership perspective, as we saw when things started going wrong in the quarter-final against France four years later.

'Still they had to all start somewhere, and that period got them up and running, with seven of them ultimately getting the job [winning the Rugby World Cup] done eight years later.'

When in the penultimate test of 2013, Carter featured in his 100th test match, he became just the fifth All Black to achieve this honour. All five were introduced during the Mitchell term: McCaw, Muliaina, Mealamu, prop Tony Woodcock and Carter.

It is testament to the foresight of the 2003 selection process that half of the 30-man squad that attended the Rugby World Cup in Australia were included again, four years later.

The squad for the 2007 tournament in France, the most experienced side in All Blacks history, featured 10 players — or 35 per cent — of all New Zealanders to have surpassed 50 test caps, to that point in the game's history.

Seven survivors from the 'class of '03' also made it through to 2011. Five appeared in the final with Carter and Muliaina, who had been first choice, being forced to watch from the sidelines due to injury.

17

TITLE YEARS (PART 4): EMERGING FROM THE FOG

Psychology plays a massive part in sport.

It provides an unseen point of difference that is often decisive in an industry more tenuous than many appreciate. The margins between success and failure can be small.

This was the case for the Crusaders during back-to-back final appearances in 2003 and 2004, both of which concluded with watching their opponents receive the trophy. While the Blues and Brumbies were worthy champions in each instance, the Crusaders were not helped by distractions on the periphery.

The shadow of that year's Rugby World Cup and the diversion it provided for the majority of the playing group undoubtedly played a part in 2003. Fourteen Crusaders attended the Rugby World Cup in Australia. While their places were all earned, most through the Tri-Nations and Bledisloe Cup wins from earlier in the year, Super Rugby had ushered in a new threat.

Wayne Smith's deputy at the Crusaders, Peter Sloane, had taken over at the Blues. Graham Henry returned from Wales to help, and had got his timing right with nine of the squad starting the year with a spring in their step, courtesy of involvement on the previous year's All Blacks tour of Europe.

Meanwhile the Crusaders' focus was probably not what it should have been. Twenty-three of the 30 players in the squad had won Super Rugby previously, most on more than one occasion. Fifteen of the All Blacks had been allowed to skip the end-of-year tour in order to get their bodies right and a proper pre-season under their belts ahead of the Rugby World Cup.

Eyes on the bigger prize?

It certainly appeared that way, to the extent that Robbie was forced to deliberately bench senior players at various stages to send out a clear message that the only thing that mattered was the present.

'While we had a few injury problems as well that year, there's no doubt that the Rugby World Cup provided a distraction, as it did again four years later.

'Comfort is a dangerous thing. It doesn't take much for standards to drop, especially if players are looking ahead and are, subconsciously at least, saving themselves for what they perceive to be the bigger occasion.'

The campaign certainly started as if normal service, following the previous year's perfect crusade, had resumed. Nine tries were scored through wins over the Hurricanes (37–21) and the Queensland Reds (34–6). Then came the shock.

Matched up against the Blues at Albany, the Crusaders uncharacteristically leaked five tries and were humiliated 5–39.

The season spluttered along from that point, arriving at crunch time entering the final two weeks of the preliminary phase. Although the defending champions had regained their mojo to some extent, boasting a six-win, three-loss record, they were by no means assured of a home semi-final. To make sure of it, they had to beat both the Stormers, whom they'd never beaten in Cape Town, and the Brumbies, away.

It was shake-up time.

Benching senior players Scott Robertson, Chris Jack, Greg Somerville and Dave Hewett while resting Richie McCaw, from such a pivotal match, was a brave move. It provoked a more stunning response than its architect had expected. The Crusaders' maiden win at Newlands was a 51–13 spectacular, featuring six tries and a standing ovation from the Stormers' faithful at the finish.

A week later, Robbie left Andrew Mehrtens, Justin Marshall, Robertson and Norm Maxwell on the bench for a 28–21 win over the Brumbies, and the Crusaders had their Christchurch play-off game.

'We were searching for a response from the whole group in each instance,' Robbie says. 'It's fair to say that we got it.'

The Crusaders advanced to their fifth final in eight seasons a week later when they saw off their former assistant coach Colin Cooper, whose Hurricanes were dispatched with ease 39–16. Cooper's men became a regular opponent for the Crusaders around knock-out time: between 2003 and 2008, the two sides met in three semi-finals and a final, with the Crusaders prevailing in all of them.

The rematch with the Blues produced a pulsating final before a capacity gathering at Eden Park. Having managed just one try against the same opponent two months earlier, this time the Crusaders scored three and only conceded two, but key defensive errors proved costly, and a late try was not enough to stave off a 17–21 defeat. It was the Crusaders' first loss from 10 semi or final appearances.

The forfeiture of the title overshadowed two key player acquisitions that year, with Dan Carter playing all 13 matches of his debut season, while league convert Brad Thorn resumed his rugby career, having sat out all 2002 for personal reasons.

Robbie, who had played inside of Carter's father Neville in the Country backline, recalls Carter junior accepting every challenge placed in front of him.

'Like Richie [McCaw] before him, we tried to manage his entry but, like Richie, at every point, he took it on and thrived.'

Thorn, who'd been tried as a loose forward during his maiden Super Rugby season two years earlier, moved into the second row where his impact was such he again attracted the interest of the All Blacks selectors, this time accepting the honour.

'What was asked of Brad [playing loose forward] when he arrived in that first year was too much,' Robbie considers. 'He had to master certain core skills first. Playing lock allowed him to do that. As it was, his value in the second row was such, he never moved.'

Thorn recalls Robbie's novel approach to his education, especially around lineout play, which was a concept that was totally foreign to the former Kangaroo and Queensland State of Origin league rep. During one session out in the country at Methven, Robbie had Thorn's 113-kilogram frame perched on a fence post, catching shoes being lobbed at him by the coach, in order to assist with his lineout technique.

Lineout jumpers have to keep their legs together so the lifters can hoist them, Thorn explains. If he hadn't kept his legs together on the fence post, he would have fallen off. It might have been unusual, but the homespun training method proved highly effective: Thorn went on to play 59 test matches and over 100 Super Rugby matches during his incredible career.

If players had been guilty of looking too far ahead when they surrendered their title, they were caught looking behind them — at least subconsciously — a year later. With nearly half of the squad having featured for the All Blacks, it was perhaps inevitable that a Rugby World Cup hangover would accompany the opening stages of the Crusaders season, and so it proved.

The year opened with a crushing 19–43 home loss to the NSW Waratahs side they'd humiliated by 77 points in the corresponding game two years previously.

Week two brought a second home defeat, 29–38 to the Blues, and the Crusaders were chasing the campaign from the start.

'One of the greatest motivations in a contact sport is the simple question: why?' Robbie says. 'What is it that excites you? Because you've got to be excited. Everyone has different motivations, different things that excite them. Identifying those things for each individual is part of the art of bringing the group together.'

To that end, as it had the year before, the Crusaders' history of success in the tournament was probably counting against the team, in the back of the players' minds at least.

'There's no doubt we took a while to warm to our work that year, and the history, both in terms of the Rugby World Cup disappointment, but also our recent success as a team, did make it harder.

'While the team was still widely experienced, that became part of the challenge because a lot of them had won Super Rugby four times to that point, so it wasn't like it was something they had never done.

'It just took a slight edge off their motivation, softening their mindset. Sometimes that's all it takes.'

After the flat start, the Crusaders finally got going with a gritty 20–17 win over the Queensland Reds in Brisbane, turning around a 6–17 deficit to gain a critical first win. This kick-started a run where they won seven out of eight, to arrive at the final round robin game with a home semi-final already secured.

Having made the semi-finals the year before, the Hurricanes had dropped back to second-last in Cooper's second season in charge, but they finished strongly, clobbering the Crusaders 37–20 in their farewell outing.

Defence is about attitude: the desire to make a tackle then get up off the ground and make another, all the while supporting your mates. If standards are lowering and short cuts being taken, mentally or physically, defence numbers are usually the first part of the game where it shows. So it was for the Crusaders class of '04.

By conceding five tries in Wellington, they ended the round robin phase of the competition having let in 38 tries — the third worst among the 12 teams, and the worst defensive statistics the Crusaders had churned out since the inaugural season, when they let in 44 tries while running last!

For a dynasty that had largely been built on its defence, the statistics were revealing, implying a prevailing attitude among the playing group of doing enough to get by and no more. The 'playing as if on remote control' feeling also pervaded their attack: the 45 tries they scored for the year was six fewer than the year before, and 15 fewer than they had scored during the perfect crusade.

'It was a tight competition that year with a lot of close results, and the statistics do reflect that,' Robbie says. 'While we had our flat patches, at the front end especially, we got back on the horse and got going, which was an insight into the resilience of the group.'

That toughness was needed on the last weekend to avert a total humiliation. Having beaten the Stormers 27–16 in Christchurch to make the final, the Crusaders found themselves caught up in a storm even more frenzied than the one they had unleashed on the Brumbies in the first Canberra final between the teams, four years previously.

After just 19 minutes of play, the Brumbies had scored five tries and converted four of them to lead 33–0! What happened?

'We just didn't start, and froze to some extent,' Robbie explains. 'Certainly, it was a night a few of the guys would like to forget. In many ways, the final reflected that campaign as a whole: a terrible start but we got back into it, only to fall short.'

The last hour against the Brumbies illustrates the point. By scoring six tries, the Crusaders achieved as many as they had in any other game all season, but a 33-point start was too big a gap to make up, even for them. The Brumbies extended out to a 47–38 win, though without the comfortable coast to the finish line that they might have anticipated at the 20-minute mark.

Throughout that year, the changing of the guard at the Crusaders had gathered in pace, both in the pecking order of the players within the squad, but also in the on-field positions in which they were used. This undoubtedly also contributed to the disjointed nature of the campaign.

'We distributed our resource, and had our best players playing, even if they were not necessarily in the positions to which they were, or would be, best suited over time,' Robbie says.

The transition was reflected by the progress of Carter, who assumed greater responsibility as the backline general in his second season, operating exclusively from second five-eighths. He called the shots, paired with either Cameron McIntyre or Andrew Mehrtens inside of him. Carter continued at second five-eighths for the All Blacks through the domestic season before making the move to first five-eighths, the position he is best known for, on that year's European tour.

'It was the right time for the change. He'd been groomed, had been able to have decision-making support around him, and had thrived, so he was well and truly ready for the increased responsibility at test level.'

The appropriate timing of the transition Carter acknowledges in his foreword to this book.

'And he brought an extra dynamic to the All Blacks' play once the positional switch was made,' Robbie claims, 'as they put 45 points on the French in Paris in just the third test Dan played at first-five.'

Another to make big strides during the 2004 crusade was No. 8 Mose Tuiali'i, who had arrived in Christchurch a relative unknown, plucked out of the Northland NPC team, where he'd played the previous season, on loan from Auckland.

'I brought Mose down based on about five minutes of footage that I saw of him playing for Northland, while I was away with the All Blacks at the Rugby World Cup.

'We were losing "Razor" [Scott Robertson] and I was looking for someone who could provide us with a similar sort of impact: athletic, a powerful ball carrier and a strong defender. So we weren't looking for much!'

Although he ultimately returned to Auckland for the following year's NPC, after having excelled for the Crusaders, Tuiali'i continued the tradition that had seen wearers of Northland's Cambridge blue thrive in the Crusaders' red and black. Tuiali'i needed just 10 games of his debut season to make the All Blacks, and went on to play nine tests, while winning three titles from his five years in Christchurch.

By the time the 2005 season started, Robbie was ready to hand the leadership keys over to the next generation. Although the squad featured 11 players who boasted in excess of a half century of Super Rugby appearances, the captaincy was bestowed on one who was yet to make it.

McCaw took over from Reuben Thorne as skipper, even though the former All Blacks leader remained a key figure for the side, and played every game of that year.

'We'd managed Richie's rise and he was ready to take it on. Making the change at that time also offered us the advantage of allowing him to learn his trade and still have Reuben alongside,' Robbie explains

Nor was the change a slight on Thorne at all. One of the team's talisman players alongside fullback Leon MacDonald, who had been missed during his two years spent playing in Japan following the Rugby World Cup, Thorne was always going to be someone the others looked to, captain or not.

In many ways the transition was made in the same unfussed manner, and for the same reason, as it had been when the captaincy had been passed to the unassuming loose forward three years earlier.

'It [the captaincy] was never going to be an issue for Reuben. He'd done a good job, he'd won a title unbeaten, but he was always going to be happy to step back and support Richie in any way that he could. That's the quality of the individual and that's exactly what he did.'

McCaw, who'd led the All Blacks in one test on the previous year's European Tour prior to taking on the role fulltime with the Crusaders, was into his fifth season in the team but still says the captaincy provided him with a solid learning curve. One of the biggest things he had to get used to, McCaw says, was being able to feel comfortable debating team-related issues with Robbie. It was one thing having a general chat, quite another discussing team issues, especially if views differed between the captain and coach.

He recalls one time, early on in his captaincy, where he debated a training field issue with Robbie in front of the team. The dialogue went backwards and forwards a couple of times, McCaw says, before he realised that having the debate in front of the team 'wasn't a good look'.

The new captain apologised afterwards, with player and coach agreeing that all such future discussions must occur in private, given the importance of the pair presenting a united front for the team. The lesson, McCaw says, is one he has never forgotten.

While he subsequently flourished as a captain, going on to be the most successful All Blacks skipper of all time, McCaw acknowledges that he learned a lot from Robbie. He also observed a subtle change in the Crusaders coaches' leadership style through this period.

There is a balance in leadership, in terms of how much a captain or coach provides, and how much is left for the players to work out for themselves, McCaw says. Robbie's strength was in convincing the team on his ideas. Over time, however, McCaw says Robbie did encourage more discussion, allowing the players to drive things, which made them more comfortable offering alternative solutions.

This reflected the maturing group of leaders the Crusaders had. It was also a product of both the coach and captain encouraging a full range of contributions from the playing staff.

Ownership in any idea is vitally important, McCaw says. While there are times, he believes, where as a leader, you just have to push on and take the team with you, this is not a practice that can be sustained fulltime. There would be no ownership from the whole group and without that the chances of success are slim.

Along with a new captain, the last Super 12 also saw Carter make the move into first five-eighths for the Crusaders on a permanent basis. Although the experienced All Black Mehrtens remained an important part of the team, and featured in all but two of the matches, he only started twice and was settled in his role.

'Like Reuben was for Richie, Mehrts was there to assist and advise Dan if and when it was needed, while contributing to the team as much as he could,' Robbie explains. 'He'd come through that barrier of being out front and enjoyed the slight decrease in his responsibilities. Just being part of the team so to speak.'

In McCaw and Carter, the Crusaders had two new leaders who were now both established test players, totally professional in their approach, and at the beginning of a period where they were the most dominant players in the world game. Even so, Robbie says the results achieved in 2005 and 2006 were the result of a team effort, with a bunch of leaders.

'The team as a whole went to another level, in terms of leadership, during that period. We had leaders who were in the prime of their careers right across the park. It was a very settled group but one that was rediscovering its hunger after having been denied in the previous two seasons.'

As the unbeaten side of 2002 had done, in 2005 the Crusaders raised the level of their game to a new level, blowing away most opponents in the process.

'We'd worked hard on our conditioning in the pre-season, and the way the players responded to the work was great. Their hunger was readily apparent, perhaps more so than it had been in the previous two years.'

This quickly manifested itself.

Although Canberra again proved a hard place to win, with the Crusaders losing the rematch of the previous year's grand final 21–32 on the opening weekend, the side lost just once more through the campaign. On four occasions the Crusaders exceeded 50 points, they topped 40 in four other matches as well, and were only held to less than 30 three times.

Such was the level of their attacking efficiency, the Crusaders final tally of 71 tries edged by one the haul that the Blues had returned during the inaugural Super Rugby competition in 1996. They eclipsed the previous record despite the final season of Super 12 being the fourth leanest overall, in terms of tries scored, from the first decade of Super Rugby.

As with 2002, the wings provided more than 40 per cent of the team's record haul of tries, with Rico Gear, Caleb Ralph and Scott Hamilton between them gathering 30 of the 71 tries the Crusaders scored — and this tally excluded the tries that Ralph and Hamilton scored from centre and fullback respectively.

The well-travelled Gear was another astute draft pick up by Robbie, being brought south to fill the sizeable hole left by the departure of Marika Vunibaka. Although an All Black himself, Gear had been forced to relocate from the Blues to gain regular game time after being restricted behind fellow All Blacks Doug Howlett and Joe Rokocoko. He'd also had a stint at the Highlanders but settled so well in Christchurch that Gear not only replaced Vunibaka, he exceeded him, crossing for 15 tries in his maiden season to eclipse the Fijian's Crusaders' record of 11.

Among the matches, one that stands out for Robbie was the 51–23 demolition of the Stormers at Cape Town, which elicited yet another standing ovation from the local faithful — as well as from a few Crusaders ring-ins among the crowd.

'We'd spent the week building up for that game in Port Elizabeth, in anticipation of their side joining the competition the following year, which was supposed to happen but then didn't, being delayed until the Southern Kings came in for 2013.

'The idea was to get a feel for the city and its training and accommodation facilities so we'd have some background if we had to come back the following year. A change like that, in terms of going somewhere new, was also stimulating for the playing group.

'The week went well, the locals really responded and looked after us. It was only once we got there that we discovered that the Eastern Province side was playing the curtain-raiser to our game in Cape Town against Western Province in the local early season competition [Vodacom Cup].

'So what happened was that all of the fans that went across with the Eastern Province team then stayed on to support us in the main game.'

Coincidentally, the Eastern Province Mighty Elephants, as they were then known, wear red and black hoops, as did their fans on this day. Their presence made the Crusaders feel right at home as they romped to a seven-try-to-two win against their former bogey team.

The second successive half century at Newlands set the Crusaders up for the run home, being the first of seven straight wins that took them to the title. Showing no charity for their former assistant coaches' new charges, the team put 87 points on the Hurricanes across back-to-back weekends, with the second game providing a 47–7 win in a one-sided semi-final.

The final promised to be closer. The NSW Waratahs arrived in Christchurch boasting an identical win–loss record as the Crusaders (nine wins, two losses), and had finished on the same number of log points, being ranked below only due to the Crusaders' superior points differential.

The Crusaders won 35–25 to secure an appropriate finish to the Super 12 era, by claiming their fifth title, but the 10-point margin flattered the Australians. It was 35–6 with 16 minutes to play before three late tries made it a little more respectable.

'While it wasn't something we spoke about too much in the build-up [to the final], we were all aware that it was likely to be the last game for some blokes who had been a massive part of making the Crusaders what they had become,' Robbie says. 'The way the players approached their work that night said all that needed to be said about how much those departing blokes meant to us all.'

Between them, Justin Marshall (105), Andrew Mehrtens (87), Sam Broomhall (56), Greg Feek (66), Dave Hewett (71) and Norm Maxwell (69) had appeared on 454 occasions for the Crusaders. Theirs was a fitting send-off.

'The situation was not that dissimilar to the point we had reached at the end of 2001 when Toddy [Blackadder] had left us, along with a couple of others. The torch was being passed to the next wave. The fact that we had leaders like Richie and Dan, who were already two of the best players in the world, along with an established core of experienced players, cushioned us to some extent from the departure of so many leaders in one hit.'

That the Crusaders were 'cushioned' is an understatement. Nine of their number went on to participate as the All Blacks made a real mess of the touring British & Irish Lions later that winter, with Carter giving one of the finest individual performances ever seen during the second of what became a 3–nil series sweep.

The first year of the new Super 14 saw the Perth-based Western Force enter to up Australia's quota to four, while South Africa's lifted to five, with the Golden Lions and Free State Cheetahs allowed to field teams in their own right after previously having being lumped together in the Cats.

If the competition looked different, its outcome wasn't, although the Crusaders sixth title wasn't quite the stroll it looks like on a report card that reads 13 wins and a draw from 15 matches.

'It was a lot of hard work just as every other season was,' Robbie says, 'and what might seem straightforward in hindsight seldom was in real time. That year was no different.'

Although the games were generally closer than in the previous year, with the Crusaders only once topping 50 points, they still exceeded 30 on eight occasions, and had opened with nine straight wins before they confronted the new Force outfit in Perth.

Coached by Robbie's former All Blacks coaching partner, John Mitchell, the Force had made heavy weather of their maiden journey in Super Rugby, with their record the exact inverse (nine losses) to that of the Crusaders, by the time the defending champions hit town. But for a hotly contested last-minute decision by Marius Jonker, the Crusaders could have been the Western Australians' first victims. The South African test referee disallowed claims for a Force try in the corner, which left the game drawn 23–23, and saw a still unbeaten Crusaders outfit board the plane for the hop over the Indian Ocean.

The winning run ended the following weekend.

After 50-pointers on their previous two visits, the Crusaders found a much sterner test waiting for them at Newlands. The Stormers wanted it badly, and their 28–17 win was every bit as convincing as the scoreline indicates.

Bob Stewart, who travelled with the team on its tour, recalls that the coach wasn't happy. The message to the players, Stewart says, was pretty blunt and unambiguous. They had gotten the team into its mess; they had to get the Crusaders out of it.

The Crusaders chairman recalls the directness of the accusation ruffling a few feathers, before the team rallied around Thorne, who was to lead them against the Bulls, and got down to the business of what became a very intense week of preparation.

Mindful of the now All Blacks captain's workload, and with him having taken a slight knock during the match in Perth, Robbie had always planned to rest McCaw from the second South African match of the tour in Pretoria. As it was, he'd had to miss Cape Town too, but Robbie stuck to the plan. This meant pitching the rookie breakaway Tanerau Latimer, who'd only made his debut off the bench in Perth, in for his first start at Loftus Versfeld.

Leaving the players to work out the Crusaders plans, Stewart says that Robbie put himself inside the mind of the Bulls coach Heyneke Meyer. He worked out how the South Africans would approach the game, and how they would try to counter the method employed by the Crusaders.

Robbie has had many head-to-head duels with the South African, and they've both enjoyed good days and bad, but this one went Robbie's way big time. The Bulls would go on to reach the semi-finals, where the Crusaders beat them again, but the damage was really done at Loftus where a lighter and more mobile visiting outfit ran the locals off their feet, with Latimer scoring two of the four tries in a 35–17 win.

It was, Stewart says, the type of planning and result that defines a great coach.

With that win in the bag, he never doubted that the Crusaders would go on to win the title. Like the rest of the capacity crowd that gathered at Jade Stadium for the final, Stewart just wishes he'd seen it.

Having taken care of the Brumbies (33–3) on their return home from South Africa, and then the Bulls (35–15) comfortably enough in the semis, the Crusaders found the Hurricanes standing between them and a sixth title. Enjoying their best-ever season, the central districts-based side had won 11 of 14 going into the final, and had got within nine of the Crusaders during an 11–20 loss in the qualifying phase. The Hurricanes ventured south with confidence, having seen off the previous year's beaten finalists, the NSW Waratahs, in their semi-final.

What no one had counted on was the fog.

As kick-off approached, a thick blanket rolled in, completely cloaking the ground on what was a crisp but still night. The mist was so dense that the visibility in most areas of the ground was no more than 10 metres. This forced the match officials, NZRU personnel and television representatives to come together with the teams 90 minutes prior to start time, to determine whether the game should go ahead.

'We wanted to play,' Robbie says, 'as did the Hurricanes. When we arrived at the ground, as we walked up the tunnel towards the playing arena, you could see how thick it was. It was suggested to me by an official that the game should be called off. I said no way.

'The teams were ready to go and the crowd had come in. There were no safety issues in playing, and to have called it off would have created a logistical nightmare. So we went ahead.'

For the coaching staff, the game proved to be the ultimate test, forcing Robbie to live a philosophy he had always preached. One of Robbie's favourite themes for the public and news media has always been around the importance of the preparation, with the performance that is produced purely a manifestation of how the players and the team has prepared. The implication is that, once the game starts, the coaches have very limited scope to impact on it. The inaugural Super 14 final was the definitive illustration of that.

'From the coaches box, we saw very little. There were yellow jerseys and red jerseys emerging from the mist and you couldn't quite see who had the ball before they disappeared again,' Robbie recalls.

'It could have been quite stressful but it was the classic symbolism of what coaching is all about. You prepare them [the players] in the knowledge that you are not out there. They can't be reliant on messaging. They can't be reliant on an intervention from someone who is not on the field.

'The ideal preparation caters for that moment so they are fully equipped, fully empowered and have the confidence, trust and belief to be able to take the initiative in real time.'

Not only could Robbie not influence the contest, he could barely see it! He had to trust his players.

They delivered.

The game was unsurprisingly close given the conditions and the quality of the two teams, but the Crusaders scored the only try through centre Casey Laulala and emerged, literally, with a 19–12 win, prevailing over the mist as well as their opponents.

With the players lost in the murk for much of the evening, and most of the pre-game planning thrown into disarray as a result, the game brought an end to the run of 104 consecutive Super Rugby games that had been played by the underrated winger Caleb Ralph.

Robbie had opted for the combination of Gear and Hamilton on the wings, with Laulala at centre, which relegated Ralph to the bench.

'We fully intended to get him out there at some stage but, with everything that was going on around us that night, for some reason it didn't happen. It was a shame but you have to leave sentiment at the door in your considerations. All decisions have to be based on what is best for the team.

'There's an endless amount of emotion involved and a variety of reasons why you might make a decision, but you've got to have an underlying philosophy that removes all of those distractions.'

Ironically, Ralph had begun his sequence playing against the Crusaders for the Blues in the 1998 final, before relocating the following year to start a run of 103 straight appearances in red and black. While the sequence came to an end, the remarkable Ralph ended his career with a record that is unlikely to ever be matched. Alongside the record run of appearances, he won six titles with the Crusaders between 1999 and 2008. He then had Robbie to thank for a seventh, popping up as an injury replacement with the Queensland Reds in 2011.

Ralph had been playing on the Sunshine Coast for local club the Stingrays when the Reds ran into injury trouble, and Robbie was happy to supply a recommendation when contacted about his former charge by Queensland coach Ewen McKenzie.

McKenzie subsequently pulled the former All Black into the squad, where one late-season appearance as a substitute qualified him for a seventh Super Rugby winner's tankard.

'In the right place at the right time,' Robbie says.

With a playing record like his, that is surely the story of Caleb Ralph.

18

SOMETHING GOLD, SOMETHING NEW

The start of the 2007 season found Robbie considering his options. Poised to embark on his eighth crusade as head coach, Robbie knew the time was fast approaching where he would need to make a change. Not only was he ready for a new challenge, either at test level or overseas, there was also the matter of the future direction of the Crusaders to consider. Just as Robbie had carefully managed the transition of the playing group from one generation to the next, so too was he mindful of the coaching line of succession.

The three-time title-winning skipper, Todd Blackadder, had returned from a stint playing and then coaching in Scotland. Robbie got the former All Blacks skipper involved straightaway, bringing him in to assist with the forwards, and specifically the lineout, taking over from Rob Penney.

This was a forerunner of Blackadder taking up head coaching roles, firstly with the Tasman Makos in what was now the Air New Zealand Cup (formerly NPC), and then with the Crusaders as Robbie's successor.

Mark Hammett was also making coaching strides, coming on board as Robbie's assistant. Forced to retire prematurely due to a neck problem, the former Crusaders hooker did two seasons with Robbie, and then another two alongside Blackadder, before cutting his teeth as a head coach succeeding Colin Cooper at the Hurricanes. Hammett had gained his start doing a year working alongside Vern Cotter as a specialist coach, before then taking over the full brief as forward coach once Cotter departed for France.

Blackadder and Hammett represented the first generation of former Crusaders players to step into the coaching arena with the team.

Daryl Gibson, Tabai Matson, Dave Hewett, Aaron Mauger and Scott Robertson have since followed in their footsteps, imparting their knowledge to the next wave of Crusaders and Canterbury players.

They have had big shoes to fill.

Moving on from the Crusaders was not something Robbie had given too much thought to prior to 2007. With three children at school and a well-established support network in place, a lifestyle that suited, and a community he loved, as well as the small matter of a successful rugby machine that he had built up, there seemed little point even contemplating change. But Robbie has never been one to allow things to meander.

A short playing stint with French club Grenoble at the conclusion of the All Blacks tour of England and Scotland in 1983 left an indelible mark, sustaining the intrigue towards further experience offshore.

Although it was prior to their marriage, Penny had been in France for a year teaching English in the town of Aix-en-Provence, four hours to the south of Robbie's club.

'I was the only one in the team who didn't speak the language, which presented its challenges, but as a life experience, it was outstanding,' Robbie says of his time at Grenoble. 'The people were great, incredibly hospitable, while I learned so much, on and off the field.'

One lesson was provided on his first day when, having just arrived, he accompanied the team to an away match against a Narbonne outfit Grenoble had beaten 28–3 at home just a few weeks before.

'I will never forget it. As we left the changing shed just before kick-off, the coach said to me, "We lose today." He was right! Narbonne won by 50 points and I was thinking: what have I got myself into here?'

It was an insight into the passion, intensity and sometimes just pure brutality of French rugby. The competitive fires burn that much more brightly playing in front of animated crowds at home to the extent that, even now in the fully professional era with overseas stars sprinkled throughout the teams, away victories are still something of a rarity in the Top 14.

'That aspect of the game in France was something it took me a while to get my head around while I was there. But what it did mean was that, when you did win away, it was a big deal.'

He saw that for himself when Grenoble beat Toulon at Toulon.

Even then, the coastal Mediterranean club was full of big names including the established test stars halfback Jerome Gallion and flanker Eric Champ, although their players were mainly French back then as opposed to the cosmopolitan line-up Toulon fields today.

'I was the last one back into the sheds afterwards because I'd been talking to my sister Jo, who was at the match,' Robbie remembers. 'When I got back, I found them [the players] all inside crying. My initial reaction was: what has happened? It was only once the penny dropped that I realised what I was witnessing was simply the emotion of the win.'

The game, like society itself, might be complex in France but alongside the culture, which he simply adores, Robbie found that aspect of French rugby highly stimulating.

'That time in France was probably my first step along the pathway towards coaching. It certainly broadened my outlook towards the game by showing me that there were many ways of achieving the same end.

'The methods involved a lot more opposed training than we were accustomed to. The French were probably the first to put an emphasis on musculature in terms of physical development via the use of weights.'

An attempt to get Robbie to return to Grenoble, which saw the club's coach come out to New Zealand, didn't materialise, largely due to its timing. This meant that Robbie was susceptible to the lure of coaching in France when approached by representatives of the Brive club during the 2007 season. The club sent personnel, including its president, down to South Africa to meet with Robbie while the Crusaders were in the Republic.

'Approaches are pretty constant, that's just the nature of the industry, and it's the same for the players, but Brive was the first one that really tweaked my interest.

'France still appealed and I was happy that the Crusaders were in good shape, which was a non-negotiable that I'd committed myself to, before I would look at doing something else.

'We'd gone through two generations of players and the next tier

206

of coaches were starting to come through. So, to that end, the timing was right.'

Brive wasn't.

In the end, Robbie opted out of discussions due to a change of president at the club, but while nothing concrete materialised from the dalliance, a seed had been planted that would germinate in an unexpected way.

In the meantime, Robbie had more than enough on his plate, dealing with the unique circumstance of the All Blacks conditioning programme, which sidelined his seven most experienced test players until the midpoint of the competition.

The scheme became known pejoratively as the 'Cotton Wool Club' after having that name bestowed on it by *New Zealand Herald* journalist Wynne Gray. The name stuck.

The plan had first been pitched to the franchises in 2006, with the key meeting of the various stakeholders being held in Wellington in the week leading up to that year's Super Rugby final.

Crusaders chairman Bob Stewart recalls attending the gathering with Robbie, and the franchise's chief executive Hamish Riach.

Ironically, given that the meeting was being held in his city, Hurricanes coach Colin Cooper didn't disrupt his ongoing preparations for that year's decider, in order to attend.

That was Robbie, Stewart says. He might have had a final to plan for but there was no way he was going to allow such an important discussion around his team to be had without having his say.

Nor was the meeting a stormy one, Stewart recalls. Robbie simply outlined why he was opposed to the idea, then stepped back.

'I actually argued that, if they were going to take the players out, it would be better for the franchises if they took them out totally,' Robbie says. 'I suspect they didn't take me seriously, but I meant it. By bringing them back, halfway through the competition [the players missed the pre-season and the first six games], it was a double-whammy. We were getting hit twice.'

Not only did the franchises have to complete the pre-season without their representatives among the 'protected' 22; they then had to assimilate the two groups at the height of the competition, when the players did return.

In laying out his argument, Robbie spoke with the authority of one who knew the level of distraction the scheme would provide the franchises. He had experienced it the last time around, when he'd had to drop established All Blacks players to the bench during the 2003 campaign because they'd subconsciously been holding back.

'The players involved were going to have one eye on the Rugby World Cup, and they would effectively be being encouraged to think that way, as they would have the knowledge that they'd already been picked.'

While this was denied at the time, all 22 players included in the 'Cotton Wool Club' were subsequently selected for the Rugby World Cup.

Aside from the impact on the franchise's Super Rugby programmes, Robbie also foresaw dangers in the scheme for the All Blacks.

'They were not preparing the players for a one-off event like the Olympics. They were going to have to play seven games to win the Rugby World Cup, and they had a lot of lesser opponents in their pool. So the programme was creating a real possibility that they could be underdone from a rugby perspective when the bigger games came along.

'The way they were structuring it was also like having an each-way bet. If they were so committed to it being the way to go, I suggested they would be better off taking the players out totally.'

Stewart says Robbie delivered his argument without emotion, but admits they both had no doubt it would be in vain.

Although the Crusaders as an organisation didn't agree, with either the concept or the rationale behind it, once the decision was made, Stewart says, it was important that they supported it 'totally'.

Robbie's concerns proved well founded — both from a Crusaders but also an All Blacks' perspective. Just as the Crusaders' All Blacks players couldn't lift with their South African opponents when the play-offs arrived, having not had the same amount of playing background, so the national team suffered when the quarter-finals began at the Rugby World Cup.

'Play-offs are a distinct beast. The stakes go up. So does the intensity and the level of pressure,' Robbie says. 'The margin for error is small.'

While there might have been some among the NZRU hierarchy who had doubted the sincerity of Robbie's case for having the All Blacks removed from the whole tournament, the progress of the Crusaders in their absence reinforced his point.

Despite having to select 13 new Crusaders, which was the most in a single season since the first year of Super Rugby, the new group came together well, and were travelling sweetly by the time the All Blacks became available.

'Given the circumstances, selection was even more critical for that campaign than usual, because we were having to involve so many new players who didn't have any background in Super Rugby, and some of whom we didn't have any background with. It meant taking a few gambles on players. Not so much on their ability, but on their temperaments, and their ability to step up.

'The situation also meant that some players were going to have to be promoted a little bit earlier than we had originally planned.'

One in the latter category was Kieran Read.

'We always knew he was going to be a gem, but the circumstances meant he ended up carrying a bigger load starting off than he might have done otherwise,' Robbie says. 'But he handled it so well, he wound up playing every game that year and hasn't looked back.'

The 2013 International Rugby Board Player of the Year had only played eight games for Canterbury across two seasons prior to his maiden selection for Super Rugby. He hadn't even met Robbie until midway through the 2006 NPC, when the Crusaders coach introduced himself, before adding that Read would be playing for Robbie the following year.

Not knowing him at all, Read admits his initial reaction was that the Crusaders coach must have been joking. Now he knows that it's just Robbie's style. He will be upfront with his players and back them all the way. The endorsement of the future All Blacks skipper was such that his first game for the Crusaders, in the 2007 pre-season, was also his first match captaining a side at any level.

Read is adamant that he owes Robbie a lot.

The then 21-year-old was included in the team's strategy group, which decides the way the side will play, from the start, and says the inclusion helped advance his game 'enormously'. It was something he enjoyed, while also fast tracking his tactical knowledge.

Most importantly, Robbie made him believe in himself.

The first time you come into any team, Read says, the biggest concern is about letting people down. The worry is that you are not good enough. Robbie left Read in no doubt that he belonged. Not only did he tell the young loose forward that he was good enough in the present, Robbie told him that he had a long future in the game at the top level. And he spoke in a manner that left Read in no doubt that Robbie really believed it, which gave him a genuine confidence boost.

If Robbie believed it, Read says, it made it hard not to at least believe that he might have a chance of 'making it'.

Entering the team with so many other new players, who were in the same situation, did make the transition easier, Read acknowledges. Everyone was learning the ropes at the same time and some boasted even less background, in terms of NPC rugby, than he did.

One selection falling into that category, of which Robbie is particularly proud, was that of the future Samoan test player Kahn Fotuali'i. Robbie first encountered the halfback during a training session in Nelson where he was assisting his former Country Colts training partner Wayne Love.

'They'd contracted a lock in from Auckland and he'd asked if he could bring a mate down with him,' Robbie recalls. 'The mate was Kahn. While I was at that training, he was kicking a ball, messing around, waiting for his mate to finish. I observed him for a bit and it was obvious that he had a bit of talent.'

Robbie backed the hunch, bringing Fotuali'i into the wider training group of players for 2007, before he became a full squad member during the following year's title-winning campaign.

At the time, Robbie believed Fotuali'i would become an All Black. Samoa got there first, and he ended up starring for the Samoan side that upset Robbie's Wallabies in Sydney in 2011, before enjoying an impressive Rugby World Cup later that year, and a highly successful career in the United Kingdom.

'The key thing was that the new players that came in weren't just happy being there. They all offered. It showed how well they did that we were right in it, as far as the competition was concerned, by the time the All Blacks became available to us.'

The week before the All Blacks returned, the Crusaders crushed the Bulls 32–10 in Christchurch to maintain their position in the top four. The significance of that result was only too clear by competition's end, by which time the Bulls were celebrating landing South Africa's first title.

Although the Crusaders won five straight after the All Blacks returned, the lack of competitive miles among those players clearly impacted at the back end of the tournament — a stage where the Crusaders had traditionally been the kings. Back-to-back losses away to the Brumbies, and then at home to the Chiefs (their first loss at home for three seasons through 27 matches), left the Crusaders in the unfamiliar position of having their semi-final destiny controlled by others.

They were in the semi-finals but had to wait to see how the Bulls fared in their final match to determine whether they finished second or third on the point's table.

The Bulls were playing the Queensland Reds, who had disintegrated as the former Wallaby boss Eddie Jones's only season as their coach came to an end. For all that, few would have expected the Australians to wave the white flag so totally at Loftus Versfeld. To secure a home semi-final, the Bulls needed to beat the Reds by 71 points to overturn a negative points differential in relation to the Crusaders.

To stress the point, their coach Heyneke Meyer, wrote the target up in his team's dressing room before the players took the field.

'We'd played on the Friday night. I can remember some of the players saying as they left the sheds "See you [at training] on Monday",' Robbie says.

'I told them not to be so sure. That anything could happen so they should keep their phones on in case we needed to round them all up on the Sunday morning to go to South Africa.'

The Queenslanders gave up. They were so abject that the Bulls had surpassed their requirement with 15 minutes to go, finishing up with 13 tries from a 92–3 rout. Damningly, 10 of the Queensland players had — or would be — Wallabies.

In the cases of winger Peter Hynes, five-eighths Berrick Barnes and Quade Cooper, lock James Horwill and hooker Stephen Moore, Robbie soon forgave them. All five were selected during his maiden season as

Wallabies coach the following year. He helped them improve to the extent that all but Cooper started when Robbie guided the Wallabies to their first win over the Springboks on South African soil for eight years, at Durban, 15 months after the Pretoria debacle.

'You could see it coming,' Robbie says of the Reds' capitulation. 'The Bulls knew exactly what they had to do and they were playing a team that had become a rabble. The signs were all there.'

It was the fourth of six wins on the trot for the South Africans as they marched to the country's maiden Super Rugby title.

The penultimate win came a week later when the Bulls beat the Crusaders 27–12 at Loftus in a try-less contest that was ultimately decided by the eight penalty goals and a dropped goal that were kicked by the South Africans' first five-eighths Derick Hougaard.

A microcosm of the campaign as a whole, the Crusaders were in contention for much of the contest but were unable to stay with the South Africans as they lifted in the final quarter of the game.

Thus the Crusaders ended a season with three consecutive losses for just the second time. They had been left with the wooden spoon the first time it happened during the first Super Rugby season.

The final saw the Bulls score a try after the final siren to beat the Sharks 20–17 at Durban. Twenty-one of the players who featured among the two teams in that game were a part of South Africa's Rugby World Cup-winning squad later in the year.

'Ultimately that was one of the biggest flaws of the whole conditioning programme,' Robbie says. 'By compromising the New Zealand sides in Super Rugby, it gave the South Africans in particular a leg up. They took the confidence out of that success into the Rugby World Cup later in the year.'

Robbie and Penny had made arrangements to go to France for the Rugby World Cup. Like many New Zealanders, their plans were based around attending the back end of the tournament, anticipating that the All Blacks would be involved. That meant watching the quarter-final weekend from afar in New Zealand, before heading to Europe.

'Because the All Blacks' quarter-final kicked off in the evening in Cardiff, and the Wallabies were earlier in the day, I watched the Wallabies before going to bed, getting up again to watch the All Blacks.

'When I got to bed after the Australians had lost to England, I joked to Penny: well that's one job opportunity!'

While coaching the Wallabies was not something he had considered at that point, Robbie says that by the time of the Rugby World Cup, he had consciously made the decision to seek a test job, if not with New Zealand, then with someone else.

There had already been interest. Wales had tried to recruit him when they removed the 2005 Grand Slam-winning coach Mike Ruddock, and enquired again following their exit from the World Cup at the pool stage.

Then France beat the All Blacks 20–18 and the door appeared as if it had opened for Robbie to return to the coaching ranks of his nation of birth.

Australian Rugby Union chief executive John O'Neill had made it clear prior to the tournament that he'd be looking for a new Wallaby coach. Robbie had agreed to meet him in Paris during his trip, not anticipating that news of the meeting would be public knowledge almost as soon as they came together.

Given the history, and the emphasis Robbie has always placed on team first as a critical dynamic within his successful outfits, the practice of doing its business through the press was an aspect of Australian Rugby to which he was never comfortable. The almost immediate public disclosure of that first meeting was a sign of what was to come.

'I was leaving the hotel after having met with John and received a text message from my daughter Annabel. She was asking "What's going on?" So it was out in the press already. It was incredible,' Robbie says, 'but unfortunately it became fairly standard!'

Having only met O'Neill in passing twice previously, Robbie had made no commitment to seeking the Wallaby job in undertaking the meeting.

'They [the ARU] contacted me before the quarter-finals had been played, to see if I would meet John while I was in Paris. Obviously by the time we met, the All Blacks were out of the tournament and the possibility suddenly existed that the All Blacks coaching position might be available.

'Given that was the case, I told John that I would try for the All Blacks position. He understood and respected my position completely.'

Robbie chose to pursue the All Blacks knowing that the timing of that appointment, in terms of when it was determined, would most likely rule out the Wallaby alternative, should he be unsuccessful in his home nation. While the All Blacks process got under way, the ARU continued its hunt for a new Wallaby mentor, with Nucifora emerging as the front-runner while Waratahs coach Ewen McKenzie also made his aspirations clear.

The NZRU advertised for a head coach.

Subsequent validations, suggesting the lack of a coaching team had counted against Robbie in the consideration process, was purely excuse making.

'It [a coaching team] wasn't a big part of the interview process,' Robbie recalls. 'They were looking for a head coach. It was later suggested that I hadn't put a coaching team together — whereas the successful candidate had, but that was a ridiculous suggestion, and pure justification of their decision.

'How can you put a coaching team together when you've got nothing to offer? Until I actually had the position, how could I start recruiting assistants?'

As it was, Robbie did offer some names, whom he had history with, and successful coaching history at that, as potential running mates should his application be successful.

'I was asked who I might look at if I was successful and suggested Vern Cotter, Colin Cooper and Wayne Smith as people I had worked well with before,' Robbie says.

'I also mentioned Pat Lam as someone who could be involved, as a young coach who had been doing a good job with Auckland in the NPC. But I stressed that I had an open mind and was prepared to work with them [the NZRU] to that end.'

Sources closer to the process than the author have provided mixed responses, when quizzed as to what chance Robbie had really had, given that the NZRU had backed the incumbents all the way and, therefore, were as liable as the head coach was for some of the controversial decisions that had been made.

Some have said it was close, others that it wasn't, and that the process was purely window dressing.

Tensions were certainly high, with the widely respected vice president of the New Zealand Rugby Union, former All Blacks manager John Sturgeon, drawing the ire of some of the union's inner sanctum when he publicly indicated his preference for Robbie. The popular West Coaster subsequently removed himself from the union offices on the day the decision was made, while union chairman Jock Hobbs, Robbie's brother-in-law, stood down from the voting process.

For his part, Robbie got the distinct impression that the outcome had been predetermined. 'You enter these things in good faith but, by the time I got in front of the panel, it was clear to me that it wasn't going to happen,' Robbie claims. 'The questions that I was asked during my interview revolved more around the past than they did the future. It felt like they had a preconceived nature about them, in terms of the responses they were looking for.

'You could see where they were heading: looking for reasons to say no.'

The interview panel was made up of NZRU board members and Robbie recalls someone raising the selection of Leon MacDonald at centre during the 2003 Rugby World Cup.

'It was almost like their minds were set. You could tell by some of the questions.'

After the All Blacks lost the semi-final to Australia in Sydney, critics charged that Mils Muliaina, who'd largely played wing in what was his first year in the squad, should have been switched to centre. Of course that conveniently overlooked the fact that the 2003 All Blacks, with MacDonald at centre, had won their Rugby World Cup quarter-final. Four years on, when Muliaina was used at centre in the quarter-final, the All Blacks crashed out against France.

The interview complete, Robbie says he left the room suspecting that he had little chance of gaining the appointment. This was confirmed the next morning by then NZRU deputy chairman Mike Eagle.

'I sought feedback, in terms of the areas that I had fallen short, but didn't get any,' Robbie says.

The NZRU reticence extended to a later enquiry from Robbie as to where he stood, in terms of future prospects around the All Blacks job, prior to opening dialogue with the ARU, who had again sought his services.

Robbie still harbours ambitions to coach the All Blacks but holds no regrets about being overlooked, saying the retention of Henry was ultimately justified when the Rugby World Cup was won four years later.

The NZRU had changed coaches after the failed 1991, 1995, 1999 and 2003 campaigns, without getting the outcome they desired the next time around.

'Obviously, it was disappointing not to have secured the position, but the decision did at least reflect growth on behalf of the NZRU. Regardless of the agendas that may or may not have been at play, retention suggested a recognition on behalf of the NZRU that they had been part of the problem.

'You can't keep chopping and changing, discarding experience as you go, because you sometimes wind up letting people go when they are at the height of their experience.

'This creates the risk of having their replacements potentially repeat the mistakes of their predecessors, which would be avoided if greater value was placed on experience.'

It is a lesson the NZRU was rewarded for when the All Blacks won the 2011 Rugby World Cup, following in the footsteps of the Rugby Football Union, which retained Sir Clive Woodward after England's disappointing quarter-final exit in 1999, and received the ultimate payday four years later.

When Robbie returned to Christchurch after his unsuccessful All Blacks interview, he didn't let the rejection keep him down, appearing the next day at the wedding of Crusaders halfback Andy Ellis. It was, MacDonald says, a strong show of his character, especially given the public nature of the disappointment. A number of the guests wondered whether Robbie would attend, MacDonald recalls, but he turned up and didn't make a fuss about it, behaving as if nothing had happened.

MacDonald acknowledges that a number of the players, himself included, were disappointed that Robbie hadn't been successful. They all would have understood if he had been bitter, and had 'gone undercover' for some private time, but he fronted 'as Robbie always had'. Everyone had a huge regard for Robbie already, MacDonald says, but the dignity he showed in how he handled that situation only added to it.

He might not have been wanted by his own country but unbeknown to all of the wedding guests at the time, Robbie included, he was still wanted.

With O'Neill off duty due to ill health, the ARU interview process had been delayed, which meant the Wallabies still didn't have a coach once the NZRU reappointed Graham Henry.

ARU High Performance manager Pat Howard, who was overseeing the process prior to his departure before resurfacing in a role with Cricket Australia, phoned Robbie a few days after the NZRU had made its choice to see whether he would allow his name to be put forward as a Wallaby contender.

To coach against the All Blacks was a big decision.

As part of his due diligence, in determining whether he was ready to take that step, Robbie spoke to the former test cricketer John Wright, who had coached against his nation of birth while in charge of India.

'He described the feeling as being like competing against your brother in the backyard,' Robbie says, 'and I'd had a fair bit of experience of that!

'John said he found it an intense experience but enjoyable and — most importantly — it was founded on respect from both sides. His words reflected my expectation as to what it would be like coaching against the All Blacks, and it pretty much lived up to that.'

Penny, son Sam and daughters Annabel and Sophie were happy with the idea. Robbie also sought, and received, the endorsement of Don Hayes and Fergie McCormick among others.

'Everyone was supportive. Certainly, if Penny, Sam and the girls hadn't been in favour, it wouldn't have happened. But at the same time, a lot was made about what it would be like for me going up against the All Blacks. Ultimately, it was never going to be about me, it was about the playing group, because you are there to support them.'

Nor was the prospect of going head to head with Henry a motivation, although Robbie acknowledges that hype around the match-up was an 'inevitable' by-product of his appointment as Wallabies coach.

'It was never about Graham or me but I don't think the media believed it when either of us said it, as it didn't make for such a catchy story.'

Having mulled it over for a few days, Robbie contacted Howard advising that he would apply.

'I was ready to coach in the test arena, and it was an exciting opportunity. Nor was it breaking new ground, coaching a major test team other than my home country. Graham [Henry] and Steve [Hansen] had both coached Wales already, while Warren [Gatland] was about to take that job. John Kirwan had done two teams [Italy and Japan]. Joe Schmidt [Ireland] and Vern Cotter [Scotland] have also since taken up international head coaching roles with other countries.

'One of the advantages of coaching Australia was that there was no other international job closer to home.'

The interview process itself was very different to the one he had just completed in New Zealand. Whereas the All Blacks conversation focused heavily on the past, the ARU looked ahead, aiming to discover what qualities Robbie would bring to the role.

'The process was more corporate in its approach,' Robbie says. 'A lot of my history, both with the Crusaders and the All Blacks, was spoken about, but only in the context of what my previous experience could bring through to benefit the Wallabies.'

Behavioural challenges, and how Robbie had helped to construct and then maintain such a strong on and off-field culture at the Crusaders, did feature prominently in the discussions.

'It was clear that it [player behaviour] was perceived as an issue, both in game but also away from it.'

It was only once he took on the job, and got inside the team environment, that the magnitude of that particular challenge, and the depth of the issues involved, became apparent.

Robbie's appointment was quickly confirmed, resulting in a trip back to Australia to be unveiled.

While he had come to terms with the prospect of coaching the traditional 'enemy', Robbie admits that he was more intrigued than anyone as to how he would feel once he first heard his name referred to as 'Wallaby coach'.

'After the appointment, I saw a news story on television announcing it, which included a clip from a past Bledisloe Cup test. When I saw the footage from that game, I felt a surge of excitement and I knew that I'd made the right decision taking the job.'

That feeling was only reinforced by the reaction to his appointment back home, which he describes as humbling.

'It was remarkable, and seemed to be across the country. I was getting friendly welcomes and encouragement in places like Auckland and Wellington that I'd never had before, well certainly not to the same extent.'

The public understanding was an extension of the view of his players who, while disappointed to be losing their coach, expressed their support. When Robbie told the Crusaders players at the completion of a training session, prior to its public announcement, the team responded with a hearty 'Aussie, Aussie, Aussie, oi, oi, oi' chant, that made it clear to onlookers what the news was that the players had just been told.

No one held the appointment against Robbie, Crusaders and All Blacks lock Brad Thorn says. Everyone was pleased for him. He was getting the chance to have a crack at being a test head coach. Such is the respect with which Robbie is held, Thorn says, the players' only real concern was how much he might improve the Wallabies, to the detriment of the All Blacks. Read and Ellis echoed Thorn's thoughts.

All of the players felt Robbie deserved the chance to coach at test level, Read says.

The team all understood why, although a lot of the players were 'gutted' that it meant he wasn't going to stick around with the Crusaders.

Ellis says the appointment did lead to plenty of ribbing from the playing group, but Robbie took it well. It wasn't like he hadn't tried to get the All Blacks job, but Ellis says there was firm support within the playing group for Robbie to see out his final year coaching the Crusaders.

As is his way, Robbie was determined to complete the agreed commitment, and had gained the blessing from O'Neill and the ARU to do so.

'Not only had I already made that commitment to the point where the preparations for the season were in place, the playing group, which was already assembled and at work, expected me to be the coach.

'This included new players [most notably locks Thorn and Ali Williams], who had signed for the Crusaders based on the expectation that I would be there.'

Although the NZRU showed initial reluctance at the prospect, the backing of both the Crusaders board and the players — most notably the senior All Blacks on the playing roster — saw the national union give way, which ensured that Robbie stayed put.

The players' feelings on the issue were made 'pretty clear' to the NZRU, MacDonald says, suggesting they may have 'dug their toes in' publicly had there been any attempt to have him removed.

Of all of the players, the All Blacks and Crusaders captain was arguably the most uncomfortable about Robbie's new job, but he too was adamant that their coach be allowed a final crusade. It was bad enough, Richie McCaw says, that the team was losing 'a very good coach'. The last thing it needed was for his term to have been cut short, which would have potentially compromised the side's prospects in a campaign that was already well advanced.

McCaw's foresight proved prophetic, with the Crusaders going on to win the title.

He does, however, acknowledge that an ulterior motive also entered his thinking. From an All Blacks' perspective, McCaw admits to believing that an early departure to Australia by Robbie would benefit the Wallabies, whereas keeping him in New Zealand for longer might have put more pressure on them, by cutting his preparation time.

As far as Robbie was concerned, the Wallabies could wait. He, and his players, had a title to win!

19

TITLE YEARS (PART 5): THE FINAL CRUSADE

When he returned to the Crusaders training base after a three-and-a-half year absence, Brad Thorn had stared up at the newly installed honours board within the team room at Rugby Park.

The panel faithfully records every player to have pulled on the Crusaders jersey, laid out in order of their appearance for the franchise. Before each name stands their Crusaders number. Placed on the other side, for the majority of the recordees, is a sword, in many cases more than one, to signify the number of title-winning campaigns in which they had played a part.

When Thorn first laid his eyes on the roll of distinction, the space to the right of his name was vacant. It was one of the levers that Robbie had used to try to prevent him from returning to Australia and rugby league at the end of 2004, and one of the reasons that brought him back.

Filling that space was also why he had signed for the Crusaders at the last moment, having been, within his own estimation, '14 hours' away from committing himself to the Highlanders.

The re-signing of Thorn, which was completed amid initial resistance from the NZRU, and then after a solid push from the national body to steer the powerful second-rower to the Highlanders, was another of Robbie's recruitment masterstrokes.

His final Crusaders playing roster was always going to be pretty powerful. The addition of a mobile ball-carrying forward like Thorn, at a time when experimental law variations were going to speed up the game, supplied a further hardened edge where it mattered most — up front.

'Brad Thorn. The man is a machine.' Robbie says admiringly. 'His career had been pretty unbelievable even prior to his return. Test matches in two codes, State of Origin selection and two Super Rugby finals. He could have retired pretty happy with all of that, but that isn't Brad's way.

'You can argue pretty comfortably now that, when he arrived back in Christchurch, the best footy of his career was still to come.'

When Thorn returned to Christchurch, he'd played 12 tests for the All Blacks. By the time he left again four years later that number had risen to 59, and he'd won both the Rugby World Cup and finally achieved the Super Rugby title that had brought him back in the first place. Yet Robbie had had to fight to get him.

'The resistance came from on high,' Robbie recalls. 'It was suggested to us [the Crusaders] that Graham [All Blacks coach Graham Henry] felt that, at 33, Brad was too old. That his return wasn't going to assist with the development of the next generation of New Zealand locks. That he'd get in the way, essentially.'

Unbeknown to Robbie, the Highlanders had gotten wind of Thorn's possible availability. With his strong Otago roots, they saw an opportunity, and their interest suddenly changed the NZRU's mind. Now Thorn was wanted, as long as he went to the Highlanders to bolster the battling southern franchise. A financial incentive was offered.

Thorn himself had thought the Crusaders' interest had cooled. They'd signed All Blacks lock Ali Williams in the time since his first contact. He'd then only been offered a place in the franchise's wider training group whereas the NZRU were sorting him a house, car and good pay to go to Dunedin. It was all but done, until Robbie heard about it and got on the phone.

Not only did Robbie know that his former charge was hungry for a title, which he realistically had a better chance of achieving with the Crusaders, Thorn already owned a house in Christchurch which made relocating easier, had a lot of mates in the team, and had earned an All Blacks jersey playing there in the past.

When it comes to selection, Robbie's a wheeler-dealer, Thorn says. He will find a way, as he did in this case.

The day before he had been due to sign for the Highlanders, a place was found for Thorn inside the protected players group, his financial security was assured, and he was now a Crusader again.

Did he feel bad about the U-turn?

A little bit, Thorn says, but professional sport is a business. He had to do what was best for himself but also for his family. Then there was playing again for Robbie, a coach Thorn rates alongside his legendary Australian rugby league coach at the Brisbane Broncos, Wayne Bennett, as the best he has encountered.

Robbie was in the zone that year, Thorn recalls.

The change was marked, he says, from his previous stint with the Crusaders in 2003 and 2004 where Robbie had arguably been distracted by the prelude and the fallout from the Rugby World Cup as much as, if not more, than any of the players.

Having made his decision to leave to coach the Wallabies, Thorn reckons Robbie was much more relaxed. He knew his method and had confidence in it. He also had total belief in his playing group. This revealed itself in the training sessions that were shorter than Thorn remembered them being previously, which resulted in the players 'absolutely fizzing' by the time it came to play.

While rugby and rugby league are very different games, Thorn says Robbie and Bennett share a large number of similarities. This includes the successful title-laden dynasties they've presided over at their respective clubs.

Both are very competitive men, Thorn says, but stress doing the simple things well. They don't overcomplicate the game, but empower their leaders and are always looking for anything — and sometimes the ideas come totally out of left field — which will give their team an edge.

Neither Robbie nor Bennett offer 'big talk' in public, Thorn says. They don't 'talk it up' in the press, but stand by their actions, and are hugely respected by their players because of it. Both have vast experience, have seen it all before and have been through the good times and the bad, so they don't panic and are always composed and clear. Importantly, Thorn says, they know what it takes to win.

The Broncos under Bennett, and Robbie's Crusaders, placed major emphasis on drumming into the playing staff that the team comes first.

A lot of coaches, and players — in both league and rugby — talk about that, Thorn says. The successful ones live it.

As well as offering hardness to the forward pack, Thorn's acquisition also provided a great foil, both on and off the field, for Williams, the Crusaders' other major off-season recruit. The All Blacks lock had gone through a spectacularly public falling out with the Blues' coach David Nucifora the previous year. In doing so, Williams had joined senior Brumbies players from the title-winning squad of 2004 in falling foul of Nucifora. By the time the Brumbies won that title, Nucifora had been advised that he would not be required beyond the end of the season.

Taking on a player sacked by a previous employer could have been considered dangerous but Robbie, who had coached Williams during his All Blacks stint, didn't see any downside.

'He'd fallen into our laps, and was keen to come, and we had a strong group with well-established habits, so there were no misgivings about any potential off-field risk.'

The investment proved worthwhile. Williams played every game, forming an imposing partnership with Thorn while adding, Robbie notes, his share of humour to the environment.

As another big and mobile athlete, he was also well suited by the law variations, which had been trialled the previous year during the sole season of the Australian Rugby Championship, and were also applied in Super Rugby before being shelved.

Although he supported the intention behind the ELVs (experimental law variations), which was to return the essence of the game to a contest played on the feet as opposed to on the ground, they failed because they actually contradicted the laws as they had been written.

'The poor quality of the games at the Rugby World Cup the year before, where teams had pushed the boundaries more and more as the stakes had increased, had highlighted the fact that the game needed to change,' Robbie says.

'The contact zone had become such a lottery, with so many players going off their feet, that the referees had been overwhelmed. Teams consciously preferred not to have the ball, and tended to kick it away when they did have it.'

Robbie was involved in the IRB dialogue around the ELVs. He says the solution that was reached didn't require changing the laws as they were written. The alteration was more in the way that they were being interpreted by referees.

'Nowhere in the laws did it actually state that, having legally entered a tackle situation, a player had to release the ball once he had played it.'

Referees had always insisted that, once a ruck had formed, the ball had to be released.

The players were reliant on the match official to tell them when sufficient numbers had arrived to make the tackle situation a ruck.

While the ELVs were not adopted long term, the trial did lead to a change in refereeing interpretation around the tackle contest. This allowed the first legally arriving player at the tackle to continue to play the ball once others had arrived and the situation had become a ruck.

'That was always in the laws. It just required a change of interpretation in terms of how the law around the tackle was being policed,' Robbie explains. 'It has led to a faster, cleaner game where the tackle area provides more of a genuine contest, although the Rugby World Cup — where the stakes are higher and the pressures are greater on all concerned — still provided greater challenge for the referees. We saw that at various stages in 2011.'

It was apparent during the early rounds of Super Rugby how much faster the ELVs were going to make the game. It was also quickly obvious how well suited they were to the way the Crusaders played.

'Tactically, they [the ELVs] didn't necessitate any change to the way we played anyway. What they did do was make it harder for teams to play negatively against us, to try to shut us down rather than playing positively themselves.'

That much was evident after the opening three matches of the campaign, which saw the Crusaders outscore their opponents by a collective 116 points to 15. After outclassing the Brumbies 34–3 in Christchurch on opening night, the Crusaders returned to Pretoria, where they'd been held try-less in losing the previous year's semi-final.

For the opening 30 minutes, the Bulls were on course for a repeat. The South Africans led 12–0 after first five-eighths Derick Hougaard punished Crusaders' errors with four penalty goals, as the visitors attempted to up the tempo of the game.

Once the Crusaders broke through, however, the dam burst totally. The defending champions were swept away by a deluge of seven tries, which left the locals absorbing a 54–19 defeat. It was a frightening performance reminiscent of the Tri-Nations 50-pointer at Loftus, during Robbie's All Blacks time.

A week after destroying the Bulls, the Crusaders held the Stormers scoreless at Newlands. This was the first time the side from the Western Cape had been shut out in its 130-game history.

The 22–0 win in Cape Town, against an opponent who had often been difficult, was satisfying. It also set up the possibility of the first unbeaten overseas tour since Super Rugby had expanded the trips to three games.

Even more importantly, the performance provided further evidence to Robbie's contention that his final Crusaders squad was his best, which was exalted praise in a class of high achievers.

'It [the Cape Town performance] was complete. There was a real composure in the group. This showed itself in the clinical nature of the decision making. That was the most exciting aspect of it.'

Although he acknowledges that the seven players who had been involved at the previous year's Rugby World Cup had taken a while to 'warm up' after that disappointment, Robbie says the squad had the depth and experience across the playing roster to get through. This was illustrated by the fact that no one started in all 15 matches.

'There was a good balance to that group, good depth. The most important factor was that we had good leadership across the board.'

Robbie's final Crusaders squad contained four of the franchise's five centurions to that point in its history, as well as eight others who had played more than 50 matches. Seventeen of the squad had or would be All Blacks. Halfback Kahn Fotuali'i, hooker Ti'i Paulo (both Samoa) and winger Sean Maitland (Scotland and the British & Irish Lions) all also went on to play test rugby.

Two who made the grade as All Blacks after starting off at the Crusaders together in 2006 were Andy Ellis and Wyatt Crockett. Their development headed the rise of the next generation of Crusaders. The underrated Ellis attended two Rugby World Cups while remaining a loyal servant for both Canterbury and the Crusaders.

Yet he could easily have been lost to rugby prior to the start of his representative career but for an intervention by Robbie. The 2011 Rugby World Cup-winner recalls Robbie turning up at his family's Harewood home in the north-west of Christchurch shortly after he had missed out on a place in the Canterbury Under-19 rugby side.

A promising cricketer, Ellis had been offered a scholarship to play in England. The opportunity could easily have led him down a different career path. Robbie, Ellis says, sat down with him and his parents in the living room of their home. They spoke about his future, where he could go in rugby, and why he should not let the disappointment of missing out on representative selection prevent him from sticking with the game. It was, he says, 'pretty cool'.

Here was the Crusaders coach making the effort to encourage a young fella who wasn't even a representative player, in order to help him advance both his potential sporting career but also his life.

While Ellis did take up the short-term opportunity to play cricket in England, Robbie's visit played a 'major part' in the decision to opt for rugby as his sporting priority.

Robbie, he says, gives his players confidence. He knows the formula: when to talk and when not to. Importantly, Ellis notes, he always acts for a reason. There is always sound logic behind it, as there was when the Crusaders coach visited his family that day.

Crockett cites Robbie's down-to-earth nature and his single-minded focus on the team as an entity, rather than the individuals within it, as the overriding feature of the Crusaders environment he entered. Everything in his coaching approach is about the team, Crockett says. It is about 14 players working to try to put the 15th over for a try.

Trust plays a big part in Robbie's philosophy. He expects his players to do all they need to do as individuals, in terms of their physical and mental preparation, to ensure they will fit in to the way the team wants to play, Crockett says.

This can sometimes lead to personality clashes, although these have usually come, Crockett notes, when individuals have put their needs above those of the team.

Robbie's genuine desire to see his players prosper, and his enjoyment of the team environment and the togetherness associated with that, helps most see beyond themselves, the popular prop says.

But while he is good at making players feel at ease in his company, Robbie is also very good at drawing the boundaries. He can be a hard taskmaster when he needs to be. Crockett recalls bearing the brunt of his coach's frustration during a training drill one day, which wasn't going well. It was a gruelling defensive session, where the players had been instructed not to put their hands on their knees to rest at any time as this would show signs of fatigue, thereby encouraging their opposition.

A lot of the guys had been 'mucking around', Crockett says, and the coach was getting 'hacked off'. Frustrated, Robbie issued a final warning: the next player to lose concentration and put his hands on his knees would be banished to watch the rest of the session from the grandstand.

Sure enough, Crockett was the guilty party, being dispatched to isolation as punishment for his sin. The only trouble was, Robbie then forgot about him, and as the session moved on to other drills and routines, Crockett was left watching forlornly from the sidelines. It was only once training concluded over an hour later and the team gathered in a huddle that Robbie was reminded the group was one short.

The coach was very apologetic afterwards, Crockett says, but the lesson was learned. It was not something he ever did again.

Robbie's love of the game was highlighted by his approach to touring, Ellis says, where he encouraged his players to work hard but also to make sure they enjoyed their experience.

This came through in his last Crusaders tour, which Ellis maintains created the momentum that set up the season. After the two big wins in South Africa where the Crusaders had simply overpowered their opponents, the final game of the trip showed they hadn't lost the ability to outstay their opposition in an arm wrestle either.

They could still tough it out, which they needed to in Perth. On a sparkling Sunday afternoon at Subiaco, the Western Force led 24–12 just after halftime and had a try pulled back for a forward pass at that point before the Crusaders reeled them in, making the right decisions under pressure to advance to a 29–24 victory.

The game illustrated one of the potential by-products of the incoming Wallaby coach still having an interest in Super Rugby: Australian players appeared to lift their efforts playing against his team.

Uncapped Force No. 8 Richard Brown was outstanding at Subiaco and subsequently won his first test jersey later in the year.

The Queensland Reds' pair of uncapped winger Peter Hynes and one-test lock James Horwill also made big impressions playing against the Crusaders later in the competition.

'It may have been in the back of the players' minds that playing the Crusaders was a big game for them individually, although we'd often found that anyway, carrying a bit of a target because of the success we'd had,' Robbie says.

'As far as test selection went, selectors watch all of the games anyway. So those games weren't any bigger in terms of the selection process than any others.'

Nor was the unique circumstance of a national coach plotting the downfall of players he would later be selecting and coaching a distraction at all.

'Clearly, in the back of my mind I knew what was coming [in terms of coaching the Wallabies]. I was conscious of that during my last Crusaders campaign but I didn't do anything differently than I otherwise had.

'You routinely study your opponents. My priority was the Crusaders and the routines remained the same.'

The results continued to come.

The three-match overseas tour was followed by four consecutive wins back in New Zealand, with Robbie spreading the player workload through wins over the Cheetahs (55–7), NSW Waratahs (34–7), Hurricanes (20–13) and Lions (31–6).

The first speed bump was provided by the high ankle sprain suffered by first five-eighths Dan Carter against the Hurricanes in Wellington. This put Carter out for four weeks, although Stephen Brett proved a more than capable stand-in for the backline general.

Two weeks later came the first defeat with the Chiefs establishing themselves as the crusade's new bogey team after completing back-to-back wins against them following an 18–5 success in Hamilton.

That result added to a fascinating background for the next home match, which was against the Blues. Williams was up against his old team and coach, while Robbie opposed one of the men he'd beaten to the Wallaby job, Nucifora, who had since been appointed as the head of the ARU's High Performance Unit.

The Blues only finished sixth in Nucifora's final year but produced one of their best performances in Christchurch, battling gamely in a 22–26 defeat where Williams proved his point with a standout display under pressure for the winners.

'It was a tough game decided on a few key moments,' Robbie recalls, 'but the habits kicked in when it mattered. Ali [Williams] had a big night and clearly enjoyed it.'

Everything continued to go to plan through wins over the Sharks (18–10) and the Queensland Reds (27–21) and with Carter returning off the bench to help spark the win in Brisbane, Robbie's fairytale finish seemed inevitable.

The Highlanders thought otherwise.

The southerners won only three matches all season, but the third of them was the upset of the competition as they came to Christchurch and totally outplayed the Crusaders, overcoming the concession of an early try to march to a convincing 26–14 success.

'We were woeful,' Robbie recalls. 'Credit to the Highlanders, they won well but although we got the response from our players in time, it is fair to say that there was a bit of bewilderment post-game in the changing room as to what had happened.'

Was he worried?

Robbie actually thinks the humbling experience helped the side go on to win the title, although that was a consideration that could only be contemplated once the task was complete.

'You don't presume anything. You are always aware of the possibility [of losing], but having that defeat at that stage was going to ensure that the team entered the play-offs with a mindset much more conducive to getting the job done.'

If it was needed, a further jolt was provided in the second minute of the semi-final when the future Crusaders winger Zac Guildford charged down a clearing kick by Carter to score, giving the Hurricanes an early advantage. It was probably the worst thing that the Hurricanes could have done, antagonising the Crusaders, and the response was emphatic.

The Crusaders always likened the challenge of playing the Hurricanes to standing up to a school bully because of the physicality the Canes brought to the breakdown contest especially. The approach was designed to disrupt their opponent's flow of quick ball.

In the semi-final, the Hurricanes didn't disappoint in attempting to bash their way to victory but the Crusaders were ready and stood up. Their collective tenacity was best typified by the effort of the 20-year-old, 87-kilogram second five-eighths Tim Bateman. The youngster, in just his second season, conceded 15 kilograms in weight and much in experience to his opposite number, the 18-test-capped Ma'a Nonu. Yet he bottled up the All Black so effectively that the Hurricanes' backline 'go-to' man barely made an impact on the match.

Recovering from the early setback, the Crusaders took control and dominated so completely that they powered to a 25-point advantage before two late tries closed the final score to 33–22.

It was almost inevitable given Robbie's upcoming assignment across the Tasman that the Crusaders' opponent in the final would be both Australian and the team coached by Ewen McKenzie, who had lost out on the Wallaby appointment.

Although the NSW Waratahs had been well beaten mid-season in Christchurch, the Crusaders had only led 6–0 at halftime before their opponents had capitulated. It was also clear that they had improved significantly in the interim, having lost just one of the eight games since in making their way to the final.

For Robbie, the priority for the build-up was to control the excitement to ensure none of the emotion involving the various farewell functions impacted on or distracted the players in any way.

As well as Robbie, Crusaders centurions Reuben Thorne and Caleb Ralph were also in the departure lounge, both heading offshore at the conclusion of the season. The spotlight inevitably focused around Robbie. He was also the focal point of the motivation of the players.

Robbie would never have allowed it to become about him from a team perspective, Leon MacDonald says, but there was 'no way' the players were going to let their coach finish with anything other than the 'appropriate' send-off. That was a win in the final.

It was a tight team, the Crusaders fullback says, that played 'good footy' and had top players in all of the key positions. So they had every reason to be confident that they could handle anything that the Waratahs could throw at them.

The build-up to Robbie's final bow had started prior to the week of the final through a send-off that was hosted by the Glenmark club at the Hornby Working Men's Club. It attracted a packed house, including some sporting identities who had flown in from around the country, one being the ever popular 'Mad Butcher', Sir Peter Leitch. The night also doubled as a valuable fundraiser for the charity Robbie had become so closely associated with, the Christchurch City Mission.

This was then followed by an official Christchurch City Council farewell during the week of the final. That event was hosted at the ill-fated Town Hall, with the once iconic building to become a casualty of the 2011 earthquake, suffering extensive damage, resulting in it being pulled down.

'I kept the playing group away from it all as much as I could,' Robbie says. 'My only insistence to the organisers of the functions was that no additional demands should be placed on any of the players.'

This was something Richie McCaw says that Robbie achieved throughout the year but most notably towards the end of the campaign. The Crusaders skipper believes that the winning of the title was indicative of the single-minded focus and commitment of both the playing group and its coach.

As it turned out, some players attended the civic function anyway, with those who went to the event finding themselves surrounded by multiple 'Robbies', as the council re-enacted a promotional stunt from the 1980s shield era their coach had starred in.

Then, the facemasks had been of 'Grizz' Wyllie. This time, Robbie found himself sitting somewhat uncomfortably in an audience surrounded by lookalikes.

'While the two functions and the whole process was very humbling, and also provided a great opportunity to reflect on all that I had experienced, sitting among the face masks at the Town Hall was a little bit unnerving. This was especially so when it was suggested to me later that the masks were better than the real thing!'

During the ceremony, Robbie was presented with the keys to the city, but they were handed over with a specific caveat attached. Should he return to his homeland and win the Rugby World Cup with the Wallabies in four years' time, Robbie was told jokingly that he would have to give them back.

If the city was going to miss him, his absence was also going to be noticed on the local rivers. Arguably one of the leading promoters of the sport of jetboating in the country, the sight of Robbie's boat parked outside of the Crusaders' training base at Rugby Park had become a regular one over the years. With no braided rivers in the vicinity of Sydney, the freedom provided by that particular pastime was going to have to go on hold, reserved for the times when he got back home.

Racing down the river with Robbie in his boat had become almost part of the initiation test for new Crusaders. Kieran Read recalls being taken out in the boat, shortly after making the team, and then being handed control completely out of the blue. A first-timer, Read says he had no idea what he was doing but remembers the boat reaching a fork in the river, at which time Robbie demanded that the nervous pilot make a choice as to which channel they took.

Read remembers asking for guidance but receiving none, being told simply to 'make a decision'. It was pure Robbie, Read says. In life as in rugby, throwing his people the rope.

Still, the novice reckons he must have done OK. They all returned in one piece.

It wouldn't have been good for the selection chances, he acknowledges, if he had wrecked the boss's boat!

Todd Blackadder is another disciple of the sport and has his own boat. He tells the story of a post-game serve Robbie delivered after a loss to the Bulls at Pretoria where not a lot had gone right. The terminology he used was quite specific and quite pointed, Blackadder recalls. It is not about how flash your boat is; it is how you guide it and the decisions you make, Robbie fumed.

The sermon confused a lot of the players but among the bewildered looks in the dressing room, there were two who knew exactly whom the spray was being directed at. Blackadder looked straight at halfback Justin Marshall and received a knowing look back. They were the only two players in the team who owned jetboats.

Although the lead-up to his last final was a busy week, Robbie still found the time for 'one last blast' down the Waimakariri River just to the north of Christchurch.

Then it was down to business.

Even though it was the last of the 119 games he had presided over as head coach of the Crusaders, Robbie says his overwhelming emotion prior to kick-off was one of enjoyment as opposed to apprehension.

'It was pure excitement,' he says. 'We'd had a good preparation that week and through the whole campaign.

'We'd just got to the point, in terms of our game, in terms of the players' understanding of what we were trying to do, in terms of their ability to initiate and to lead, and to cope with any adversity within the game, that I had total confidence in them whatever the circumstance they faced.

'So I was determined to make sure that I enjoyed it that one last time.'

The Waratahs, 16 of whom would be named in Robbie's first Wallaby squad two days later, made a good fight of it. Two tries by speedy winger Lachie Turner, the first of which was created by a 'Carter-esque' pinpoint crossfield kick from the precociously talented first five-eighths Kurtley Beale, saw the visitors jump to a 12–3 advantage after 26 minutes of play.

Robbie had snarled at his players at the start of the week that there was no such thing as fairytales. Anything worth getting would have to be earned. His players heeded the warning. By halftime, they had worked their way back into the game, closing to a one-point (11–12) deficit after a try by No. 8 Mose Tuali'i three minutes before the break.

It was the only try the Crusaders scored in the final but it was the fifty-third for the campaign and symbolised their artistry with clever deception plays and wide flat passing being used to shift the ball to the width of the field at pace, thereby outflanking the opposing defensive line.

The home side could have had a second 15 minutes after the break, but Crockett's effort was rubbed out by South African referee Mark Lawrence after the touch judge spied a Thorn punch on Waratahs lock Dan Vickerman. The flagman hadn't seen the wily Vickerman's earlier punch which had provoked the response but the incident saw the try overturned. Thorn was sent to the sin-bin.

Having crept ahead 14–12 just after halftime, the try would have skipped the Crusaders clear 19 or possibly 21 to 12 (with the conversion), heading into the final quarter. This would have, in all probability, been game over. Instead, while a distraught Thorn watched from the naughty chair, the Crusaders soaked up the time, holding the Waratahs scoreless through the period where they were short-staffed.

'We'd prepared for the adversity. When it came, being a man down, I was comfortable that the players would respond,' Robbie says. 'They knew what to do, in terms of how to play under those circumstances and executed to the extent that we held the ball for much of that time and the Waratahs didn't threaten during the 10 minutes without Brad.'

Once a very relieved Thorn returned, the Crusaders camped on the Waratahs line before advancing beyond penalty goal range with a Carter dropped goal. The game was then put to bed by his fourth penalty goal of the evening, seven minutes from time, which put the score beyond reach at 20–12.

In many ways, given the somewhat chaotic nature of the post-game celebrations, it was almost appropriate that there was still drama to come when one of the Crusaders' horses, who are a much-loved part of the pre-game activity, spooked. The steed broke free of its stall when upset by the fulltime fireworks. It galloped at full throttle around the field while the players celebrated in the middle and officials were readying the post-match presentation. Fortunately, no one was hurt before the startled horse was recaptured, but its adventure added a surreal element to the evening as the Crusaders completed their now traditional post-title ritual.

The players gather in a tight circle around a large ceremonial sword, which is placed in the ground on the field of play. The attractive sword was gifted to the team by a wealthy Durban-based fan.

Those gathering in the tunnel outside of the changing rooms after the trophy and medallions had been presented could then have been excused for wondering which changing room was which, as the Australian national anthem was belted out with gusto — in the Crusaders changing shed!

The impromptu rendition, to help Robbie learn the words, kick-started celebrations that continued when the team gathered for brunch the following day. The function, which included all of the partners and wives, marked the end of the era, as the final get-together of Robbie's last crusade.

'It was all rushed, but that's what we had chosen to do, knowing that if we made it through to the final, the turnaround into the next campaign would be pretty quick,' Robbie says.

'The speed in which it ended was all part of it. All of the experiences that I'd had over the years had prepared me for that moment.

'You go from one campaign to the next. It's all part of the industry and is the same for players and coaches alike.'

Not all endings are like this though.

When he returned home from the function that night, Robbie would be on the phone to Australia, finalising the names of his inaugural Wallaby squad, which was to be named on his arrival in the country the following morning.

Even so, he still had time and counsel for the group he was leaving and it was special, Read recalls. The up-and-coming loose forward was being touted for an All Blacks call-up but suffered the disappointment of not hearing his name when the squad was announced the morning after the final.

He might have been about to start as coach of the opposition, but Robbie was still prepared to pull his disappointed player aside and offer encouragement. Read was told that he didn't need to be named as an All Black, just to play like one. It meant a lot and is something the future IRB Player of the Year, who eventually made his test debut at the end of 2008, will never forget.

Nor will Robbie's contribution to the Crusaders ever be forgotten.

The first Super Rugby coach to surpass 100 matches in charge of a team, Robbie's last final produced the 88th win of his 119-game, nine-season tenure as head coach. This represented a 74 per cent success rate, which is unlikely to be repeated by any coach who is involved for more than just a few seasons, given the intensity of the annual competition.

Staggeringly, at the time of his departure, the 88 wins the Crusaders had achieved under his stewardship represented more wins than all but the Blues and the Brumbies had achieved among the teams, through the 13 years of Super Rugby — and Robbie had given them all a four-season head start.

His association with the team, which had started off as manager, meant Robbie had been involved in all but the first 11 of the 153 games that the Crusaders had played by the time of his departure.

But maybe his influence was best summed up by the years that immediately followed his departure. The Crusaders made the play-offs in each of the five years he was Wallaby coach without winning the title once.

20

A TALE OF TWO CITIES

Picture this. One moment, you are in the dressing room, enjoying the moment with your players. The victory celebrations after seven months of hard Super Rugby graft have reaped the ultimate harvest.

Less than 36 hours later, you are in another room, addressing another playing group that features 16 of the players your previous team has just beaten in the final.

Such was the whirlwind nature of Robbie's introduction to the Wallabies and Australian Rugby.

Out of necessity, Robbie went straight into camp with his new charges, after a 6 am flight out of Christchurch on the Monday morning following the Super Rugby final.

After introductions to the media, which included an interview on the high-rating breakfast radio show of Alan Jones, the former Wallaby coach whom he'd beaten to the job, Robbie got down to team business. Ironically, his first team meeting was held in the same conference room at Sydney's Manly Pacific hotel where the Crusaders had established team protocols during the pre-season of their successful campaign.

'It was in at the deep end, but that was the best way to do it, to just get on with it,' Robbie recalls. 'I had encountered a few of the players over the years but didn't really know any of them. It was a new experience for all of us.'

It was new also for his assistant coach, the ex-Wallaby Jim Williams, who had been appointed by the Australian Rugby Union. Williams was fresh to the position, having returned home from a successful stint playing and then coaching at the leading Irish club Munster, where he won the Heineken Cup in both capacities.

Michael Foley's contract had carried over from the previous coaching team, although he moved onto the Waratahs staff after Robbie's first year.

The core of the previous year's Wallaby squad was retained.

'We went for stability [in selection] where we could, largely out of necessity. The team had already lost a lot of leadership capacity through the departures of George Gregan, Stephen Larkham and Chris Latham in particular. They were a huge part of the team's brains trust. They had all occupied pivotal playing positions.'

One of the most important initial decisions was around the captaincy. This saw Australia's Rugby World Cup leader from the previous year, Stirling Mortlock, retained in the role despite a solid push from both within and beyond the ARU for the long-time Waratahs skipper Phil Waugh.

ARU chief executive John O'Neill, who insisted on signing off all major team decisions including the playing squad, was keen on Waugh before accepting the rationale behind Robbie's argument.

'Our options were limited given the leaders that Australia had lost, so the incumbent, Stirling, was given the first opportunity,' Robbie says. 'Phil [Waugh] was the most able leader available to us in terms of his extended history leading New South Wales, but he wasn't guaranteed a starting position as we also had George Smith.'

As it turned out, Waugh didn't feature for the Wallabies beyond the mid-year tests of 2009, playing his 79th and final game as a replacement during the win against France, having fallen behind both Smith and the emerging David Pocock. Waugh was one of 10 players whose test careers were completed in 2009 as Robbie's overhaul began in earnest during his second year in charge.

By the end of that campaign, over two-thirds of the players who had been eliminated in the quarter-finals of the 2007 Rugby World Cup had been phased out of the team.

Given the hype that had been drummed up regarding his appointment, results were the main priority in the first instance, taking precedence over the longer-term development of players.

'Right from the start, the expectations were obvious. It was important that we hit the ground running. While some new players who we felt were ready to go were introduced from the start, we largely relied on experience first up, giving the incumbents licence.

'They had the first shot, although it became apparent as that first year unfolded that we were going to have to move some of those players on.'

Two weeks of mayhem characterised the preparation for Robbie's first test as Wallabies coach. He was getting to know the players, they were getting to know him, while the ARU propaganda campaign was in full swing. It sought to capitalise on the credibility of their new man while creating the expectation that Robbie would turn the Wallabies into an international version of the Crusaders.

'They [the Crusaders and the Wallabies] were totally different environments with totally different challenges so any comparisons or expectations based on that were naive.

'There were some aspects [from his past] that I could bring forward but the Wallabies group had to establish its own culture, drawing from their identity and their history. There were never going to be any quick fixes.'

It soon became apparent to the new coach that it was going to be a long-term rebuild for a side that had finished the previous year ranked at the all-time low of fifth on the International Rugby Board ratings.

'You arrive with a perception but once you are there on the ground you get to see it for real. That's what those first two weeks were all about,' Robbie says. 'There were a lot of behaviours that reinforced my existing perceptions. It was obvious from the start that [physical] conditioning would be a big part of our challenge. That proved to be the case, and it takes time and cooperation [from the states] to sort out.'

While vast improvements were made, an across the board approach to the physical preparation of players was something that Robbie was never able to fully achieve, reflecting the nature of the Australian game where the state programmes are run totally independent of the national side.

Off-field behaviours, attitudes and priorities also quickly drew his attention. The work needed in this area was highlighted when the senior players called a meeting at the start of the week prior to the Wallabies' opening Tri-Nations test against South Africa in Perth. The team's recent history had been dogged by off-field incidents. The motivation behind the Perth gathering indicated that attitudinal change was needed and had to start with the senior players.

'When the meeting was called, I thought: "Great, they are being proactive as far as their match preparation goes",' Robbie recalls. 'It turned out that they were organising their social requirements for the week, their access to transport and the like. I thought to myself: "We've got some way to go here. This could be harder than I thought."'

For all of the challenges ahead, Robbie's Wallabies made a flying start, racking up successive wins over Ireland (18–12) and then France (34–13 and 40–10) to build up confidence levels prior to the start of the Tri-Nations.

The Irish always had the potential to be a banana skin first up. They had a history of troubling the Wallabies and didn't disappoint, although an 18–7 advantage just after halftime proved enough despite an edgy final 15 minutes where the visitors were within a converted try of stealing the result.

It was a strong Irish combination. They went on to win their first Six Nations Grand Slam in 61 years the following March and would provide Australia with further difficulty, both in thwarting the Wallabies' own 2009 Grand Slam attempt, but also in providing one of the upsets of the 2011 Rugby World Cup.

'That game was always going to be a real hard slog. The Irish are always confrontational. The pleasing thing was that we found a way to win against an experienced side reaching the height of its powers.

'We had provided a new philosophy in terms of playing the game, that the players were having to adapt to. There was a lot more licence for them to take the initiative within a simple framework, but I quickly sensed that the prospect excited them.'

The approach was tagged 'playing what you see in front of you' by the Australian press. It reflected a shift in mindset from where the Wallabies had been before.

'It [playing what you see in front of you] was an obvious statement, but it highlighted how different the approach was. The historically prescriptive method that had been the way previously was an issue we had to get beyond. We had to train the players to think for themselves and make choices as opposed to relying on what had been pre-programmed.'

Part of the process was the introduction of greater competition at training. The players were split into mini teams to compete in various drills and games. These were designed to improve individual aspects of their skills while also fostering teamwork and cohesion.

The increased competition also ensured the players remained fully focused at training while sending out a clear signal that no one was guaranteed their place in the side.

Of course, not all of Robbie's initial challenges were on the field.

The Australian national anthem had to be mastered, although he had come well prepared, knowing that the spotlight would most likely be on him when 'Advance Australia Fair' was sung prior to his first test.

The anthem also doubles as the Australian team's victory song. It is belted out by the players and the staff in the changing room afterwards, so it wasn't just the news media who were watching with interest to see if he knew the words on that first night.

Dealing with Australian dignitaries was also part of the brief, although Robbie's skills of recognition failed their first test after Prime Minister Kevin Rudd visited the changing sheds following the win over France in Sydney.

The PM was waiting patiently with O'Neill when Robbie returned to the changing room following the post-game press conference, only for the coach to brush straight past the pair as he headed to congratulate his players. The incident provided much amusement for the team afterwards, with a stunned Rudd and a bemused O'Neill having to wait their turn for Robbie's attention.

Robbie still claims not to have initially seen the Prime Minister, who had his back to him in conversation with the ARU head when Robbie returned to the sheds, although one management member was quick to point out that Rudd needn't have worried about the slight as Robbie wasn't eligible to vote anyway.

Playing South Africa in Western Australia has always been somewhat problematic for the Wallabies. Not only do the Wallabies have to journey the five hours across the country, which gives up some of their advantage in the travel stakes, Perth also boasts a large expatriate South African population, who invariably turn out in numbers to back the Boks.

It has made a difference.

The 38–12 defeat of Ewen McKenzie's side in Brisbane in 2013 was the first time the Springboks had won at any Australian venue other than Perth since the annual southern hemisphere championship began in 1996. In 2008, not only was the Bok side that arrived in the west the reigning Rugby World Cup holders, they'd also just knocked off the All Blacks 30–28 to record South Africa's maiden test win in the southern city of Dunedin.

The match, which was Australia's introduction to the Tri-Nations after the three test wins gathered in June, was always going to be tight, but the Wallabies showed the greater creativity while standing up to the usual physical assault.

The tries scored in the 10 minutes either side of halftime, firstly by winger Lote Tuqiri and then by Mortlock, proved the difference as the world champions were held try-less in a 16–9 defeat.

'It was an important result for us as a group,' Robbie says.

'There was a vibrancy to the team. You could see it in the way we defended. We soaked up a lot of Springbok pressure before taking the try-scoring opportunities when they presented themselves.'

The win was a headline writer's dream ahead of the back-to-back Bledisloe Cup tests against the All Blacks. That week was to be a tale of two cities, and two vastly different outcomes, with the contrast of the results in Sydney and Auckland indicative of the boom–bust mentality that has embedded itself in the Wallabies' culture through the professional era.

Naturally, much of the focus beforehand was on the rival coaches — Robbie and Graham Henry, although both refused to be drawn into any pre-game sniping. If Robbie had still harboured any doubts about the decision to take on the Wallabies, the first game in Sydney was to be the night when they would have surfaced. Not only did the contest isolate him from his nation of birth, it also divided his family, with brother-in-law Jock Hobbs the chairman of the NZRU.

As had been the case previously, the family simply compartmentalised the potential division, although Robbie's sister Jo made it clear where her loyalties stood when interviewed by the media at Christchurch airport prior to her departure to Sydney for the game. Family comes before country, she declared, happily advertising that she'd be supporting her brother.

Having prepared for successful Bledisloe Cup tests during his career as an All Blacks player and then coach, Robbie knew the sensation and sensed it in the excitement of the Australian players. This manifested itself in a fast start, which saw the Wallabies score tries through the Bledisloe Cup first-timers Ryan Cross and Peter Hynes to jump to a 17–5 lead after 30 minutes, taking advantage of an unusually nervous All Blacks effort.

A try right on halftime, and another five minutes after, then saw the All Blacks assert themselves, edging ahead 19–17.

Fuelled by the confidence of their unbeaten start under Robbie, the Wallabies kept coming. Some verbal subterfuge by lock James Horwill, who fooled Sione Lauaki into believing that another New Zealand defender had Rocky Elsom covered by shouting words to that effect at the All Blacks No. 8, allowed the Australian flanker to cross for a vital try. A dropped goal by first five-eighths Matt Giteau, and a try by Horwill himself then iced a remarkable 34–19 win from a pulsating game played in front of 80,000 fans.

Yet while the jubilant Australian players celebrated, their mid-game lapse highlighted a vulnerability that would be seized on again and again by the All Blacks in the matches to come.

Robbie says of the six-minute period when the All Blacks scored 14 unanswered points: 'It was indicative of the lack of genuine belief within the playing group when it came to the games against New Zealand. Our decision making would drop off the radar under pressure when we were right in the games.'

Certainly, physical conditioning was an issue. This helps to explain why the Wallabies could lead the All Blacks at halftime in six of the 10 matches they subsequently lost in sequence from the second Bledisloe of 2008 up until the final game of the 2010 series.

The belief levels within the respective groups also played a big part in the outcomes. While the Australian players consistently doubted their ability to get the job done, and lacked the on-field leaders to help overcome the uncertainty, the New Zealanders simply hung in and waited for the opportunity, knowing that the chance would come to put their opponents away.

'It was frustrating for sure, but there were numerous elements at play, physical, mental and just as importantly, historical. That was why the issue was predominantly one that was exclusive to playing New Zealand. When we established an advantage against anyone else, we nearly always got the job done.'

The Wallabies had not won more than one test in a year against the All Blacks since 2001. Australia had only twice won a series against New Zealand through the professional era. This meant the elder generation were too used to losing, and deep down expected it, while the younger ones took their lead from what was going on around them and then in turn struggled to genuinely believe that they could beat the All Blacks when they moved into the leadership positions in the side.

'The lack of expectation internally, especially against the All Blacks, proved a pivotal factor over time. It was a chain that kept pulling us down,' Robbie acknowledges.

Admittedly, the All Blacks dominated everyone through this period, winning 40 of the 49 tests they played between the 2007 and 2011 Rugby World Cups. And with four games a year through the 2008, 2009 and 2010 seasons, the Wallabies were more exposed to the world's number one ranked team than anyone else.

By the time the term of the Wallabies' most capped test coach was done, games against the world champions had made up 24 per cent of his 74 tests in charge. This was a higher ratio than for all but Greg Smith (1996–97) among Robbie's five immediate predecessors, and Smith's career encompassed just 19 tests, where he lost all five that were played against New Zealand.

The fact that Australia began to master the South Africans on Robbie's watch while rising to number two in the world rankings only increased the sense of frustration at being unable to take the final step on a consistent basis.

While oblivious to what lay in store from future All Blacks contests, Robbie admits he had been fascinated by how he would feel if the time came when he coached the Wallabies to a win over the national side he had once represented, both as a player and as a coach.

'I was excited by the contest,' Robbie recalls, 'but it was founded on the respect I had for the All Blacks as an opponent. There were some outstanding men in that team, men I'd done a lot of yards with, both as their coach and their friend.

'I knew how much they had put into that game [in Sydney] but, by the same token, I also knew how much the outcome had meant to my playing group, and to the nation as a whole. So I was fulfilled.'

The night was not without its awkwardness.

All Blacks halfback Andy Ellis says it only really hit home 'properly' that his former Crusaders coach was now guiding the opposition when he saw Robbie in his Australian team suit during the pre-game warm up. It just didn't seem or look right.

Brad Thorn is another who acknowledges that the presence of his former mentor made an impact. Thorn's wife Mary Anne and Penny Deans are good friends. Thorn regards Robbie as a mate, so to suddenly be playing against a Robbie Deans-coached team was a strange feeling, even for an All Black who'd previously represented Australia at rugby league, although Thorn feels that his old coach never received the credit he should have for his work with the Wallabies.

Thorn says he had always expected Robbie to improve the Wallabies and he did, making them the second best team in the world, and the main rival for the All Blacks during the powerful lock's second stint representing New Zealand. If they couldn't consistently beat the All Blacks, Thorn says, then they were in good company and the Wallaby games were usually closer than any others.

All Blacks skipper Richie McCaw, who was a spectator that night in Sydney due to injury, admits he didn't enjoy the experience, saying the significant improvement by the Wallabies while they were in Robbie's care was what he had always feared.

It's no coincidence, McCaw contends, that two of the All Blacks' best performances of that era — at Eden Park in 2008 and again in the 2011

Rugby World Cup semi-final — were reserved for the Wallabies.

The All Blacks knew Robbie so well, and knew what a good coach he was, it was only natural that they saw the threat the Wallabies posed as having increased with him in charge, McCaw says.

As he acknowledged in his foreword to this book, All Blacks first five-eighths Dan Carter held similar concerns about how much more competitive Robbie would make the Wallabies. The defeat in Sydney only added to those, and to the discomfort when Robbie came across Carter, who had just played his 50th test, in the player's tunnel after the game.

'I said hello but there was awkwardness around the interaction,' Robbie recalls. 'You could sense that they [the All Blacks players] weren't comfortable. That probably wasn't surprising.'

What was surprising was a comment made to Robbie by second five-eighths Berrick Barnes after the game.

'Berrick told me that he'd never been in a side, at any level, which had won five games in a row, as we'd just done. The comment shocked me,' Robbie says.

It also probably helps to explain what came next.

A week later in Auckland against an All Blacks side under huge pressure, the Wallabies came up short. Well short.

It has been suggested since that had the All Blacks been defeated, it would have been the end for Henry.

McCaw, who returned to duty for the game, acknowledges the extreme pressure the whole side was under. It showed in their collective response.

While the Wallabies briefly threatened to make a game of it when a try by Adam Ashley-Cooper closed them to a 10–18 scoreline after 30 minutes, the visitors fell away in the second period. The All Blacks piled on 21 unanswered points to complete an emphatic 39–10 victory.

The Wallabies had been intimidated. A number of players, including some of the more experienced team members, appeared out of their depth and unable to respond to the pressure that was exerted by their All Blacks counterparts.

Although the first return to his homeland hadn't produced the result he was chasing, Robbie wasn't about to panic.

'I knew when I started that there was going to be some rapid learning, as there was that night at Eden Park. As you have to do in those situations, we took what was of value out of the game and moved on.'

Often the best gauge as to how a group is coming together is how it responds to adversity. The Wallabies responded superbly at Durban during the first of their two matches in South Africa before falling in a heap at Johannesburg the following week.

Once again, it was a tale of two cities.

Robbie's love of touring South Africa is something he transmits to his players. This was important for the Wallabies who badly needed a reason to approach visits with confidence in their ability to perform.

The positive way that Robbie embraces the challenge of South African tours is reflected by his record in the Republic. It stands at 54 per cent (11 wins from 19 with the Crusaders and three wins from seven with the Wallabies). It is a record few visiting coaches can match, especially when it is considered that Robbie took teams to South Africa for 13 straight years between 2000 and 2012.

While the Wallabies were in credit historically against the Springboks from home Tri-Nations matches, their away record was dire. There had been just one win (19–18 at Durban in 2000) from 11 matches to that point of the competition's history.

'The record was horrific. I just couldn't comprehend it,' Robbie says. 'It was a priority for us to address not just in South Africa but around the world because the recent record on the northern tours to Europe hadn't been too flash either.'

To that end, Robbie made a statement of intent when he omitted long-serving lock Nathan Sharpe from the 26-man touring group. Sharpe was a popular tourist but Horwill and Dan Vickerman were the settled starting second-row combination, and with the need for additional blindside flank cover, the Western Force skipper missed out to the utility value offered by Hugh McMeniman and Dean Mumm.

The selection raised eyebrows but served notice that reputations counted for little.

As it turned out, the Australian pack largely outmuscled the Springboks on a day that their blindside flanker won't forget in a hurry. It started with Elsom missing the beginning of the pre-game team meeting due to the slow nature of the lifts at the team's Durban hotel, and ended with the hard-nosed flanker both winning the man-of-the-match award and being cited following Australia's convincing 27–15 win.

The first Australian win on South African soil in seven years, which reclaimed the Nelson Mandela Challenge Plate, was never in much doubt as the Wallabies raced to a 20–3 lead after an hour before two late tries by centre Adrian Jacobs allowed the Springboks to close the scoreline.

At fulltime, a militant King's Park crowd roundly booed the home side from the field. The noise and the hostility that was directed at the home players should have served as a warning to each of the Australians as to the lift they would require individually if they were to repeat the dose a week later.

Instead, they got comfortable. And, as had been the case in Auckland four weeks before, they failed the test.

Regardless of the outcome in Johannesburg, the players knew that both the Tri-Nations and the Bledisloe Cup would still be within reach. The former was going to hinge on the final tournament game against the All Blacks, to be played in Brisbane.

The players had also already created history by snapping the wretched 14-game losing run from away Tri-Nations matches.

Robbie himself had distractions. He spent much of the week defending Elsom from a dangerous play charge relating to interference with the lineout jumper. After a prolonged and demanding process, the Wallabies finally won the case. It was their only victory for the week.

In an attempt to provide fresh legs at altitude, changes were made to the team.

'It all proved to be an explosive cocktail,' Robbie says of the various factors that surrounded the 8–53 defeat. 'Once the South Africans got their foot in the door and got momentum, there was no coming back. The circumstances of our situation were such that we were learning a lot about our players on the fly. Like Auckland, we had to take what we could from it and move on quickly.'

As with the Eden Park defeat, the afternoon exposed limitations in players, which ultimately ended their Wallaby careers, while casting doubt over others.

249

The Springboks scored four tries in each half with the Cheetahs winger Jongi Nokwe scoring half of them as the Wallabies conceded a half century of points for just the third time in Australia's history. Ironically, the previous instance had been by an All Blacks side Robbie was helping to coach.

New Zealand quickly became the focus again with the tournament-deciding Tri-Nations game following two weeks after the Johannesburg flop.

An Australian win at Suncorp Stadium would also have taken the Bledisloe Cup series to the fourth game, which was being played in Hong Kong as the two unions attempted to grow the profile of the game and their respective bank balances with a foray into the Asian market.

When Australia led 17–7 five minutes after halftime, the game was there for the taking.

New Zealand took it. As they had in Sydney, the All Blacks took charge, posting three converted tries in 22 minutes, before conceding a late try two minutes from time which closed the Wallabies to a 24–28 defeat.

'When the ante goes up in game, the ability to think on your feet suffers if you can't go with it,' Robbie explains. 'That was what was happening to us. It became a recurring theme: our skill execution and decision making would taper off under pressure.'

The simplicity of the errors made was a result of the mental and physical fatigue that crept into the Wallaby effort. Once again, the All Blacks capitalised, this time sustaining the effort, which they hadn't been able to do in Sydney.

'It was hugely frustrating as it was a game we could have — and probably should have — closed out. What was becoming evident was how much we had to do across Australian rugby, both in terms of physical conditioning, but also in overall alignment of the states and the national body, if we were going to close the gap on the All Blacks and ultimately overtake them.'

The Wallabies might have been denied, but progress had been started with a view to closing the gap.

An appreciation of this was shown by Robbie's old Canterbury teammate and Crusaders colleague Wayne Smith. He obviously could sense Robbie's frustration as history repeated itself in the Brisbane and Hong Kong tests. His sense of fair play and respect were also evident after the All Blacks had won the match at the Hong Kong International Stadium, which ended that year's Bledisloe series, 19–14.

Once again, Australia had a halftime advantage (14–9) overturned, although the New Zealand victory owed much to an error by Irish referee Alan Lewis and his assistants. A clearly forward pass between winger Sitiveni Sivivatu and McCaw was missed as the All Blacks skipper scored to break the 14–14 deadlock.

As the dust settled, the All Blacks assistant coach approached the Wallaby coach on the field to offer some positive feedback on the way ahead.

He said simply that the Wallabies 'hadn't deserved to lose'.

21

WINDS OF CHANGE

The conclusion of Robbie's maiden year as Wallabies coach heralded the start of a transition within the playing group, which should continue to serve Australian Rugby well through the next two Rugby World Cups.

By the time the process was complete, Australia would head away to the 2011 tournament fielding a squad whose average age, at 24, was at least two years younger than any of its major rivals. The Australian roster was three years younger on average than that of New Zealand and South Africa respectively.

While Australia's mid-year performances in that first season against New Zealand and South Africa had already raised its place on the International Rugby Board rankings from fifth to third, the shortcomings the Wallabies had shown told Robbie that he had to make personnel changes.

With a six-match tour of the northern hemisphere to conclude 2008, there was no time like the present to get started.

'While the players had done well in that first campaign and we had wound up beating everyone who had been ranked above us at the start of the year, it was evident that we couldn't perform to that level consistently with the [playing] group that we had,' Robbie says.

'We had two choices. We could take the conservative approach, stick largely to the same player group and be happy to come close.

'Or we could try and add in a few ingredients. This would mean accepting that there might be some suffering, in terms of inconsistency, in the short run. But it was necessary if we were going to make the team genuinely better through the longer term.

'We had to find a way of taking that final step [towards a consistently dominant team]. That meant getting the next generation [of players] started.

'Some of them got their opportunity before their time, in terms of earning it. But there had been enough evidence there, in the case of each of the players that we selected, to suggest that they were clearly going to be part of the next generation of Wallabies.'

One of the newcomers to receive his maiden Wallaby boarding pass for that tour was first five-eighths Quade Cooper.

Ironically, given the generally held perceptions of subsequent events, Robbie was actually warned by a number of Queensland officials and identities about Cooper's behavioural issues at the time. It was suggested that it would be a mistake to include the New Zealand-born Queenslander.

Robbie brushed aside those misgivings, believing that as the then 21-year-old matured, both as a player and in life, his self-destructive instincts would lessen. He would develop into a leader, both on the playing field and away from it.

It was a further irony that Cooper sought Robbie's counsel prior to making a decision, midway through 2009, on whether to stay with Queensland for whom he was off-contract, or whether to ink a lucrative deal with the Western Force.

Robbie advised Cooper to factor in family considerations and think about what he wanted out of his life as part of his decision-making process, as opposed to mere financial deliberations.

Shortly after their discussion, Cooper knocked back the Force to remain at the Queensland Reds.

Flanker David Pocock, prop Sekope Kepu, loose forward Peter Kimlin and winger James O'Connor were others Robbie introduced at this point. Pocock, Kepu, Cooper and O'Connor all made their test debuts on the trip while Kimlin gained a brief introduction during the 18–11 defeat of a powerful Barbarians outfit at Wembley.

From a results perspective, the tour provided a more than satisfactory return. Four of the six games were won, including the tests against Italy (30–20), England (28–14) and France (18–13).

Robbie's policy of giving young players an opportunity also reaped its reward, most notably when Cooper came off the bench to score the try which broke a 20–20 deadlock during the test against Italy on a significantly smaller than regulation-sized pitch at Padova.

The Italian test represented the first start in the career of Ben Alexander. His rise that year had been so rapid that he hadn't even started a game for his Super Rugby side prior to running out against the Azzurri. The Brumbies prop went on to become a mainstay for the Wallabies, playing his 50th test during the 14–13 win over the British & Irish Lions at Melbourne in 2013.

He doubts he would have made the grade had it not been for the belief instilled in him by Robbie. Alexander admits his head was 'spinning' when he was selected in Robbie's maiden Wallaby squad, saying that he didn't feel deserving of the honour until his first one-on-one meeting with the new national coach.

Like so many of his New Zealand counterparts before him, Alexander found the strength of Robbie's belief and encouragement so persuasive that he began to believe for himself. Robbie, he says, is the only coach he has ever experienced to be so committed to making his players believe in themselves and the part they play in the 'bigger picture' of the team.

There is never any indecision with Robbie, Alexander notes. Regardless of the circumstances, both personally and for the team, Robbie was always calm and measured in front of the playing group.

This included following the passing of his father Tony in 2009, when Robbie joined the team late before its Tri-Nations match against South Africa in Cape Town, but got straight down to business, focusing on the team and the game ahead. The players involved admired him enormously for that, Alexander says. He was selfless and put the team first.

Alexander can only recall one occasion where Robbie allowed his feelings to openly surface. It came at training before the game against England on his first European tour when Robbie tore into the players for their lack of concentration in what became a tough session.

The eruption had an effect, with the Wallabies going on to beat England 28–14, recording Australia's second highest winning score in London.

The win at Twickenham, where the Wallabies had won just twice in the seven previous visits, provided a firm indicator of the progress the team was making, especially as the side had to show plenty of resilience after falling behind 12–14 with less than 30 minutes to play.

Whereas England had humiliated the Australian scrum during the Rugby World Cup quarter-final defeat the previous year, this time the Wallaby eight stood firm.

Robbie's ploy of bringing Stirling Mortlock in one place in the backline to second five-eighths, in order to utilise his physical prowess more efficiently, also paid dividends. The tactic had first been employed in the final two All Blacks tests, working most notably in Hong Kong where Mortlock's size and strength had allowed Australia to play more directly off first phase.

'He [Mortlock] was a good foil for "Gits" [Matt Giteau] who was still really learning how to play first five-eighths at test level, having been used at halfback the year before,' Robbie says.

'It was a steep leaning curve. Stirling playing immediately outside gave him organisational support, a calming influence and a frame to use both offensive and defensively.'

Unfortunately, a succession of injuries brought the curtain down on Mortlock's career the following year. He played just four tests of the 2009 campaign before being sidelined and never made it back, robbing the Wallabies of both his experience and his sizeable physical attributes in the backline. The latter aspect proved to be a particularly heavy loss.

It was not until Robbie defied the misgivings of some of the critics by speeding the introduction of the high-profile league and Australian Rules football convert Israel Folau against the British & Irish Lions in 2013 that he finally found a frame to fill that void in what had previously been a lightweight backline by international standards.

Australia built on the win over England by securing its first win in Paris for eight years before slipping up in Cardiff. On a surreal night, injuries saw the Wallabies led by four different players through the 80-minute duration of the match, losing Mortlock after just two minutes following a sickening head clash with his Welsh opposite, Jamie Roberts.

The 18–23 loss to the Warren Gatland-coached Welsh, who had won the Six Nations Grand Slam earlier in the year, represented the third time in four visits to the Millennium Stadium that the Wallabies had failed to win. Unfortunately for Gatland and Wales, it proved to be their last post-Wallaby celebration during Robbie's tenure.

Although Gatland, as Lions coach, would claim Robbie's final test series two matches to one, and Wales won the Six Nations on three occasions during this period (including two Grand Slams), the Welsh had lost eight games in succession to the Wallabies by the time Robbie concluded his tenure. This was just one short of the record nine won by Australia between 1990 and 1999 against an infinitely weaker Welsh outfit which failed to win the then Five Nations once through this time.

The Welsh defeat was followed just four nights later by the tour finale against a Baabaas outfit coached by Jake White and Eddie Jones that included four of the previous five IRB Players of the Year, as well as Wallaby legend George Gregan.

To the surprise of many given the strength of the opposition, Robbie fielded a changed combination, allowing a number of younger players within the squad their chance.

Such was the inexperience within the group, O'Connor and Cooper held a competition at the captain's run to determine who would goal kick in the game. O'Connor won and succeeded with all three of his attempts as the Wallabies scored two tries to one in overturning an 11–13 deficit after an hour to claim an 18–11 win.

Traditionally, Barbarians matches are festive with the focus on running rugby but there was nothing festive about the White–Jones approach. On three occasions, the Baabaas took penalty shots at goal, which indicated how serious their coaches were about claiming the win.

As well as being a revenue-raiser for the Australian Rugby Union, which was provided with a healthy fee for agreeing to play, the game was also promoted as a celebration of the centenary of the Olympic gold-medal-winning Wallabies. Their 1908 title stands alongside the American win of 1924 as the only time where 15-aside rugby union had featured at the world's largest sporting event.

Unfortunately, the match will be remembered more for the unsatisfactory nature of the Wembley Stadium playing surface that its historic commemoration. The pitch came apart under the pressure of a 46th-minute scrum, resulting in nasty injuries to both Matt Dunning and Sekope Kepu.

While the popular Dunning did make it back from his ruptured Achilles in time for the following year's European tour, he managed just two more test appearances for Australia before being forced into retirement.

The pectoral injury suffered at the same time by Kepu cost him a domestic season, slowing the former loose forward's development as a test front-rower as a result.

By the end of the 15th Wallaby game of an exhaustive and unique year, which had also included 15 games of Super Rugby for Robbie, Australia's new coach had reason to be satisfied. His team was showing improvement and he now had time, both to draw breath, but also to finally set up accommodation and other requirements for his family as they prepared for their first Aussie summer.

Robbie had lived out of the Manly Pacific hotel for the first six months of his time in Australia. The end of the rugby season enabled the family to set up house in the Sydney suburb of Mosman and saw Penny and youngest daughter Sophie relocate across the Tasman.

Her elder sister Annabel stayed behind in Christchurch initially to complete her final school year before joining the family at the end of 2009 when she enrolled at Sydney University. Elder brother Sam also stayed on in Christchurch to conclude his studies at Canterbury University prior to completing his Masters at Sydney University.

'It was a hectic time but we'd all been prepared for that. The family were well used to me being away on rugby duty anyway, so while our circumstances had changed, it was nothing that they hadn't all seen before.'

As far as the Wallabies were concerned, the changes he had initiated on the European tour were already offering cause for optimism.

'By the end of that tour, I felt we were really on the way. They [the players] had a clearer understanding of what was going to be required and we'd got some players started who were going to offer us points of difference, although it was evident that there was a lot of work to do.'

Robbie couldn't have realised then just how much.

With a full season of Super Rugby to absorb prior to his second test campaign, the Wallaby coach was able to spend the time getting around the Australian franchises. This allowed him to formalise the communication lines with his state counterparts while broadening his knowledge of the player base through observation, both at training and in matches.

The link between the states or provinces and the national teams, in terms of the effects and consequence, is one usually overlooked by most observers. Yet it forms a critical part of both the national team environment and its evolution.

We are products of our experience. Players bring forward both what they have learned, but also their habits, out of each and every experience they have, whether it is at state or international level.

These were not always positive. At times a marked difference in behaviours and attitude could be detected between the different state groupings of players within the Wallabies.

This has long been an issue for the Australian national team, such is the depth of the rivalry between New South Wales and Queensland in particular. The most successful Wallaby teams have generally only been able to overcome this threat to unity through the leadership skills and positive approach of the senior player group.

But while the establishment of a strong player leadership had been a key component of Robbie's Canterbury and Crusaders teams, with the key Crusaders directors continuing to provide the leadership backbone for the All Blacks after his departure, the same was not true of his Australian experience.

In Australia, there was a genuine reluctance among the senior members of the playing group to lead in the truest sense of the word, in terms of rallying the team by action on the field, but also by pulling into line those not adhering to team standards off it.

The situation reflected an astute observation made by the former Crusaders fullback Leon MacDonald. As a former All Black, MacDonald says he was nervous because he believed that if anyone was going to genuinely bring the Wallabies together, it was going to be Robbie. The Australians had always had talented players, MacDonald explains, but he'd never felt that they had possessed the strong team-orientated culture and ethic, which has been the bedrock of all successful New Zealand teams, at test, Super Rugby and NPC level. If Robbie could achieve that, MacDonald believed the All Blacks would have their hands full.

Just how big the task of changing the existing off-field culture was going to be was highlighted by two different incidents during the early part of 2009.

The first occurred in Canberra after the Wallabies had opened the year with a 55–7 win over the Barbarians at the Sydney Football Stadium. While the game had been a public relations stunt to some extent due to the inclusion of the high-profile code-hopper Sonny Bill Williams in the Baabaas, it had provided the Wallabies with a valuable workout prior to the June tests.

The importance of the exercise was to be seen not only by the clean sweep of the June tests that the Wallabies achieved after the Baabaas game, but also by the subsequent defeats that were suffered against Samoa (2011) and Scotland (2012). In each instance, the team was locked into first-up tests with a wholly inadequate preparation time allowed beforehand.

Any pleasure regarding the benefits of the Baabaas outing was quickly overshadowed a few days later when, in the lead-up to the first of two tests against Italy, an allegation of serious misconduct was laid against the 67-test-capped winger Lote Tuqiri.

While ARU chief executive John O'Neill bravely and quite appropriately refused to publicly disclose details of the incident, despite extreme provocation from certain quarters, the matter left the union with little choice but to terminate the high-profile player's contract.

'It wasn't pleasant but the decision was made [by the ARU] to terminate and it was the right decision,' Robbie says. 'The frustrating aspect from a team perspective was that we had put a lot of work in with Lote, most notably around his physical conditioning, and the ability to repeat effort. We felt like we were making progress. He had been part of our plans but it wasn't to be.'

The Tuqiri incident aside, June was a productive month for the Wallabies. O'Connor became the youngest scorer of a test hat-trick during the 31–8 win over Italy at Canberra, which was followed by a 34–12 success in the second test at Melbourne a week later.

The mid-year programme was completed by a 22–6 win over a full-strength French outfit that had arrived in Sydney fresh from a shared series in New Zealand, having won the first of those tests 27–22 at Dunedin.

The opening game of the Bledisloe Cup and Tri-Nations was at Eden

Park where George Smith became just the 10th player in the history of the game, and the fourth Australian, to play 100 tests. For a while, it seemed as if Smith was going to get the appropriate celebration too. The Wallabies grabbed a fourth-minute try through Berrick Barnes and led 13–3 when the Australian second five-eighths sliced through the All Blacks defence again.

A try looked certain but Barnes didn't see the oncoming Mortlock, who was unmarked. Instead he tried to link with Smith, who wasn't expecting the pass, spilt the ball and the scoring opportunity wasn't taken.

On such moments, test matches are won and lost.

A 20–3 advantage would have been hard to peg back, even for the All Blacks. While the game remained tight, the All Blacks scored shortly after the blown try and eventually overturned a three-point halftime deficit as they eased to a 22–16 win.

'It's easy to look back and wonder how it might have turned out, even understandable I guess, as a win at Eden Park would have been a huge deposit [of belief] for our group. But it's not a fair approach because you can't be totally certain what would have happened.

'It's cause and effect. One act alters everything. It was certainly a tipping point against us as far as the All Blacks were concerned, though, one of the many we experienced.'

In close matches, everything must go right. That wasn't how it panned out for the Wallabies through this period against the All Blacks. After the forward pass had been missed for the winning try at Hong Kong the year before, the Wallabies had the agony of the one that got away at Eden Park. This was followed by a contentious 78th-minute All Blacks penalty, which denied the Wallabies during an 18–19 loss in the year's second Bledisloe. There were then a number of incorrect refereeing decisions during the 2010 Bledisloe test in Sydney, which the All Blacks again won by one point.

'Sometimes you have to be so deserving that those little moments, which go against you, get swamped,' Robbie says.

'When that happens, the tide turns and you start getting the rub of the green — whether that be in terms of luck or on-field decisions. The fact that we kept falling just short was indicative that we weren't quite there.'

The Wallabies weren't quite there off the field either.

Although the team had won in South Africa the year before, it was still hard to escape the feeling that the visit to the Republic remained as much about the off-field activity as it did the rugby, for some of the playing group.

The squad convened prior to its Tri-Nations trip to Cape Town to discuss how it would plan out the preparation, and in particular how it would handle the weekend before, given that the side was flying into the Republic eight days prior to its engagement at Newlands. While it was agreed that light days through that weekend would allow the players to recover from the 20-hour journey, there was disagreement over the ground rules.

Robbie asked the playing group what was acceptable, knowing that the imposition of ironclad parameters wouldn't work if the players didn't buy into them. Astonishingly, when one of the younger players suggested the imposition of an agreed curfew time, there was resistance from senior players who argued that they should be 'trusted'. Having been to South Africa many times, Robbie knew the later the hour the higher the risk, and wanted more from his leaders off the field.

Ultimately, there were no off-field indiscretions to distract from the test preparation but the debate again reinforced the shift in attitude that was required.

Subsequent to the discussion, Robbie returned to New Zealand to be with his family for the passing of his father. He only rejoined the team in Cape Town two nights before the test. When Robbie arrived, he found a game of elimination, an off-field amusement that had been enjoyed by the Crusaders, in full swing, having been introduced to the Wallabies.

The activity, which is a useful source of humour to break the monotony prevalent for the players given that they spend so much time away from home, is a version of hide and seek. Only it has a catch: the target is instructed as to the nature of his exit which he is then required to act out or stage in front of his teammates. The departures invariably provide plenty of amusement. On this occasion George Smith was required to sit through dinner at a restaurant without talking to anyone, including the waiter taking orders.

Robbie first remembers encountering the exercise on a Crusaders tour, and recalls Scott Robertson being a source of amusement among the locals when he emerged out of a luggage conveyor belt following a domestic South African flight.

Given that humour was never in short supply within the Wallaby environment, the players attacked the game with relish and creativity. They had all contributed an entry fee, which would go to the player who unmasked the perpetrator, or to the culprit should he successfully eliminate all of his teammates from the game.

Such was the level of creativity involved, Giteau and Tatafu Polota Nau were instructed to exit during a mock wedding between the pair prior to a team meeting, to which the whole group was required to be present, with the service presided over by Drew Mitchell as the minister. The players all dressed appropriately for the occasion, with the quick-witted Mitchell excelling as the priest, in an episode that produced great humour before the newly-wed couple departed the game.

Although he arrived late, there was still time for the coach to be among the victims, receiving a visit from the eliminator shortly after he made the team hotel. Robbie was instructed to go ballistic at the players during a team meeting, haranguing them for their lack of preparation in his absence, before then appearing to get too excited, collapsing and dying of an apparent heart attack.

'I think I probably acted it out a bit too well,' Robbie recalls, 'judging by the looks on some of the faces, which suggested they thought that the whole thing was for real.'

He didn't know it at the time but the perpetrator of all the mayhem, who was eventually unmasked, played the 80th and final test of his illustrious career that weekend, succumbing to an injury-enforced end. So one of the closing acts of the Mortlock career had been to take out most of his teammates!

For all the off-field amusement, there was precious little on it at Newlands. The Wallabies had three players sin-binned, at one point playing eight minutes with just 13 men, during a 17–29 loss.

They returned home to an agonising loss to the All Blacks at the Olympic Stadium in Sydney — the first of three straight one-point losses the team was to suffer at the ground — before being outplayed by the

South Africans again during a 25–32 loss in Perth.

With the pressure building after four straight Tri-Nations losses for the season, Robbie made four significant personnel changes for the final game against South Africa at Brisbane. They were to shape the future direction of the team.

Pocock and Polota Nau took over from Smith and Stephen Moore respectively in the forward pack, and largely retained their first-choice ranking for the rest of Robbie's time as Wallaby coach.

Utility back Adam Ashley-Cooper was also on the move, ultimately settling in as Australia's long-term centre, after having previously been employed at wing, fullback and second five-eighths.

The biggest change was at halfback where Will Genia, who hadn't even been first choice for the Queensland Reds when Robbie had selected him earlier in the year, took over from Luke Burgess after recovering from a broken hand.

The alterations inspired as the Wallabies swept to a 21–6 win over a South African outfit that was playing for the Tri-Nations title. The Boks did go on to win the tournament but they had to do it the hard way by beating the All Blacks in Hamilton the following week.

Such was the discipline the Wallabies showed at Suncorp Stadium, the Springboks' goal-kicking maestro Morne Steyn was restricted to just one shot at goal, having kicked 23 out of 23 in his previous four games.

It was the Wallabies' only win of a Tri-Nations series where they had been more competitive than the final table showed. Three of their five defeats had been by the margin of a converted try or less.

In the Wallabies' case, the saving of the worst performance till last did not help the perception of their overall tournament performance. On a difficult night in Wellington, the visitors capitulated in the final quarter, which allowed the All Blacks to blow out a 13–6 halftime advantage into a humiliating 33–6 final score.

'We'd brought a lot of blokes in, and tried to do it in a way where we wouldn't suffer, but it had been a conscious decision at the end of our first year that if we were going to come up short, we'd be best getting started on the future.

And that's pretty much how it had unfolded. You learn the most about your players in adversity and it's fair to say that we'd suffered some growing pains. But we'd learnt a lot about them and they'd learnt a lot about themselves in what were tough circumstances.'

The conclusion of the Tri-Nations brought with it another shock for many in the Australian rugby community when Robbie appointed Rocky Elsom as captain for the end-of-year tour, which included an attempt at the Grand Slam of the United Kingdom and Ireland. Maligned by some, Elsom had been granted a 10-month release from his contract the previous year, in order to play for Irish club Leinster where he had excelled during the province's run to the Heineken Cup.

While some within the ARU hierarchy were uncomfortable with his appointment as captain, Robbie was able to convince them that Elsom was the best candidate, given Mortlock's injury and the fact that Smith, who had deputised in his absence, wasn't comfortable in the role.

'Rocky was the only guaranteed selection in the whole group on a week-to-week basis. He was also a bloke who consistently stood up against the tide in-game. They were two good starting points in terms of appointing someone whom the group would look to.'

Elsom's debut tour as leader produced some useful if not earth-shattering results. The trip again began with an Asian stopover, this time in Tokyo, where a stadium that was only three-quarters full saw the Wallabies run over in the second half for the third time in the four Bledisloe Cup tests that year.

After establishing a 16–13 halftime advantage, the Wallabies couldn't stay with the All Blacks in the third quarter. They were restricted to just three second-half points as New Zealand drew out to a 32–19 victory.

Less than three days later, the Wallaby midweekers played the English Premiership side Gloucester after Robbie requested two additional tour outings against club sides in order to fast track the development of the emerging player tier.

The move, which was repeated on the 2010 European tour, has since become impractical due to the additional volume of rugby that was added to the schedule through the extension of both Super Rugby and the Rugby Championship.

It proved its worth at the time. Not only did the Wallabies beat both

Gloucester (36–5) and the Cardiff Blues (31–3) during the trip, the midweek matches ultimately provided the starting point for 15 new test players through the five-year period where Robbie was Australian coach.

Four days after winning in Gloucestershire, the test side conquered Twickenham for the second time in 12 months, holding England scoreless in the second half as Australia overturned a four-point halftime deficit to prevail 18–9. The win, and the manner in which it was achieved, provided a great boost as the tourists headed to Dublin with the Grand Slam tilt well and truly on.

'The team was excited by it [the Grand Slam possibility] and the players took to their work well,' Robbie says.

'Ultimately, we were denied by the Irish in the last minute at Croke Park, but the defining moment of that game was earlier when [referee] Jonathan Kaplan sin-binned Cliff Palu for what was a perfectly legal tackle on an Irish ball carrier.

'We were all over them at that point. That one decision changed the momentum of the game.'

The 79th-minute try, which allowed Ireland to force a 20–20 draw, killing off the Grand Slam hopes, was scored by Brian O'Driscoll. It was the Irish captain's 100th test appearance. His try allowed Ireland to continue towards an unbeaten calendar year, having earlier won their first Six Nations Grand Slam since 1948. Ireland completed the 11-game undefeated sequence for 2009 a week later when they beat the reigning southern hemisphere champions, South Africa.

The draw put a dampener on the tour ahead of the next test, which saw the Wallabies fall to an 8–9 defeat at Murrayfield in a scrappy contest in which Scotland registered its first win over Australia in 27 years. Australia could have stolen the game at the end, but Giteau was unable to convert the 80th-minute try scored by Ryan Cross and the game was lost.

'We didn't play well. The weather and playing conditions were difficult as they always seemed to be when we played Scotland, but we didn't adapt as well as we should have. Perhaps the result the previous week, which had ended the Grand Slam attempt, had an impact. It's difficult to say.'

The unexpected defeat was not received well back in Australia where the critics of the Wallaby coach were getting louder. While, in isolation, the reverse didn't put Robbie's position under threat, there is no doubt that a loss the following week in Cardiff would have.

As they were to do so often when the knives were out for their coach, the playing group responded. The trip was finished with a 33–12 carve-up of Wales, which featured standout performances from the flankers Smith and Pocock, who were used in 40-minute bursts for the first time. The winning margin was the second highest Australia had achieved in Cardiff but it was the emphatic nature of the performance that offered the most promise.

'It was our most complete game of the year by far,' Robbie says. 'You could sense that we were on the cusp of taking that next step. Having the two top-class opensides operating fresh for 40 minutes each opened up the game. It allowed us to play to our strength by utilising the full width of the field. The Welsh couldn't cope with it.'

The style of the performance provided a preview of what was to come the following year when the Wallabies played a game based on all-out attack.

Defensively, however, 2010 saw the side fall away from the well-organised screen of the previous year, where just one try had been conceded across the four European tests. This was in part due to changes in personnel.

While the introduction of Cooper at first five-eighths opened up the edges of the field for the Wallabies on attack, offering threat both with the ball and via his kicking game, opponents soon came to realise his lack of appetite for defensive duties and began to target him.

Robbie had tried Digby Ioane at centre during the European tour, looking for his physical presence to replace Mortlock. While Ioane did well, advancing his skills in the position with every outing, a dislocated shoulder the following year sent him to the sidelines after just three tests. This saw the experiment discontinued as the preparation time left before the Rugby World Cup was minimal by the time he returned.

'We didn't have a lot of luck on the injury front, especially among the midfield and five-eighths. Those are the key directing positions in the backline but ours became a revolving door, denying us continuity.

'Whereas the All Blacks had a set midfield pair in Ma'a Nonu and Conrad Smith, who had a deep connection and understanding due to the games they'd played together, and the Springboks likewise benefited with Jean de Villiers and Jaque Fourie, we were constantly having to make changes.

'There was never any lack of effort on behalf of the players who were used but the lack of stability was unsettling for the whole group.'

The numbers highlight the difficulty. Across his 74 tests in charge, Robbie was forced to utilise 14 different midfield players in 23 combinations with the frequent changing largely necessitated by injury. In effect, this meant that the Wallabies fielded a different midfield partnership on average once every three tests.

The instability had a flow-on effect one place further in, given that Barnes, Giteau and Cooper were all employed at both first and second five-eighths through his tenure. As a consequence, the Wallabies required 15 different bodies operating the first and second five-eighths' channels, fielded in 21 different combinations. This averaged out as a change in that combination every three and a half tests. All of which inevitably contributed to the side's inconsistency through the period.

The elevation of Cooper into the starting XV at the end of 2009 saw Giteau pushed back to second five-eighths, the position from where he had originally started his Wallaby career.

Although the working relationship between the coach and Giteau was cordial, elements around the player tried to make it difficult by creating the perception of a serious breakdown between the pair.

'Gits was working hard. He's got a great work ethic. We had a real need in the position when we started [in 2008] and didn't have a solution at that point,' Robbie says. 'He was never a natural first five-eighths but got close to cracking it.

'It is a tough position to master at test level. The balance of the playing group impacts on it as well, in terms of what is outside him.

'Gits played his best rugby from 10 when he had a powerful ball carrier in Stirling alongside, who also sealed up that channel defensively.'

Giteau would go on to France at the end of 2011, hooking up with the glamour French club Toulon where he primarily played second five-eighths outside of the English star Jonny Wilkinson.

22

HIGH VELDT HEROICS

If there was one player through Robbie's coaching tenure who best summed up the extremes of rugby in Australia, it was Kurtley Beale.

The indigenous kid from Sydney's west, who has carried the burden of expectation since his days as a schoolboy star at the prestigious St Joseph's College (Joeys), is a special talent. He is also exasperatingly prone to hitting the self-destruct button, delivering the good and bad in equal measures through a five-year period where the Wallaby coach went to extraordinary lengths to help him thrive, both as a player and a person.

Guy Reynolds, the Sydney-based financial executive, who has acted as both a mentor and a minder for Beale, speaks glowingly about the extent of the personal commitment that Robbie made to his young charge. Reynolds says that Robbie's involvement with Kurtley was well beyond the call of duty, especially considering how busy he already was with all of his commitments as Wallaby coach.

The work showcased Robbie's values, and the fact that his motivations go beyond the playing field, Reynolds says.

He seeks to help his players thrive as people too.

Robbie encouraged Beale as a player, but also offered him genuine respect with off-field support and advice around his habits. The extended level of support was not something the youngster had ever had from any of his coaches before. This trust even went as far as leadership responsibilities within the team, which gave Beale confidence and allowed him to flourish playing for the Wallabies.

It was a two-way street, Reynolds says. Robbie made Beale attain goals in terms of his physical conditioning that he had never reached before.

The level of encouragement helped the young Waratahs first five-eighths shed eight kilograms following the 2009 Super Rugby competition. A leaner and more motivated Beale was rewarded with an introduction to the Wallabies, and his test debut, at the end of that year.

Like many young players, Beale's behaviour often reflected the influences of those around him. His difficulties with alcohol were well documented, although this tended to be more of an issue away from the Wallaby environment than inside it.

Even in the aftermath of Beale's ill-judged, well-publicised and heavily criticised 4 am appearance at a hamburger restaurant, alongside James O'Connor, four days out from the second British & Irish Lions test in 2013, it was largely overlooked that the pair had not been on the drink. They had adhered to the team's abstention from alcohol for that series.

'Kurtley's biggest challenge is his lack of self-reliance,' Robbie says. 'When placed in an environment where he lacked sufficient support, it was nearly always detrimental.'

This was most obviously exposed during his spectacular fall from grace while with the Melbourne Rebels in South Africa earlier in 2013, where a booze-filled team night following a humiliating loss in Durban ended in a dust-up between Beale and fellow Wallaby, Cooper Vuna.

'While his signing for Melbourne [having previously played Super Rugby exclusively for the NSW Waratahs] could have been advantageous as he had to leave home and develop some independence, it also exposed him to risk,' Robbie explains. 'He didn't have the support mechanisms that he needed.'

The incident didn't paint a positive picture of the Rebels' culture and the level of leadership that was being shown by the team's senior players, who'd been quite happy to lead the party, appearing to take no responsibility for what had been an abject on-field performance. Its aftermath saw Beale stood down from rugby by the Australian Rugby Union. He voluntarily entered a private clinic at this point to gain help in dealing with his alcohol-related problems.

It was a testament to Robbie's commitment to Beale, and the player's appreciation of it, that the national coach was one of the few people who was allowed to visit the clinic during his rehabilitation.

'You've got to care about these blokes as people, not just as rugby players. It's part of the territory. I'd been having dialogue with Kurtley, trying to help him to thrive, long before he even became a Wallaby.

'The key is to be motivated by the right reasons, not the wrong ones. For me, the wrong ones are the win–loss balance sheet.

'The game offers its participants so much because it is a fast track of life every week, in terms of all that you experience. I care about the people on my watch. Whether, in this instance, Kurtley was selected [to play the Lions] or not was another matter completely.

'This was about seeing the player thrive in life. He'd only be playing the game for a short time. I didn't want to be in the position where I'd look back and think that I didn't make a difference for him when it mattered.'

Once Beale completed his time at the clinic, Robbie introduced him to early morning paddle boarding off Sydney's Balmoral Beach as help for his physical preparation. The sessions also provided the opportunity for face-to-face dialogue between the pair on a regular basis.

While the level of the personal commitment Robbie made was significant, he brushes it off, having assisted players with off-field challenges, albeit in less high-profile circumstances, routinely through his coaching career.

'Anything that takes time and distracts you from your core purpose with the [playing] group becomes a burden — sometimes an unnecessary one — but that's the nature of the [sporting] industry.

'The players all come into your team at various states of readiness, physically and mentally, so the demands are constant. It's just a matter of what the demands are.

'There's not a lot of difference from a management perspective between campaigns. People from the outside looking in see win–loss, but the work that goes on within that is constant. The difference is just the areas of particular need that you have to tend to. There's always a need.

'When you are winning routinely the need might be different from when you are losing routinely, but it's always there.'

In Beale's case, even his introduction to the Wallabies wasn't straightforward. It set the tone for his career as it developed.

'We'd been waiting on Kurtley to master his physical state. He just lacked the wherewithal to do it himself,' Robbie says.

'Pete Harding [the Wallabies strength and conditioning coach] worked hard with him and Kurtley made the effort. Then, once we took him on the 2009 tour, we drove him hard in his physical load, and worked with him closely off the field so that we could get him started.

'Clearly, some of his demons from past experiences were coming forward with him. He needed support to master them and succeed. But it was an ongoing challenge.'

When Beale was good, he was a match-winner.

A kick from his own side of halfway after the final siren created a slice of history for the Wallabies on a momentous night at Bloemfontein in 2010, snatching a 41–39 victory over the Springboks. The win put an end to a 12-game losing sequence for the Wallabies at South African high veldt venues which dated back 47 years.

Interestingly, Robbie nominates a moment other than the dramatic penalty kick as defining in that match, although it did involve Beale.

'When we fell behind after having sat back on a big lead and seen it easily swallowed up, the players were trying urgently to get back into it. At one point, off a turnover, a wild pass from Quade [Cooper] hit Kurtley in the head before he could turn and get his hands up to receive the ball. Talk about total humiliation.

'It was his reaction that said it all to me about where both he and the team was at on that night. He didn't become a victim. Instead of thinking of himself, he reacted instantly, scrambled back, chased, and made the tackle to prevent them from scoring, while getting the ball back.

'Within two minutes of that moment, we'd got the penalty and Kurtley didn't hesitate in stepping up to take it. But it was his earlier action that really won us that game.'

The result, and the manner in which it was achieved, made for an appropriate end to one of the more remarkable weeks in Wallabies' test history. Across two high veldt encounters, Australia and South Africa shared 17 tries and 155 points in a frantic try-fest, which provided fast and furious entertainment, if not the bloody-minded defence normally associated with test rugby and, more significantly, Rugby World Cup rugby.

A year later, the two would feature in an equally frantic Rugby World Cup quarter-final that touched the opposite end of the spectrum, with just one try scored as two points again separated the teams.

In the week prior to the Bloemfontein match, Australia had jumped to a 21–7 advantage after just 10 minutes at Pretoria, only to be gradually pegged back by the Boks, who'd closed to 24–28 at halftime. They overpowered the Wallabies in the second period, which they won 20–3 to complete a 44–31 victory.

The match marked the 100th test of the Loftus Versfeld favourite Victor Matfield, but while locals celebrated with their hero, it was a decidedly flat Australian party that trooped off to sea level at Durban for the week to try to work out what had gone wrong. That process started on the Monday before the second test of the trip, firstly at a players-only gathering proactively called by the skipper Rocky Elsom, and then during a full team meeting.

'We knew that we were capable of doing it [beating South Africa at altitude]; we could have done it at Pretoria. We spoke about that and said that it was unacceptable to have built up the advantage like we'd had, to then let them back into the game. If we got into that situation again, we had to close the game out.'

As it was, Bloemfontein almost mirrored Pretoria, at least to start with, as the Wallabies scored four tries in a surreal opening 25 minutes to lead 31–6 before again getting the staggers.

A combination of Springbok pressure and Australian short cuts which were ruthlessly punished by Morne Steyn (who kicked six penalty goals), brought the home side back to the extent that they went ahead 33–31 entering the final quarter of the match.

'In many ways, the manner in which both games had unfolded captured the stage of development the team had reached. It illustrated the player's habits: they enjoyed doing the things they were good at, primarily with the ball, but didn't always turn up to do the other stuff.'

This included defence, cleanouts at rucks and generally putting their bodies on the line in contact.

This time, though, adversity brought the best out of the Wallabies and they responded after replacement hooker Saia Fainga'a had been yellow-carded, which saw the Boks move ahead 36–31.

Quick thinking from replacement halfback Luke Burgess, who tapped a penalty before the South Africans had time to reset their defence, allowed Drew Mitchell to charge over to score, damaging his hamstring in the process, which ended his 50th test appearance. The conversion made it 38–36 to Australia, but a Steyn penalty four minutes from time looked to have won it for South Africa.

This was until the home side failed to heed repeated warnings from English referee Wayne Barnes not to seal off ruck ball, which presented Beale, and the Wallabies, with their chance.

'With the ball, we could go toe to toe with anybody; those two games in South Africa showed that,' Robbie says.

'But when the tables turned, and our opposition had possession, we struggled to contain them.

'And there was no way it was going to be all one way at the Rugby World Cup the following year when the intensity and physicality was always going to step up significantly from regular test matches, as it had in 2007.'

This observation was backed up by a comparison of the try-scoring statistics from the matches between the Tri-Nations teams in 2010 and 2011. The 2010 championship yielded 52 tries across the nine matches, with Australia contributing 17 of them (with 21 against). A year later across eight matches, which included the Rugby World Cup quarter-final between Australia and South Africa and the semi-final between Australia and New Zealand, just 28 tries were scored (with Australia scoring 12 and conceding just eight).

One of the biggest contributors to the shaky nature of the Wallaby defence in 2010 was the comparative lack of size among the backs. This impacted on individual enthusiasm towards defensive duties. None of Will Genia, Quade Cooper, Matt Giteau, Drew Mitchell, Kurtley Beale or James O'Connor could have been considered as strong defenders and they made up six-sevenths of Australia's starting backline. This meant that the Wallabies had to employ width at all times and rely on scoring more points than they conceded.

It worked sometimes, and was certainly exhilarating to watch (if you weren't the coach), but it was also clearly not going to succeed in the more pressure-cooked environment of the following year's Rugby World Cup. More defensive grunt was needed.

As well as creating history, the result at Bloemfontein regained for Australia the Nelson Mandela Challenge Plate, gave it second place in the Tri-Nations and also lifted it above South Africa on the International Rugby Board rankings.

Thus the Wallabies stood second only to the All Blacks, just two and a half years after they had been rated as the fifth best team in world rugby.

The rest of the year allowed Australia to consolidate that ranking, which the Wallabies retained through until the final stages of Robbie's time as coach. Part of that consolidation came against the All Blacks, although more frustration was ahead when the two teams met in Sydney after the Wallabies had returned from South Africa.

The game was the third between the two for the year.

The Bledisloe Cup had already been retained by New Zealand courtesy of a 48–29 win in Melbourne, which was backed up by a 20–10 success in Christchurch a week later.

Game one had been notable for Mitchell becoming the first player in 161 trans-Tasman tests to be sent off. The Wallabies winger had been dispatched by referee Craig Joubert after the receipt of two yellow cards.

While the Wallabies hadn't capitulated, the prospect of winning while playing 37 minutes with 14 men was always an unlikely one and the two tries they scored in this period couldn't prevent a heavy defeat.

Robbie's return to his hometown as Wallabies coach yielded a warm welcome, and a competitive effort from his team in what was to be the only test played in front of the new grandstand that had been named in honour of the Australian coach's family.

Beale scored the opening try, but while the All Blacks recovered to lead 17–10 at the break, they couldn't get away in the second period, with just a penalty goal added to the total as New Zealand prevailed by 10 points.

That win was New Zealand's ninth in succession against Australia. There shouldn't have been a 10th.

Buoyed by the performance at Bloemfontein, the Wallabies started the third match strongly in Sydney, with tries by O'Connor and Adam Ashley-Cooper securing a 19–6 advantage after 46 minutes.

The pivotal moment came with 14 minutes remaining, at which point Australia led 22–9. All Blacks skipper Richie McCaw had detached early from a scrum earlier in the match and not been penalised. He did so again in the 66th minute and South African referee Mark Lawrence again missed the infringement, which had the ultimate consequence as McCaw took No. 8 Kieran Read's pass to score the All Blacks' opening try.

The referee's mistake was inexcusable, especially in the age of television match officials. It was to have far-reaching consequences, both for the game, but also for Lawrence whose poor overall performance on the night contributed to him missing selection for the Rugby World Cup referees panel the following year.

In conceding the try, the seed of doubt was sewn among the Wallabies. The All Blacks didn't miss the opportunity, with Read scoring himself six minutes later to get his side home 23–22.

Referee issues aside, fluffed goal-kicks also hurt the Wallabies. Giteau missed four of his eight attempts while the All Blacks were successful with all five of theirs.

The below-par return completed an unhappy double for the Wallabies' lead-off kicker at the Olympic Stadium: he'd also succumbed to the pressure when he missed four of eight, including one from in front of the posts, as Australia had also gone under by a point to England at the ground earlier in the year.

After Giteau's costly performance in the loss to the All Blacks, the change was made to O'Connor as the goal-kicker for the end-of-year-tour.

'Out of all of those pieces of adversity that we'd had against them [the All Blacks], the key thing for our players at that point was to heed the message,' Robbie says.

'Clearly, it [beating the All Blacks] was achievable for us. We had to get our playing group to the point where they expected to win when they played them, as opposed to just hoping to.'

That the gap was closing became clearer when the Wallabies beat the All Blacks in two of their next three meetings. The sequence of 10 straight trans-Tasman defeats was finally broken in a thriller when the teams returned to Hong Kong en route to their respective northern hemisphere tours.

O'Connor scored an after-the-final-siren try and then converted it from the sideline to snatch a 26–24 win. In what was almost a role reversal from previous meetings, this time it was the All Blacks who wobbled under pressure after they had appeared in command while overturning an early 0–12 deficit to lead 24–12 with 25 minutes remaining.

Although Australia closed to 19–24, New Zealand still held the winning of the match but first five-eighths Stephen Donald missed a penalty goal attempt that would have sealed it, four minutes before the end. He then failed to find touch after the siren had gone as Australia attacked furiously.

The Wallabies kept coming and ultimately got their reward when O'Connor wriggled over in the corner following a quickly taken tap penalty by prop Ben Alexander.

One could have been excused for believing that the Wallabies had just won the Bledisloe Cup, such was the emotion exhibited by the players after O'Connor's conversion had sailed over. The spontaneous celebration didn't sit especially well with the All Blacks.

'The reaction simply showed how much the run of losses had hung over the players,' Robbie explains. 'You could sense that the belief was emerging as we'd kept attacking in those final moments and hadn't simply accepted that the game was lost.

'By doing that, we put the pressure on them. It wasn't a position they'd been used to and it showed.'

Nor was this a dead-rubber as far as the All Blacks were concerned. The loss pulled them up three short of the world record of 18 consecutive wins against all-comers. It was the first of two occasions where the Wallabies denied them on the cusp of this achievement.

The busy programme in Europe which followed saw two midweek matches played, for a 26–15 win over English champions Leicester, alongside a 6–15 defeat to the European champions Munster. The latter match was played out on a night where gale-force winds and rain rendered Limerick's Thomond Park almost unplayable.

There were also four tests, with the Wallabies beating Wales (25–16), Italy (32–14) and France (59–16) alongside a loss to England (18–35), which surrendered the Cook Cup.

Australia and England had shared the earlier June series Down Under, with an under-strength Wallabies side winning in Perth (27–17) before England levelled with success in Sydney (21–20).

The subsequent experience at Twickenham was a reminder for the Australian players that even though they had now finally broken through against New Zealand, they weren't good enough to be able to relax against anybody.

England feasted off Australian errors, which became more numerous as the Wallabies tried unsuccessfully to play catch-up once they had conceded a 20-point deficit just after halftime. The cause wasn't helped when O'Connor missed four of his seven attempts on goal, but the youngster had showed courage even in playing, having been informed of the death of a close friend on the morning of the match.

O'Connor subsequently returned to Australia for the funeral, and missed the Italian test before rejoining the tour for its spectacular finale in Paris where he underlined his class with a Wallaby record 29 points.

'They [the players] knew they could win the [England] game but lacked the maturity at this point of their development to recover when things went against us,' Robbie says.

'A side that's really able in its intent, as the All Blacks generally are, gets through those games. We weren't there yet.'

The Wallabies weren't, but you'd have struggled at the time to make the then Six Nations champion French team believe it. France was on the receiving end of a withering six-try, 46-point scoring burst in the second half of the final game of the year, which was played in temperatures that were so cold in Paris that the ice had to be mowed off the pitch pre-game.

Whereas the players had become rattled in adversity at Twickenham, this time the Wallabies worked their way out of it after falling behind 13–16 just after halftime while having Alexander sent to the sin-bin for repeated scrum collapses.

'It was a culmination of what had been coming through the year. The game was fast and open, which suited the personnel we had and they showed what they were capable of.

'The players' understanding of the way that we wanted to play was coming together. There was also greater application on defence that night. Having a full [player] muster to select from for one of the rare occasions that year helped too.'

In piling on the last 46 points of the game, the Wallabies set a new Australian record for winning margin and total score against the French, while the 29 points by O'Connor was the most totalled by an Australian player in a test on foreign turf. The win also equalled the Australian record for consecutive wins over the French, being the fifth to have been delivered on Robbie's watch.

Paris provided the close to an exhausting six months where the Wallabies played a record 15 tests, won nine of them, and required 34 players. Twelve new Wallabies were introduced, which was the most since Robbie's maiden season, due to the large number of injuries that had been sustained through the campaign.

Robbie hoped Rugby World Cup year would provide relief on that score at least.

He was to be disappointed.

23

QUAKES, INJURY BREAKS AND MISTAKES

The tragedy of 22 February 2011, was an event that no one who has any association with the city of Christchurch and the greater Canterbury region will ever forget.

The force 6.3 earthquake struck with such ferocity just after lunchtime that within seconds much of the central city area was reduced to rubble, taking with it the lives of 182 of its people.

Christchurch Cathedral, the city's iconic landmark, was left in ruins.

So too was the future of the newly erected Deans stand at Lancaster Park. It was rendered useless by a crack through the structure that made it unsafe. Extensive liquefaction and other damage put the entire stadium out of commission permanently. At the time of writing, the famous old ground still stands in eerie silence in the shadow of the Port Hills, as it awaits demolition.

For the rest of their lives many New Zealanders will recall where they were at 12.52 pm when the quake struck.

As a prominent member of the expatriate population, and a leading figure within the Canterbury community, Robbie had reason to feel more estranged from Christchurch than most. He was in an ARU planning meeting in Sydney when the news broke.

'It was horrific seeing the first images that came through on television. It was an emotional experience.

'You felt so far away, guilty in fact that you weren't there. You weren't going through the heartache along with the people of Christchurch and you could do nothing to help.'

Few escaped untouched by the tragedy. Such is the size and closeness of a community like Christchurch it was inevitable that almost everyone would know someone who had lost their life. As the lists of the deceased were confirmed, news of the passing of Crusaders board member Philip McDonald, who perished when the PGG building collapsed, was released.

'The impact was immediate and it was real for everyone,' Robbie says. 'It is a testament to the strength and spirit of the community that the city and the region has bounced back strongly so quickly.'

Although unable to help immediately, Robbie returned to Christchurch shortly after the quake. He visited the army of student volunteers that were assembled, to provide encouragement. Robbie also worked alongside Salvation Army personnel to assist with the initial clean-up, providing a motivational address at the end of the day.

His Balmoral touch rugby mates later contributed sufficient funds to purchase a bulldozer to aid the liquefaction clean-up.

The Wallaby coach was involved in numerous fundraising drives. He also ensured that the stricken city got a taste of the Rugby World Cup even though the disaster had given tournament authorities no choice but to relocate the scheduled games out of the city.

Given the connection with Robbie, Rugby World Cup organisers had planned to base the Wallabies in the city. While the games had to be moved, Robbie took advantage of a break in the schedule following the team's third match to take the Wallabies to the rural North Canterbury resort of Hanmer Springs, one and three-quarter hours north of Christchurch. As well as holding an open training session and mixing with the locals, the Wallabies spent a day in Christchurch en route to their final pool match. The players split into groups to cover the city.

Events included a fundraising lunch, visits to a children's hospital and a retirement home and also a coaching clinic at inner city Hagley Park.

The welcome the team received was genuine. The effort, appreciated.

The tragedy might have reminded all of the frailty of human existence and provided perspective in terms of the significance sporting outcomes should play within it, but life had to go on.

And Robbie's was getting more complicated by the day as a raft of injuries to key players through Super Rugby threatened to throw a serious spoke into his Rugby World Cup plans. By the time the team departed for New Zealand six players were being nursed back from injury and were going into the tournament without prior background with the Wallabies earlier in the year.

Although Drew Mitchell, Berrick Barnes, Rob Horne, Wycliff Palu, James Slipper and Tatafu Polota Nau had all been starters at their most recent test outings and were certainties for the squad if deemed fit, none of them had played a part in the Tri-Nations. Nor were they the only fitness concerns.

Rocky Elsom and Dan Vickerman were both managing long-term injuries. Vickerman had just returned to the Wallabies after a two-and-a-half year gap for study purposes in England. Robbie had stayed in touch with the lock around the prospects of a Wallaby return, providing encouragement as he worked on his conditioning unsupervised.

'Dan was highly motivated to do it [return] but it wasn't without challenge. He had been dealing with the consequences of his leg problem when he left [Australia] and his body was starting to founder.

'This was particularly so once he lifted his training rate. If you have an injury history, once you taper in terms of your conditioning and training, it gets harder to get back to previous levels,' Robbie explains.

For a 32-year-old, the idea of returning to test rugby after a 27-month absence was asking a lot of both body and mind. Understandably, doubts surfaced at various stages on the road back, but while Vickerman expressed misgivings, Robbie was positive that he would both make it and provide plenty of impact when he returned. The perseverance of the player and the faith of the coach paid off.

'I was always confident about his mental state to succeed,' Robbie says. 'Dan was well motivated, which he had to be to even contemplate the idea. The challenge was going to be whether his body would stand up to it.'

The hard work gave Vickerman one final year and eight more test appearances. By the time another injury forced him to concede and retire at the start of the following season, the former South African age-group player had represented Australia on 63 occasions, winning a first Tri-Nations in his final campaign. The title was a significant achievement for a player who had begun his test career a decade earlier. So too was his appearance at three Rugby World Cups.

'Dan showed his value without a doubt,' Robbie says. 'It wasn't without frustration for him throughout that campaign, but he showed what we had lost through those previous two years when he hadn't been available.

'While it is simplistic to say that we wouldn't have won the Tri-Nations without him, he was undoubtedly a point of difference player for us. He added physicality and mental hardness to the group.'

Even the success of the Vickerman return was overshadowed by arguably the most astonishing comeback in test history. That was the story of Radike Samo. Officially aged 35, although many close to him only half joked about that figure being a little on the low side, Samo returned to the Wallabies when named on the bench against South Africa at Durban.

The appearance was the loose-forward's seventh in tests but came an incredible 2456 days after the sixth, which had occurred on the 2004 Spring Tour.

'Radike offered us something extra, both with the ball but also without it. You've got to have an ability to break teams open, especially when you are playing against well-structured and disciplined units like the All Blacks. You've got to find a way to unlock them.'

Samo certainly did that, most notably when he scored a brilliant solo try, outpacing a startled All Blacks cover defence, during the first half of the Tri-Nations decider at Brisbane. It was the signature moment of the first Australian Tri-Nations title in 10 years.

Earlier that year, the remarkable Fijian had become the first Australian player to feature in three Super Rugby-winning teams, adding a title with the Queensland Reds to the two he had won previously with the Brumbies in 2001 and 2004. It was only 12 months after he had come out of semi-retirement to act as an injury replacement for Queensland.

The three Super Rugby titles sat alongside a Top 14 he won with Paris club Stade Français as well as a club title during the first of his two stints in Japan. With that pedigree, and having proved that he could still cope in Super Rugby, Robbie decided Samo was worth a try.

'Radike's been a winner wherever he has travelled and for good reason.

His influence among the group is good, he's a got a wide-ranging skill-set, an outstanding work ethic and is hugely respected by his teammates.'

The respect for Samo was only enhanced by his contribution that year. It included two appearances on the wing where he had played during his younger days, after injuries stretched playing resources to breaking point at the Rugby World Cup.

Samo was one of 16 members of Queensland's title-winning Super Rugby squad to earn Wallaby selection in the aftermath of the state's thrilling run to the competition summit. Eleven of those had featured on the previous year's Wallaby end-of-year tour. Super Rugby saw their growth continue at pace.

'The potential [among the playing group] was starting to come to fruition. The year before, the Wallabies had done a couple of things [beating South Africa at Bloemfontein and the record win over France in Paris] that held historical significance.

'The belief was growing and the indicators were good. There's no doubt that off the back of the recent experience — both in Super Rugby and with the Wallabies — the players assembled for the first time that year in a positive frame of mind.'

The euphoria of Queensland's success provided plenty of feel-good about the game with the public, but it also presented Robbie with a quandary. A one-off test against Samoa had unhelpfully been tacked onto the front of the Wallabies' pre-Rugby World Cup programme, seven days after the squad assembled. Given the compressed nature of the preparation, could he afford to play the Reds players when their minds might not necessarily have been on the task at hand?

Having been through the title aftermath and its distractions seven times himself with the Crusaders, Robbie opted to leave the Queenslanders where they were. While the rest of the squad assembled in Sydney to get started, the Queensland players were given extra time at home so they could participate in the public and private post-final celebrations prior to joining the Wallabies midweek.

That restricted selection options for the test to the extent that just five Reds players were involved, and only two started. And one of those, debut winger Rod Davies, was only brought in after James O'Connor strained his hamstring during a sponsorship promotion two days out from the test.

In contrast to the underdone Wallabies, the bulk of the Samoan group had played in and won two Pacific Nations Cup tests prior to arriving in Sydney. Their side was drawn almost entirely of professional players based mostly in Europe. Seven of the cast were well known to Robbie, having previously been under his charge at the Crusaders.

'They were a useful team and showed it later in the year at the Rugby World Cup where they got within seven points of Wales and eight of South Africa, and could have beaten both of them with a bit more luck on their side.

'To be exposed to meeting them without a meaningful preparation was a recipe for disaster.'

So it proved.

The damage was done in the opening half an hour when Samoa romped to a 17–0 advantage. The visitors always had the Wallabies' measure from there as they finished off a 32–23 success.

Only a few of the Wallabies had stood up to the physical and mental stress. This had consequences when the 30 names were jotted down for the Rugby World Cup squad two months later, with six of the side that played Samoa not making the cut.

First five-eighths Matt Giteau, who'd already fallen behind Quade Cooper in the rankings at the end of the previous year, was the biggest name casualty. Although he scored a try and missed just one shot at goal, the playmaker struggled to assert himself and provide the team with direction in the face of the aggression employed by the Samoans. This proved his downfall given the number of five-eighths options that were available to back up Cooper. Kurtley Beale, Berrick Barnes and O'Connor were able to perform a similar role and were all coming forward with their careers at a time when Giteau was tapering.

Industrious flanker Matt Hodgson was another casualty, although he did eventually make it to New Zealand as a replacement. It was clear that physicality was going to be critical at the tournament. Hodgson's lack of size and power had made it hard for him to compete with the bigger Samoan players.

This led to utility forward Ben McCalman acting as the back-up openside behind David Pocock when the squad was named. McCalman subsequently had to start in the position against Ireland at Eden Park when a back injury forced Pocock to withdraw.

The selection of the stand in, and his performance, was heavily criticised in the aftermath, although the lack of application and physicality of the entire Australian pack was the major contributing factor in the loss.

As with the Samoan defeat earlier, the Wallabies didn't respond well to the physical approach of their opponents, with the failure of the tight five largely denying the back row a platform to be effective.

McCalman again had to replace Pocock at halftime in the end-of-year test against Wales at Cardiff.

In this instance, the whole pack lifted, shifting bodies around the breakdown, which resulted in the Wallabies being more effective in this area once McCalman took the field than they had been before he came on.

'The need for three specialists both at hooker and at halfback, because you have to have two of each in a match night squad, impacted on the balance when it came to selecting the Rugby World Cup squad,' Robbie explains.

Due to the logistics of the tournament, there is a stand-down period between a replacement player being requested and that player being able to arrive. This is to equalise the timelines for teams on both sides of the equator so that where the tournament is being played becomes irrelevant. Once a player is replaced, he cannot rejoin the squad even if he recovers from his injury.

'The delay in the ability to bring in replacements meant that we couldn't risk not having three halfbacks and three hookers, so that we had an extra specialist in those positions on hand if one went down on game day.

'It was just as well we went that way as it actually happened when we lost [hooker] Stephen Moore an hour out from the Ireland game.'

The flow-on effect of the six specialists required meant that versatility became key for the remaining 24 positions on the plane.

Elsom and Nathan Sharpe were others for whom the Samoan test did no favours. The skipper struggled off the back of very little Super Rugby playing time while Sharpe found himself pushed into the background due to the more forceful presence that was provided by Vickerman and James Horwill.

One who did excel was Pat McCabe. Introduced to the test side on the previous year's tour of Europe, McCabe stood up to the Samoan's brute force when others around him wavered. The underrated second five-eighths quickly set himself up as the rock of the Australian backline, providing solidity and continuity as he featured in 11 of the 13 tests for the year. This included a heroic Rugby World Cup semi-final performance where McCabe battled with a shoulder injury that later required surgery and only participated for 50 minutes but still topped the Australian team's tackle count.

'Defence had been a major issue for us the previous year,' Robbie says. 'Pat shored up the channel [between first and second five-eighths] while offering us the ability to play direct through the middle of the field.

'The biggest indicator of how a player is performing is the esteem in which he is held by his peers. Pat was widely appreciated by his teammates.'

Although the loss to Samoa put the squad on the back foot, optimism returned following the opening game of the Tri-Nations where South Africa was outclassed 39–20 in Sydney.

Australia scored five tries to two in the win and led 39–6 at one point, although the need to give everyone in the squad match time did disrupt the back end of the game.

It was a good performance but the All Blacks at Eden Park, who were up next, were always going to give Robbie a better indicator as to where his players were at mentally and physically a month out from the Rugby World Cup.

Given New Zealand's then 16-year unbeaten run at the venue of the major Rugby World Cup play-offs, the All Blacks were always going to come out hard. They did — providing the Wallabies, and particularly those who had enjoyed Super Rugby success earlier in the year, with a timely reminder that test rugby was a big step up.

In attempting to play to the width of the field prior to going forward, which they had largely got away with for their states, the Wallaby playmakers made it too easy for the home side. The All Blacks simply fanned out their defence to shut the attacks down, profiting from the turnovers that were created while playing narrower and more directly themselves.

It was a play-off mentality and it led to a 20–0 advantage after 47 minutes, which meant the game was all over well before the Wallabies scored their two tries to close to a 14–30 defeat.

'We played a lot of rugby without any profit. There was no appreciation shown by the players to the fact that you can't have a one-dimensional approach against a good opponent and expect to get an outcome.'

Ominously, the Wallabies were dominated in the physical exchanges. Robbie believed that was at least in part due to the attitude taken into that game.

'It seemed like we were in a hurry to get an outcome that night. There was a lack of substance around the physical realities that were required to get the job done.

'You can't approach test matches frivolously, regardless of who the opponent is. You can't expect to skin them out wide without having earned the right [through the physical exchanges] to go to the edge. That was essentially what happened in that game.'

The players had plenty of time to absorb their failings as the team had a 5 am start the following morning for the 24-hour trip to South Africa ahead of the second Nelson Mandela Challenge Plate match.

Their performance in Durban, and in the subsequent rematch with the All Blacks in Brisbane, showed that the lessons of the Auckland defeat had been absorbed, both in terms of their directness, and their patience.

While it lacked the tries of the previous year's epic win at Bloemfontein, the Wallabies' 14–9 win over the most experienced Springbok combination ever fielded sits alongside it in terms of significance.

The Bok side was reinforced by a number of experienced hands who had been allowed to miss their overseas tour, yet the Wallabies essentially beat the South Africans at their own game. The most emphatic statement of intent was delivered seven minutes from the finish when the visitors, having overturned a 0–6 halftime deficit to lead 11–9, earned the match-sealing penalty via their much-maligned scrum.

The work the Wallaby forwards had put in under the tutelage of scrum coach Patricio Noriega provided the ultimate payday when they targeted South African skipper John Smit. The usual hooker was playing out of his best position on the tighthead side of the scrum. As soon as Springbok halfback Fourie du Preez fed the ball, the full force of the Wallaby pack came through on Smit, who buckled under the pressure.

O'Connor kicked the goal to complete the win.

'We got the balance of our game a lot better that day as opposed to in Auckland. While there was only one try, that simply reflected the intensity and desperation of the rugby that is played in a Rugby World Cup year. The game wasn't too dissimilar to the quarter-final the two teams played two months later.

'The key thing with Durban was that we went forward first before opening them up on the edge of the field. We got the win as a result. That gave the guys a lot of confidence.'

A week later, the Springboks beat a much-changed All Blacks side at Port Elizabeth. This gave the Wallabies a shot at the Tri-Nations just three weeks after one Australian newspaper, in light of the Eden Park loss, had declared that their tournament was all over.

The All Blacks certainly intended to finish the job in Brisbane. They showed their resolve by leaving their key players behind to rest, prepare and focus exclusively on Australia, while the rest of the team made the trek to South Africa. As a result, there were 11 changes to the side that had lost to South Africa for the Tri-Nations final, with the All Blacks bringing back, among others, Richie McCaw and Dan Carter.

But while the All Blacks were making alterations, so too was Robbie. His was a big one, opting to promote Horwill to skipper the Rugby World Cup squad in place of Elsom.

While he had excelled in the physical slog that had eventuated in Durban, Elsom was still battling a chronic hamstring complaint. It was impacting on his overall performance. Robbie had already concluded that a change was required.

Horwill was the obvious replacement after his recent leadership experience with Queensland.

Robbie made the decision prior to the Durban test but didn't communicate with Elsom until the following day, sticking with it even though Elsom had been one of the Wallabies' best at King's Park.

'The motivation was to relieve him of the demands of the captaincy because he was going through a struggle with his body to get in the right physical shape,' Robbie explains.

'That didn't change as a result of the Durban test. If anything, his performance only reinforced our decision as it had shown what Rocky might be capable of with the additional help we were giving him.

'By minimising his off-field demands as well as taking away what can be a big mental focus in terms of the on-field demands of the captaincy, we felt that it would provide the greatest opportunity for him to get back to somewhere near his best.'

While disappointed, Australia's fifth most capped test captain reacted inspirationally.

'He was outstanding. He lived his commitment to the team by the way he subsequently played against the All Blacks in Brisbane.

'All of the players were looking to see how he would respond and he did it by showing that he would still lead in his own right as a player, while supporting the new captain.

'The decision wasn't in any way a reflection on Rocky and all he had contributed as Australian captain. It was actually an endorsement. We wanted to provide him with the best opportunity to do well at the Rugby World Cup.

'We felt Rocky would continue to show leadership within the group and continue to take the initiative because that's what he had always done. That is the way Rocky Elsom played the game.'

A change of captain after the team had just won in South Africa was a bold move. It wasn't the only off-field talking point provided at the time.

O'Connor let himself and his teammates down badly when he failed to pitch for the Rugby World Cup squad unveiling and official team photo as the result of a night on the town the previous evening.

While Robbie was criticised for his handling of O'Connor towards the end of his tenure, those critics conveniently overlooked the fact that the ARU acted swiftly to punish the wayward winger's no-show.

It had also been decisive in its disciplinary actions two years earlier when O'Connor and Cooper copped heavy fines after a food fight in their hotel room.

Despite the fact that he was fast evolving into one of the team's genuine points of difference, O'Connor was suspended by the ARU for the Tri-Nations decider. The sanction had Robbie's full support.

Shortly after, a story emerged with regards to misbehaviour by O'Connor along with Cooper and Beale on the previous year's European tour. Representatives of a disgruntled player planted the tale, which was promoted by a journalist. It told of an incident where senior players within the team had acted to keep details — both of what had happened and the punishment — in house. Even team management was unaware of what had happened until it was placed in the press.

'The players put the protocols in place to deal with misdemeanours. This was quite normal and has been a feature of every team that I have been associated with. Everybody agrees on the standards and the senior players ensure that they are adhered to.

'If the police or public property was involved, which wasn't the case in this instance, then it escalated beyond the team as a case of misconduct and the team management and/or the ARU became involved.

'Otherwise, under the protocols the players had agreed to and were living, it was up to them to sort the matter out, which they had tried to do in this instance.'

Given the difficulties Robbie experienced through his tenure due to the lack of proactivity and general leadership exhibited by most of the senior players, it was something of an irony how this incident played out, as the team had dealt with it themselves and censured the players involved.

If the intentions of those behind the sideshow had been to distract the team, the ploy didn't work. The Wallabies beat the All Blacks 25–20 to claim just Australia's third Tri-Nations title.

Such was the determination of the All Blacks, not even the concession of the biggest halftime deficit in their 477-test history could guarantee the Wallabies victory. Although Australia led 20–3 at the split after tries by the close mates Will Genia and Samo, the All Blacks had gobbled up the 17-point deficit by the hour mark and appeared set to sail on by the Wallabies, as they had done so frequently.

This time, the Wallabies were not to be denied. The lead was reclaimed within four minutes of the All Blacks drawing level when Beale posted Australia's third try.

The home side then held firm during a frantic final 15 minutes to hand the Rugby World Cup hosts and favourites their second loss from the three most recent matches against the Wallabies.

'We did all of the things that we hadn't done against the All Blacks when we'd played the earlier game at Eden Park. In both our attack and our defence we were squarer and a lot more direct. The first half of that match was one of the best we had in my time in terms of the substance of our play. It was just relentless.'

So too was the Wallaby defence, and aggression in the contact area.

'They [the All Blacks] were always going to lift. They'd been waiting for that game. You could see that in their selection. The main players were held back [from South Africa] so that they were fresh and focused for us.'

All Blacks centre Conrad Smith subsequently relayed the impact the loss had on his team in an interview for a Sky Television documentary about New Zealand's Rugby World Cup campaign, which aired the following year.

The Brisbane loss, Smith said, had caused anxiety because it had indicated that the Australian threat was such that the All Blacks could play well against them and still might not necessarily win.

All Blacks No. 8 Kieran Read concurred with the assessment, saying the loss had created genuine fear within their playing group. It ultimately drove them on.

Australia had always been viewed by the team as its biggest threat, Read says, partly because of the respect the All Blacks players all had for Robbie, and their first-hand knowledge of what a good coach he was. To that end it was not coincidental, Read contends, that the All Blacks' two most complete performances of the year were both against the Wallabies at Eden Park.

The All Blacks threw a lot into the Brisbane match. But while the result was disappointing, the All Blacks captain believes the reverse ended up doing his side a favour. It exposed the danger that the Wallabies posed, McCaw says. The Tri-Nations defeat reinforced to the All Blacks that they could not allow the Wallabies to gain any sort of belief if they met in the upcoming tournament, because if the Australians got momentum, their capability was such that they would be hard to stop.

McCaw found himself on the wrong end of a boot from Cooper after an altercation during the Brisbane test. It was not the first time the two had clashed.

Robbie's persuasive argument got his player off the subsequent citing at the following morning's judicial hearing but the incident had far-reaching consequences. The New Zealand public didn't take too kindly to what was perceived as an unprovoked attack on their national skipper. This resulted in the Tokoroa-born Cooper becoming public enemy number one for the duration of the tournament and beyond. The booing and jeers at matches made for great media fodder, although it didn't present an entirely accurate picture.

Cooper's popularity among the children of his homeland was such that he was still the most in-demand Wallaby at any public events.

'The judicial process might have resulted in a win but there was still a conversation had between Quade and myself around the nature of the event and how that, regardless of the judicial outcome, what had happened was still not appropriate,' Robbie says.

It was the second time that Cooper had fronted the judiciary during the Tri-Nations. He'd earlier been exonerated for an alleged dangerous tackle on his South African counterpart Morne Steyn.

When the Rugby World Cup began, Australia opened with a hard-fought 32–6 win over Italy on a wet Sunday afternoon at North Harbour Stadium. While the scoreline sounds comfortable, the plucky Italians held the Wallabies to 6–6 at halftime before the shackles were finally broken by a three-try burst in nine minutes after play restarted.

As was becoming the norm, the win came at a cost, sidelining winger Digby Ioane for the rest of the pool matches due to a broken thumb. Preparations for the following week's clash with Ireland were also hindered by injury, with Pocock succumbing on the morning of the game while an ill Moore withdrew after the team had arrived at the ground.

Centre Anthony Fainga'a also played while suffering from a virus but didn't report this until after the match, which the Wallabies lost 6–15 in front of a ground filled with excited emerald-clad Irish. Although the game was level six apiece at halftime, it showed similar traits to the Bledisloe Cup defeat at the ground earlier in the year. Shaken by the physicality of their opponents, the Wallabies seemed in a hurry to make big plays while the Irish were prepared to graft their way to a result.

As had happened against the All Blacks, the team's directors played as individuals under pressure, trying to make things happen on their own while the Wallaby forwards were outmuscled.

'The significance of the occasion got to us a little bit,' Robbie concedes. 'We'd come a long way as a group but we were still a young team in most positions and that showed. Under pressure, we were overwrought and lacked the composure that was needed to find a way out of the situation.'

The loss virtually ceded top position in the pool to Ireland. This placed the Wallabies against the Springboks in the quarter-finals with the winner expected to play the All Blacks in the semi.

'A lot was made of having to play the All Blacks a week earlier than the final but it wasn't that relevant. Whoever was going to win the tournament was almost certainly going to have to beat them anyway. Whether that was in the semi-finals or the following week was immaterial.'

Australia completed its pool obligations with wins over the United States (67–5) and Russia (68–22) but faced a rising injury toll as it did so. The win over the Americans ended Palu's participation at the tournament as he tore a hamstring. The futures of Horne (facial fracture), Beale (hamstring) and McCabe (shoulder) were also placed in doubt on a night where Australia ran out of back replacements. Things got so desperate, the game finished with Samo on the wing and Moore at second five-eighths.

The final pool match at Nelson brought more of the same with a torn hamstring during the win over the Russians ruling Mitchell out of the remainder of the tournament.

While the fitness of both Mitchell and Palu had been compromised prior to the tournament as they'd raced to recover from injury, the battle damage that was sustained in New Zealand also reflected the intensity even the supposed minnows brought to the tournament.

'Both the United States and Russia were incredibly physical in their approach. That took its toll and compromised some of our selection options as we headed deeper into the tournament,' Robbie says.

The next phase saw the Wallabies produce one of the finest defensive efforts that Robbie has ever been associated with, ranking up there with his maiden Super Rugby final when the Crusaders beat the odds in Canberra.

Despite being taxed to the tune of 147 tackles to the mere 53 that were required of the Springboks, Horwill scored the only try as the Wallabies eliminated the defending champions with an 11–9 win at Wellington.

Australia led 8–0 just before halftime but fell behind by a point entering the final 20 minutes before showing tenacity to overcome statistics which saw the Boks gain 76 per cent of the territory and a 56 per cent share of possession.

'They [the Springboks] held the ball well throughout the game and sapped us enormously. But the belief of the recent wins that we'd had over the Springboks, especially in adversity over there [in South Africa], kept us in it.

'The physicality that we'd added to our defence made a difference. To hold them try-less was a remarkable effort.'

Inevitably, there was criticism of referee Bryce Lawrence afterwards, although the Springboks were generous in their praise of the Wallabies, possibly still disbelieving that they had been unable to break the Australians down.

Australia's advance was followed later that evening by New Zealand's 33–10 win over Argentina, which set up the much-anticipated trans-Tasman showdown.

Unfortunately, the opportunity to force the pressure of the country's expectations to weigh heavily on the tournament hosts was lost from the kick-off when Cooper showed his nerves, over-hitting his kick to the extent that it cleared the touchline easily.

The mistake was just what the All Blacks had been seeking. The opening handed them a scrum feed, field position and most importantly momentum. They maintained it until Ma'a Nonu crossed to score what would be the game's only try in the fifth minute.

Although the Wallabies clung onto hope and still had a foothold while trailing 6–11 after 30 minutes, the All Blacks skipper never doubted his team had their opponents covered. The power of their preparation for that game was such that the possibility the All Blacks might lose never entered his mind.

There was an edge to the build-up, McCaw says, that he had never seen before. Outside pressures were never allowed to come into it. He was convinced that his team would play well and it would win.

'The All Blacks were always going to be at their best for the start of that game. The key for us was to start with composure and deny them, getting them to that tipping point where frustration and doubt might creep in,' Robbie says.

While the kick-off handed the All Blacks the advantage, for Robbie the defining moment came later in the first half when Jerome Kaino made a critical defensive play.

The All Blacks flanker hauled Ioane back from the goal-line when the powerful Australian winger appeared likely to score.

'It was a remarkable piece of defence,' Robbie muses. 'Had Digby scored then, and he did everything he could, it would have brought us back into the game while denting their psyche and bringing those outside pressures into their minds.

'We saw that a week later in the final where the nerves kicked in and the All Blacks nearly got tipped over by the French.

'But when Kaino stopped Digby, it just reflected how they had played as a group really. Out of their skins.'

Although the 20–6 defeat closed the door on the possibility of Rugby World Cup success in 2011, Robbie left Eden Park that evening believing that the Wallabies could get to the point the All Blacks had just reached.

'There were actually a lot of similarities between the two groups,' he says. 'The difference was just that our group was at the front end whereas the All Blacks had reached the point of fruition. They had developed composure and depth. Their core group of leaders had been hardened off the back of two previous tournament failures in 2003 and 2007.

'The All Blacks performance had shown that they had leaders across their entire playing group who were prepared to take the initiative and do what had to be done. If you look back, that has been arguably the key trait of every side that has won the Rugby World Cup.'

It was to the Wallabies' credit that they rallied to win their final three matches of the year, beating Wales 21–18 to finish third at the Rugby World Cup, which provided Sharpe with an appropriate outcome to mark his 100th test.

The side then beat Wales again 24–18 in Cardiff, having outclassed the Barbarians by a record 60–11 the week before, on the short money-making tour the ARU had arranged which closed the year.

'It was frustrating that we hadn't played as well in New Zealand as we'd aspired to. If you've played to your potential and come second, it's a lot easier to accept.

'There were elements within our performance where we learnt a lot about individuals within the team, but that was possibly not surprising. The Rugby World Cup is a unique context.'

He remained undaunted.

'Regardless of the outcome in New Zealand, the job was always only going to have been half done and I'd communicated that along the way.'

Australia had fielded the youngest side of the top eight nations at tournament, giving it a core of players with valuable Rugby World Cup experience on which it could build its challenge in four years' time.

'The age profile of our players showed that the 2015 tournament was more likely to be the optimal timeline for this playing group to fulfil its potential. To that end, the experience they'd just had in New Zealand was going to be invaluable,' Robbie says.

That had certainly been the case for the All Blacks, who had gained the benefit of retaining the spine of the 2003 and 2007 sides that had been eliminated in the semi and quarter-finals respectively.

England reaped similar reward for staying the course with a beaten team. After exiting at the quarter-final stage in 1999, the RFU had stuck with Clive Woodward and he stuck by the core of that squad, taking them to success against Australia in the final four years later.

'It didn't mean that 2011 hadn't been a possibility for us. We'd all worked hard to try to get it done in New Zealand, but there was no doubt in my mind that the team's best was yet to come.'

The Rugby World Cup was a triumph for New Zealand not only on the field but, even more importantly, off it. The manner in which the country embraced both the event and all of the competing teams more than repaid the faith the International Rugby Board had shown by awarding the tournament to New Zealand.

Robbie says its success highlighted that there was still scope for smaller nations to aspire to host the Rugby World Cup, which had previously been considered the almost exclusive remit of the more economically powerful countries.

The Wallaby coach's brother-in-law Jock Hobbs was central to New Zealand's selection as host by the governing body, but the event provided the last major international stage for the NZRU's former chairman. After having been treated for leukaemia in 2006, Hobbs was subsequently diagnosed with non-Hodgkin's lymphoma four years later.

The aggressive nature of the illness forced Robbie's former school, flat and Canterbury teammate to resign from his positions at both the NZRU and as chairman of the Rugby New Zealand 2011 boards, in order to undertake a six-month course of chemotherapy.

He was still able to attend the tournament, poignantly presenting McCaw and fullback Mils Muliaina with their caps as they became the first two All Blacks to play 100 tests. The presentations were his last major public appearances. He passed away in March the following year.

Hobbs was 52 when he died, leaving behind his wife, Robbie's sister Nicky, alongside Robbie's nieces Emily, Penny and Isabelle, and his nephew Michael.

'He was one of the best,' Robbie says of his long-time mate, 'as a father, a friend and a teammate. Jock was the first to commit and the last to relent.'

It is indicative of the tight bond between the pair that even when they occasionally found themselves in opposing camps with relation to rugby matters, it wasn't allowed to interfere with their relationship.

'It was an unusual situation to some extent after Jock became chairman of the NZRU, but it was all fine. We didn't really talk about rugby matters a lot. Family is family. If necessary, you compartmentalise, which we did when we needed to.'

This was illustrated the first time that the pair found themselves with conflicted interests, in the immediate aftermath of the lost 2003 Rugby World Cup semi-final, when the NZRU chairman informed incumbent coach John Mitchell that he would have to reapply for his position. Not only did the decision spell the end of the line for Mitchell, it meant that Robbie's time as All Blacks coaching coordinator would also finish.

Less than a month later, Robbie, Hobbs and their respective families were spending the Christmas holidays together in Hanmer Springs.

Robbie, and his nephew Michael Hobbs, were among the pallbearers at the funeral along with former Canterbury captain Don Hayes. NZRU chief executive Steve Tew, who'd worked closely with Hobbs during his time as the union's board chair, also helped to carry his casket.

The memory of Jock Hobbs was subsequently honoured by his old school, Christ's, with Robbie, Nicky, her children, and Hayes all in attendance as the college unveiled the Jock Hobbs Memorial Trophy. This is now at stake in matches between the Christ's College and Christchurch Boys' High School first XVs. Incredibly, it had taken over a century for a trophy to be struck in association with the historic inter-school fixture.

There could be no more appropriate name than that of Jock Hobbs with which to have filled the space.

24

MATTERS OF ALIGNMENT

'One Team'.

It was hard to escape the irony of the slogan used by the Australian Rugby Union to market the Wallabies Rugby World Cup campaign. While the refrain, which had actually been suggested by Robbie, held the best of intentions, rugby in Australia is far from united. And the lack of alignment between the states and the national body remains the biggest hurdle that has to be overcome if the Wallabies are to advance beyond their current state of aberrational success.

Robbie was the first major appointment undertaken by chief executive John O'Neill as he bedded in for his second term running the game.

There was much to be done to get the national body's house in order. For the ARU's hard-pressed community rugby team, the attitude of the new coach offered huge encouragement. He would do anything, anywhere and at anytime if they thought it would foster the development of the game. This meant the maintenance of a very busy schedule attending coaching and development events all over the country, but Robbie insists the effort was worth it.

'There were lots of demands whether they were public events, media, ARU staff requirements or team-related, but that was all part of it. We [the Wallabies] had a responsibility to the rugby community who had created the history. It was important that both I, as the head coach, and the team as a whole, embraced that.'

Robbie's tireless community and development work far exceeded the commitment the ARU had gained in that domain from any of its previous national coaches.

'There are some incredible people involved in Australian Rugby,' Robbie says. The geography of Australia is very hard. We call it domestic rugby, but the fact of the matter is that most parts of New Zealand are closer to the east coast powerbases of the Australian game than Western Australia or the Northern Territory is.

'That presents some unique challenges, but there are some fantastic people in the game in Australia who are every bit as passionate and committed as their counterparts in New Zealand. I was fortunate to be able to get out and see them and really enjoyed the experience of their company.'

Such was the level of his commitment, a few hours after the meeting where his contract as national coach was terminated, Robbie still fronted for a club rugby development discussion he'd agreed to attend at the Moore Park base of the NSW Rugby Union.

'I was always immersed in the community aspect of the game and I always will be. Not only is it important to reach out and encourage the next generation, it's rewarding as well.'

While some of the challenges might be different, the game at community level is no different in Australia to its counterpart in New Zealand.

'Rugby is a tie that binds,' Robbie says, 'it brings people together.'

Binding elements of the game back together was one of the earliest moves of the first foreign-born Wallaby coach.

Robbie gave back to the club game by frequently releasing squad players not required for test duty so that they could appear in their local competitions. It provided the players with valuable game-time while also re-establishing a link to club rugby that had largely been severed by his predecessors.

That first season also saw him move to bring into line the 15-a-side national programme with its seven-a-side counterpart, which had largely been run in isolation from the Wallabies previously.

Both linkages are strongly maintained in New Zealand at franchise and even national level. Their previously dysfunctional relations with the Wallabies were symptomatic of the lack of alignment prevalent in Australia.

At ARU headquarters, the issues relating to moving the game in one direction were not limited to events beyond the walls of the St Leonard's, Sydney offices. O'Neill's second move after the recruitment of Robbie as Wallaby coach was to hire David Nucifora, who'd missed out on the Wallaby job, as the union's new High Performance Unit (HPU) manager. Nucifora succeeded the former Wallaby player and Leicester Tigers coach Pat Howard, who'd departed and ultimately took up a similar role with Cricket Australia.

'You have to presume the best,' Robbie says of the Nucifora appointment, 'but I was always aware that his first passion was coaching.'

That preference was made clear when the former Brumbies and Blues coach took charge of the Australian Under-20s in 2009, which was an unusual situation given the extensive HPU commitments he already had. He was also installed by O'Neill as a Wallabies selector and travelled intermittently in that capacity with the team on its European tours.

'If you follow actions, you gain a great insight. It's not so much what people say but what they do that tells the real story,' Robbie says.

'Some of the decisions that were being taken were consistent with an intention to take control of the programme. Over time, it wasn't hard to work out that the way was being cleared for the future.' That meant a Nucifora-coached Wallaby team.

The Nucifora influence was expanded even further when he took over management of player contracting, which had been the domain of the long-time O'Neill confidant Peter Friend in Robbie's first year. While this rather ridiculously left the Wallaby coach without the final say in the contracting process, Robbie could live with that provided he was being 'kept in the loop'.

'A system is only as good as the way it is lived. As long as I knew what was going on, it wasn't an issue.'

Unfortunately it increasingly became one.

Robbie had been briefed on the circumstances involved in the releases that were granted to Rocky Elsom and Dan Vickerman during his first year. He was also party to the departure of George Smith at the start of 2010. The last was a massive decision especially given its timing, as the emergence of David Pocock as a test regular the year before offered the chance to relieve much of the burden the 110-test veteran had previously carried.

Smith was released from the remaining two years of his contract so that he could join French club Toulon. The decision recognised his unprecedented service to Australian Rugby.

'The cumulative effect of a decade of travel to play the game while managing the needs of a young family had taken its toll,' Robbie explains. 'He'd chosen an option [in terms of a club contract] that allowed more time for his family.'

Although it was not to be the last that the Wallabies saw of Smith, his departure did deny the opportunity to combine the two gun openside flankers. The combination had produced a devastating result on the one occasion where Smith and Pocock had been able to be used in the same game during the 33–12 rout of Wales on the previous year's European tour.

Over time, the consultation Robbie was afforded around contracts waned. The drying up of the information flow resulted in players he wanted to retain slipping through the net. Towering lock Sitaleki Timani was the most obvious example. Despite having had to move around the states in order to get an opportunity, the big Tongan was a player in whom Robbie had long shown an interest. Yet he was twice allowed to sign for overseas clubs without the Wallaby coaches' knowledge. Timani was released to go to Japan for a year in 2011 and was then allowed to leave for France two years later, even though Robbie had developed him as a critical part of the Wallaby forward pack in the interim.

Explosive winger Digby Ioane, who eventually departed for France in 2013, could have gone earlier too but for an intervention by Robbie. The Wallaby coach flew to Victoria to meet with the player's family, which helped convince Ioane to stay after the negotiations had broken down.

The exciting Brumbies winger Henry Speight is another who would have represented Australia earlier had he not been released, without Robbie's advanced knowledge, to play provincial rugby in New Zealand.

The decision to allow Speight to return to Waikato on a short-term contract, after he had settled in Canberra, compromised his eligibility for the Wallabies.

While Robbie was happy to take Nucifora on board for the 2011 season as an extra coaching resource, the sense of encroachment was continuing at pace.

Although the Wallabies won their first Tri-Nations for a decade, the reward for the rest of the coaching team of assistant Jim Williams, defence coach Phil Blake and scrum coach Patricio Noriega was their removal at the end of that year.

Outside of the author, and Crusaders analyst Andrew Sullivan, who both accompanied Robbie across from New Zealand in 2008, the Wallaby coach did not have the power to appoint his staff. This was specified implicitly when Robbie renegotiated his contract for beyond the 2011 Rugby World Cup. O'Neill justified the decision for the purpose of organisational structure, but it appeared to represent an each-way bet on behalf of the union boss.

As a consequence, Robbie was powerless to intervene when Nucifora removed the existing coaches for the 2012 season and beyond. While Robbie had no previous history with any of the replacements, they were largely associates of Nucifora from his days at the Brumbies, as were other management staff appointments that were made.

Of the staff appointments process, Robbie says, 'Initially it wasn't an issue but players and observers beyond the team began to pick up on the connections. It was another dynamic that created an imposition we didn't really need at a time when the team was travelling well.'

The end of the first O'Neill term had seen the Wallabies under the stewardship of Eddie Jones increasingly operate in a silo separate from the national body. The ARU head's determination to avoid a repeat of that scenario undoubtedly led to the usurping of many of the responsibilities that should have sat with the Wallaby coach but were instead controlled by Nucifora.

'John liked his head of the HPU to be a coach, so that presented challenges,' Robbie says. 'In many ways he [Nucifora] became the CEO's eyes and ears with the accompanying influence. John was such a busy man and was involved in so many things, it could be challenging at times getting his ear.'

Yet for all of the difficulties he experienced, Robbie remains an admirer of the man who brought him to Australia. He will always be grateful for the opportunity that O'Neill gave him to have the privilege of coaching the Wallabies.

'John O'Neill is a quality bloke. There's no one more passionate about Australian rugby and the Wallabies than John O'Neill. He doesn't get the credit he should do for that, and for all the good that he has done for the game in Australia.

'We had some great fun along the way and shared in some fantastic moments. While he could be hard to pin down sometimes, we had some forthright discussions that we both enjoyed.

'John didn't mind a debate and he was prepared to listen. Our conversations were always well founded.'

Inevitably, the O'Neill management style polarised opinion. The canny political antennae that had served so well during his first term lost its acute sensitivity to some extent the second time around. This was especially so towards the end of his time when some of his allies turned against him and some of his advisors came up short.

But O'Neill was a tough negotiator who was determined both to develop a successful Wallaby team from the new generation of players but also to ensure that high off-field standards and a strong culture was maintained.

Contrary to the attempts by some to create a public perception of disorder with regards to the Wallabies team culture, O'Neill, supported by Robbie, twice acted swiftly to punish Quade Cooper and James O'Connor for their public misconduct.

The pair also acted in concert around Lote Tuqiri's swift exit following his incident of serious misconduct.

'John is a very good administrator; you don't build up his performance history by accident,' Robbie says. 'He more than anybody mastered the splintered, factional nature of the game in Australia. He understood the politics but was usually decisive in the way he managed that dynamic.

'Whether you agreed with him or not, you couldn't ever doubt that John got things done.'

There's no doubt that the autocratic style O'Neill employed was suited to the landscape.

Above: Robbie gets to know his new skipper Stirling Mortlock (right) as the pair take a walk along the waterfront at Manly Beach during the Wallaby coach's first official day in the job.

Left: Pressure, what pressure? Robbie is in relaxed mode at the Wallabies' captain's run, just over 24 hours out from his maiden test against the All Blacks in Sydney in 2008.

'What's that you're wearing?' Robbie is joined by his title-winning Crusaders captain from earlier in the year, All Blacks skipper Richie McCaw, during a pre-test function at Sha Tin racecourse in Hong Kong ahead of the first Asian Bledisloe Cup game in 2008.

Regular squash opponents Pat Wilson (left) and Joe Ryan (to the right of Robbie) join World Champion David Palmer and the Wallaby coach for a hit. No score disclosed.

Robbie and Berrick Barnes (right) oversee a skills session during a Wallaby fan event in Canberra. The sight of the Wallaby coach inspiring the next generation was a familiar one during Robbie's five-year term.

Robbie (far right, front row) joins a number of NSW sporting stars and personalities for a celebrity Twenty-20 cricket match under lights at the Sydney Cricket Ground.

In the good times. John O'Neill (left) and Quade Cooper (centre) are all smiles as they join Robbie at a press conference announcing Cooper's re-signing with Australian Rugby in 2010.

Destiny awaits. The Wallabies line up for the national anthem at Bloemfontein in 2010 before the historic 41–39 win over the Springboks that broke a 47-year drought of wins by Australia over South Africa on the high veldt.

The excitement is evident as the Wallabies celebrate moments after James O'Connor's after-the-siren try and conversion had broken a 10-game losing streak against the All Blacks by sealing a 26–24 win in the 2010 test in Hong Kong.

All smiles as the Canterbury-born Wallaby coach joins Christchurch students who had been relocated to Adelaide in the aftermath of the 2011 earthquake.

Right: Arguably the most underrated Wallaby of all. Robbie joins the versatile Adam Ashley-Cooper (left) at training prior to the 2011 Tri-Nations final at Suncorp Stadium. Ashley-Cooper was a constant through Robbie's tenure, being described by the coach as the Wallabies' glue.

Below: End of days. Despite winning Australia's first Tri-Nations title in a decade, Robbie's assistant coaching team of (from left) Jim Williams, Phil Blake and Patricio Noriega were all moved on shortly after the 2011 season concluded.

Robbie acknowledges the All Blacks' performance in the World Cup semi-final, congratulating Graham Henry after the match.

David Pocock (right), one of the key leaders in the future of Australian Rugby, whom Robbie got started, naming him captain in 2012. The star flanker's loss through injury was a huge setback for Robbie's final two years as Wallaby coach.

The beauty of New Zealand's Southern Alps supplies a spectacular backdrop as Robbie hurtles down the river in his jetboat. The pursuit has always provided a welcome escape from the world of rugby.

The graduate. Robbie, Penny, Sophie and Sam join Annabel (front centre) to celebrate the occasion of her university graduation in Sydney.

'It's the nature of the way the game is set up in Australia that it is all about control. Essentially, it mirrors federal and state politics. Everyone functions in silos, not necessarily pulling in the same direction.

'If Australia is to become genuinely the number one team in the world, and is to retain that ranking consistently over a period of time, a way has to be found whereby the game achieves alignment across its many existing fault lines.'

This is something New Zealand was forced to address following the All Blacks' shock semi-final exit from the 1999 Rugby World Cup. The New Zealand Rugby Union cleverly set up a system of central contracting for players and coaches in Super Rugby, which Australia still doesn't have, from the start of professionalism in 1996. Even with this in existence, the galling defeat by France forced the country's various stakeholders to come together to reassert the national focus.

The view that the All Blacks jersey must come first was reinforced even if it meant that provincial interests would be perceived to be compromised on occasion. It is a philosophy New Zealand has steadfastly lived in the time since, even though mistakes have inevitably been made, most notably through the flawed 2007 player-conditioning programme.

'They [New Zealand's administrators] realised that if they didn't do everything that they could to sustain the excellence that the All Blacks jersey represents, everyone would suffer,' Robbie says.

'That hasn't been achieved successfully in Australia yet, but it needs to be for Australia to become a consistently high achiever.'

While ARU chairman Michael Hawker did successfully lead a change of the game's governance structure as the result of an external review, the recommendations from that review have yet to be fully instituted. This includes the installation of a board comprised of members who are fully independent of the states.

Alignment between the states and the national union over the workload of the players as well as transparency in player conditioning are two urgent requirements. While injuries are an inevitable by-product of a contact sport, Robbie was constantly hamstrung by player unavailability during his tenure, to the extent that by 2012 the casualty rate was simply ridiculous.

'We worked hard on our systems so that we could support the franchises in terms of making decisions around the management of player workloads and injury prevention. But it was slow going making progress in a system where the states run their own programmes entirely independently of the national body.

'Over time, we did make progress. Some of the franchises responded in terms of the way they approached their work. Their systems with regards preparation and conditioning and their policies around the management of player workloads did improve.

'It didn't prevent a number of issues with players coming off significant injuries, though. Many of these were avoidable given the performance and workload data that was available.'

One franchise in particular was frightening in terms of the low level of intensity with which it conducted its training, with the players then expected to function at a far higher level in matches on the weekends. It was a recipe both for underachievement on the field, because the players weren't properly prepared, but also for disaster off it. The number of soft tissue injuries that came out of that programme was alarming. They had been caused by obvious and avoidable reasons.

Prior to his departure, Robbie finally achieved his long-time goal of getting a fulltime rehabilitation coordinator employed by the ARU. The role was to coordinate the rehabilitation of players from injury with the states but also to monitor their progress to an agreed set of standards. This was to ensure that injured players weren't pressured by their coaches into returning too soon.

'The key is to provide an overall system that functions in the players' best interests because they are the most important resource in the game,' Robbie explains. 'But they are also the meat in the sandwich between the state and Wallaby programmes.'

It's what you get with the peculiar contract system Australia operates, whereby the players are separately employed by both their states and the ARU, even though the states' professional arms are predominantly funded by their income distributions from the national union.

Yet if Robbie could have been forgiven for suspecting that certain state coaches were compromising the national team at times by the manner in which they managed their Wallaby players, the ARU executive didn't necessarily help with some of its decisions either. By the time the Wallabies concluded their extraordinary 2012 season, which had required 41 players and four different captains, the team had played a staggering seven more games across the calendar year than had South Africa, and four more than New Zealand. The game-load, which encompassed the period from the semi-finals of the 2011 Rugby World Cup through until Australia's 2012 test against Wales at the beginning of December, was undertaken despite Australia's smaller base of credible test players compared to its major rivals.

'The biggest issue was the lack of consultation,' Robbie feels. 'We wouldn't learn about the extra games until after the agreements were in place. There was no possibility for input yet we were being asked to do things that other international teams wouldn't even consider. It was clearly compromising us.'

That neither the NZRU nor South African Rugby are exposing their flagship teams in such a manner was highlighted in 2013. The All Blacks were withdrawn from an end-of-year revenue-raising test with Wales (which was subsequently picked up by the ARU) after the players voiced their concerns over the workload. The South Africans opted not to seek an additional revenue-raising test and haven't on their recent European tours, for the same reason.

At a time when its major rivals are scaling back commitments to ensure that they don't impact on their Rugby World Cup prospects, Australia is once again pushing ahead with money-making tests added on to their existing tour obligations in 2014.

During Robbie's term, each of his five European tours featured tests or Barbarians matches that were added on outside of the existing IRB schedule. The two-game 2011 tour itself was an add-on. Ironically, it was the two tests imposed at the front end of the domestic test calendar that provided the most graphic examples of how to compromise your own national team.

The fact that an Australian team might qualify for the Super Rugby final, thereby complicating a preparation that was already limited to a week, was clearly not factored into the thinking when the one-off test against Samoa was put in place in 2011. Nor, one suspects, was it ever considered that Samoa could field a strong team, and therefore could be a threat to an Australian side that had been afforded a totally inadequate preparation time.

The lesson was not learned. The scheduling of a midweek test against Scotland the following year, which allowed the full Wallaby squad just two days together beforehand, was even more outrageous. While players from the Western Force and the Queensland Reds had the bye in Super Rugby on the weekend before the Tuesday night test, and so were able to assemble eight days prior, the Brumbies, NSW Waratahs and Melbourne Rebels all played games. This meant their representatives could only join the Wallabies on the Sunday, 48 hours out from the test.

Even the attempt to get the players from the three teams in for some organisational time during their training-free day in the week before the test was resisted by their states.

'It was simply ludicrous scheduling. There was no consultation at all. It was negligence bordering on arrogance. The Scots must have been rubbing their hands together with glee, and for good reason.'

The losses to Samoa and Scotland represented two of the low points of Robbie's time as Wallaby coach.

But it was the lack of respect that was accorded to their opponents by the scheduling, and the way it compromised the opportunity for his players, that was the most frustrating. In denying the Wallabies a proper preparation, the team was set up to fail.

'The game is founded on respect,' Robbie says. 'It doesn't matter what the level is, if you don't respect your opponents, the chances are that you will pay for it.'

History shows that the Wallabies did.

25

LIVING ON THE EDGE

Overcoming challenge is the very essence of sporting competition. But adversity is not always confined to within the perimeters of the field of play.

After coming out of Rugby World Cup year filled with optimism about the path ahead, Robbie found that the biggest test of 2012 was simply being able to put a competitive side on the field. It is testament to the resilience of both the playing group and its coach that Australia was able to win nine and draw another of its 15 test appearances. In doing so, the Wallabies retained their seeding as the game's second-ranked nation for all but the final few weeks of an extraordinary year.

While the capability of the side to open opponents up when granted front-foot possession had never been in question, Australia's ability to consistently win tight contests had. Despite the multitude of personnel changes dictated by injury, the Wallabies' performance throughout the year indicated that the habits of hanging on during times of stress, and finding a way to get the job done, were becoming ingrained. Ten of the tests Australia played were determined by the margin of a converted try or less. The Wallabies won eight of these, alongside the draw with the All Blacks.

For sure, there were three occasions on which the Wallabies lost decisively but that was possibly to be expected in a year where 41 players were required and four different captains had to be named.

Eight regulars including the originally appointed skipper James Horwill and the influential James O'Connor failed to even make the starting line due to injury. The loss of O'Connor, whom Robbie had got started at first five-eighths on the brief European tour that followed the

Rugby World Cup, had implications beyond 2012. His injury-enforced absence erased valuable development time, both on and away from the field, after the 21-year-old had made significant progress in the position during the previous year's wins over the Barbarians and Wales.

Such was the extremity of the situation, Robbie was never once able to select the same backline combination. The 13 new test players he summoned represented the most for a single year of his tenure as Wallaby coach.

Yet even after the disastrous start against Scotland, heads didn't drop. The Wallabies quickly regained their poise to see off Wales, claiming a three–nil win from a compelling series against the best team in Europe.

If the preparation, or more accurately the lack of, prior to the Scotland test had been bad enough, the sense of foreboding as to what might be in store deepened with the arrival of a major storm that hit Newcastle on the New South Wales coast an hour before kick-off. The conditions turned the city's first test into a lottery but one where the Scots, who had the greater experience playing in such weather, held the lucky ticket.

It was somehow almost inevitable that a test match where, from an Australian perspective, almost everything had been wrong should be decided by a penalty goal after the final siren that gave the Scots a meritorious 9–6 win.

It was a tough night for all of the Wallabies but none more so than the first-time test skipper David Pocock. After scrambling tirelessly on the floor in the unforgiving conditions, he required post-game treatment for the effects of hypothermia. Defeat was also a bitter pill for the six players who were representing their country for the first time.

Four days separated the Newcastle match and the first of the three tests against Wales at Brisbane. It was a quick turnaround but at least allowed the Wallabies time for two full training runs in between, which seemed luxurious compared to what had gone before. The preparation proved enough to assist the side to a 27–19 win over the Six Nations champions. Australia scored three tries, which was one more than Wales had conceded throughout the five wins from their Grand Slam earlier in the year.

The composure that had been growing within the side was evident throughout the Welsh series but especially in the conclusion to the second test. Australia manufactured the opportunity to secure the game-winning penalty on that occasion after the final siren had blasted in Melbourne.

The New Zealand-born Mike Harris, who'd endured a difficult test debut against the Scots, showed the strength of his character when he stepped up and kicked the goal that snatched the 25–23 win. He had only taken the field as a replacement eight minutes earlier.

With Quade Cooper in the early stages of a comeback from the ruptured ACL in his knee that he had sustained at the end of the Rugby World Cup, and O'Connor and Kurtley Beale also sidelined due to injury, Berrick Barnes was the last man standing among Australia's options at first five-eighths. He responded with the two best performances of his test career in the second and third games, winning the man-of-the-match award on each occasion.

The level of Barnes' commitment was such that he had rushed back to Melbourne from Sydney after his son Archie was born on the eve of the second test. He returned just in time to make the team bus to the game and then calmly directed operations as the Wallabies came from behind for the dramatic win.

A week later, Barnes held his nerve again in the third game to land the match-winning goal five minutes from the end of a 20–19 win in a daytime test played in front of a full house at the Sydney Football Stadium.

'Both teams played some great rugby in that series,' Robbie recalls. 'There was a lot of ball movement and plenty of width; it was pure quality. To win the line-break contest, three-to-one, against a team who'd shown their defensive strength in that year's Six Nations was particularly satisfying.

'Our players had stood up, especially considering that in Cooper, O'Connor and Beale we had been without three of our most capable players, in terms of our capacity to play with width.

'It was a good period of growth both in terms of the composure shown by the players but also in the maturity tactically in our game.'

Veteran lock Nathan Sharpe, who had planned to retire at the end of that series, played a big part through the June tests. He enjoyed the experience so much that he decided to keep going into the inaugural Rugby Championship.

Pocock's development as a leader, especially in the level of his proactivity with teammates, also came to the fore. This was most notable during the second test where he didn't panic as Australia was awarded a penalty in its own territory with time almost up and the Wallabies trailing by a point.

Rather than rushing a quick tap, Pocock ordered a kick to the sideline. The resulting lineout win and drive sucked the penalty out of the anxious Welsh defenders, which Harris goaled to seal the series.

Unfortunately for the captain, and the team, injury intervened in the opening Bledisloe Cup test, which the Wallabies dropped 19–27 in Sydney. Although Pocock made it through the game, he damaged cartilage in his right knee and was ruled out until the final test of the year. It provided a deflating postscript to a contest lost in the opening half an hour.

The world champions wound up scoring 50 tries across 14 tests that year, which was 27 more than the tally achieved by anyone else, yet they managed just three in three tests against Australia.

Two of those were the result of one-on-one missed tackles by Beale as the All Blacks established a match-winning 18–3 lead in the opening game. Back after having missed all but the third of the Welsh tests due to injury, the inclusion of the game-breaking fullback should have advantaged the Wallabies. It did later in the year, especially when he took over at first five-eighths and shouldered the responsibility admirably, but the first of the Bledisloe tests wasn't a night Beale will remember with any fondness. He was enduring a period of troubled times off the field. The distraction clearly hadn't helped.

While the Wallabies battled back, closing to 19–24 with four minutes to play, the All Blacks never looked like losing and a last-minute penalty goal completed the scoring.

The far-from-ideal opening to the new four-way Rugby Championship was made worse by a 22–0 shut-out at Eden Park the following week as the Wallabies were simply overpowered by a rampant All Blacks side.

While it was of small consolation, such was the All Blacks' total domination, there was genuine surprise in their dressing room afterwards that they had been held to one try. After a point-a-minute scoring burst between the 25th and 47th minutes, it was to the Wallabies' credit that the score didn't blow out to record proportions. The All Blacks were held scoreless for the first 25 and the final 33 minutes of the game, with the Wallabies shunning goal-kicking opportunities in the latter period in an understandable but futile effort to try to gain a foothold in the game.

Nor did the All Blacks find the Wallaby defence any easier to crack during the third test between the two sides at Brisbane in October, which saw New Zealand held try-less for the first time in 106 tests dating back eight years.

Despite fielding a combination featuring six players who had never faced the haka before, and just seven of the same faces who had started the first of that year's Bledisloe tests only eight weeks before, Australia was again able to thwart a New Zealand winning streak short of the IRB record.

The 18–18 stalemate, which produced a frantic finish where both sides could have won it in the final moments, pulled the All Blacks up at 16 straight wins. This was one short of New Zealand's best-ever winning sequence and two astern of the IRB record.

'Our inexperience cost us. It was a much-changed team. We'd lost so many players, I think some of our selections might have amused them [the All Blacks] privately but they were out of necessity. No one who put on a jersey let us down.

'Even though they had already retained the Bledisloe, the All Blacks put out a full muster. It was obvious how much it [the winning sequence record] had meant to them. Their frustration was pretty clear in the body language when the two teams spent time together in the sheds afterwards.'

The denial of the Bledisloe after the loss of the first two tests had ramped up the external pressure on the Wallabies. This didn't ease despite back-to-back home wins over South Africa (26–19) and Argentina (23–19) that in each instance saw the Wallabies courageously overturn halftime deficits to succeed.

The win over the Springboks in Perth retained the Nelson Mandela Challenge Plate for the third year in a row while also setting a new Australian record of five consecutive wins against South Africa. Even though it lacks the history and accompanying publicity of the Bledisloe Cup, the Mandela trophy had gained in significance for the Wallabies by the dramatic manner in which it had been reclaimed three years previously at Bloemfontein.

Unfortunately, the duty of its receipt post-game was virtually the last act for the team's third captain for the year, as halfback Will Genia was hobbling on crutches after sustaining a knee injury that ended his season.

'We'd showed a lot of anxiety especially in the first half against South Africa which reflected our circumstance at the time. It manifested itself in both of our five-eighths [Cooper and Barnes] kicking away a lot of possession, which is not the way we had talked about playing before the game.

'The kicking gave them [the South Africans] a lot of ball to play with but the guys hung in, defended well and kept coming at the end to get the job done.'

Criticism of the team mounted through this period with the agendas of the factions seeking to remove Robbie becoming more blatant through the media. Some of it danced a fine line between criticism and defamation.

One former Wallaby and television commentator accused Robbie of being a 'Trojan horse' on behalf of the All Blacks. Another later claimed through the English press that Robbie was 'destroying' the game in Australia, while a former Queensland and test skipper wrote in a newspaper column that the Wallabies' injury toll was not an excuse for the coach.

It was also suggested by another television commentator and ex-Wallaby that Robbie's nationality was an issue. Strangely, the critic made no reference to the fact that a third of the team had been born outside of Australia. Applying the same logic, those players shouldn't have been involved either. He was also apparently oblivious to the fact that he resided in a country whose most recent census had revealed that 26 per cent of its population had been born overseas! This tally included over half a million Kiwis, some of whom have provided a significant contribution to rugby union in Australia.

Despite the increasingly personal nature of the criticism, the Wallaby coach remained unflustered, earning praise for the dignity he showed under extreme provocation.

How did he handle the criticism?

'It is not a particularly enjoyable part of the role but it goes with the territory,' Robbie says. 'It's a constant. It doesn't matter what you do or how you act, you will never have unanimous support.

'Even when you are humming along, there's always someone who — for whatever reason — doesn't agree with a component, or believes that they could do it better. Its just part of the industry.'

Given the relatively small numbers of media personnel dedicated to rugby in Australia compared to other sports, and the incredibly competitive nature of Australian media, coverage of the game is heavily coloured by a system of patronage. This manifests itself in some within the game feeding compliant journalists with unattributed information from behind the scenes in return for their loyalty. The client journalists respond by promoting their patrons' interests at every opportunity while disparaging those of their rivals.

The advent of social media, which has given athletes the ability to control and release their own news, has intensified tabloid tendencies in the written and televised press. This is because platforms such as Twitter further reduced the news-breaking capacity for these forums, which had already been severely compromised by the advent of the immediacy of the internet.

While Robbie didn't buy into the media game, endeavouring to treat all journalists and the various mediums equally, it wasn't difficult to understand the motivations behind particular reports.

'More often than not, when there was activity in the press, it wasn't hard to work out where — and on whose behalf — it was coming from. The footprints were always pretty easy to spot.'

One of the main perceptions fostered by the critics was that the Wallabies kicked too much. The Perth test undoubtedly provided the basis for this argument, although the performance data from the year simply didn't back it up. From the 15 tests that the Wallabies played, they kicked on more occasions than their opponents only six times, winning four of those matches. One of these was during the 20–14 win against England at Twickenham, where Beale and Barnes controlled the game superbly using the boot to pin the home side down as the Wallabies produced one of their best performances of the year.

In all but three of the games, Australia made more line breaks than its opponents, and this was despite an injury count that saw the combinations within the side changing regularly. This was especially so among the directors in the backline where Australia was forced to use three players at halfback, three first five-eighths and five different fullbacks.

'The adversity galvanised the side,' Robbie says. 'With three of the leaders [Horwill, Pocock and Genia] gone, the rest of the team stepped up and began to take initiative. We saw that in the performance.'

The Wallabies found a way back from a 6–19 deficit to beat Los Pumas on the Gold Coast and then showed courage to win the return match 25–19 at Rosario on what was the first visit for all but one of the squad to Argentina.

On an eventful night, where Harris kicked seven goals from eight despite the attempts of a local fan to put him off by shining a laser into his eyes, the Wallabies tamed the Argentine pack and largely controlled the game.

The win enabled the Wallabies to claim second in the Rugby Championship despite having lost the return match to South Africa (8–33) at Pretoria where they were reduced to 13 men at one point due to a mistake by the sideline officials over injury replacements.

Sharpe, who took over the captaincy, played a big part in rallying the side, both on and away from the field. This included an effort to address internal standards, which precipitated one of the year's biggest controversies.

A team meeting was called prior to the test against Argentina on the Gold Coast where the new skipper sought to achieve greater adherence to requirements around time keeping, attendance at medical checks and general habits that senior players felt needed improving.

'We'd been waiting on some initiative from within,' Robbie says. 'Peer pressure is the most powerful habit changer. While as management we can be as punitive as we like in trying to drive behaviours, until it starts happening at ground level, until the expectations of the standards are being driven by the players, then nothing is going to change.'

While the dialogue wasn't intended to single out individuals, fingers were pointed. Cooper was one of the players whose habits were singled out.

'Quade did become a focal point among the discussions and he didn't enjoy that, which probably manifested itself in his public reaction later.'

An unhappy week for Cooper ended with an indifferent performance during the four-point win over the Argentines, where Australian errors conceded two tries and a 13-point deficit before the Wallabies rallied to get the win. Inevitably, after the match Robbie was quizzed by the media on his first five-eighth's performance. He was asked whether he had considered substituting Cooper during the game.

'I answered yes, because we consider personnel changes routinely through a game with all of the players. It was not just a case of isolating Quade.'

That was not how one Brisbane-based journalist, who had spent five years trying to undermine Robbie, chose to represent the conversation.

'He wrote that we had been going to pull him. This was a complete distortion and misrepresentation of what I had said,' Robbie says. 'The fact of the matter was we hadn't. We'd left Quade out there and he'd worked his way through the adversity alongside his teammates.'

The situation was inflamed further the following week after Cooper was ruled out of the tour to South Africa due to an aggravation of his previous knee injury. With the team having moved on to Johannesburg, Cooper appeared on a televised rugby show and proceeded to heavily criticise the Wallaby environment, sensationally labelling it as 'toxic'. While the outburst incensed the majority of the players, Robbie brushed the comments off, telling the media that Cooper was still welcome within the team.

'It was a reflection of his state of mind to some extent and to what had happened on the Gold Coast. While those with an agenda to follow were happy to interpret it as a personal attack [on Robbie] because it suited their ends, it wasn't if you read exactly what he had said. It was all very general.'

A subsequent meeting with Cooper in Brisbane during the lead-up to the final Bledisloe test confirmed Robbie's suspicions around the confused state of his head space, with the player both receptive and emotional during the course of the discussion.

'My immediate reaction when I heard about it [the television interview] was that he was being used by the people around him.'

Robbie had experienced the complexities of Cooper's associates first hand on the morning of the test in Auckland during a chance meeting with the player's manager Khoder Nasser.

Robbie had failed to select Cooper for the Rugby Championship and Bledisloe Cup opener in Sydney the previous week because he was short of background with the team through not having been involved in the Wales series. Having copped heavy criticism for sticking with the in-form Barnes on that occasion, Robbie then found himself under attack from Cooper's handler for having selected him this time.

'It was a remarkable conversation, especially given what had gone on around the non-selection of the previous week. He [Nasser] felt it was unfair that Quade had been picked for the Auckland test given what had happened the previous year at the Rugby World Cup,' Robbie recalls.

'We'd deliberately held him back from June even though we were threadbare in his position at the time. We then kept him back from the first of the Bledisloe tests.

'Quade just wasn't ready physically or mentally at either point. When we first assembled in June, he'd only had two Super Rugby games after a long layoff from what had been a serious injury. The motivation was to do the best we could by both Quade and the Wallabies.

'By the time of the Auckland test in late August, he'd had three weeks' training with the team, knew the method, was better fitness wise and was ready to go. So we threw him the rope. It was a great opportunity for him.'

Interestingly, the following year, Robbie's successor Ewen McKenzie chose to pitch Brumbies youngster Matt Toomua in on debut during the first two tests against the All Blacks.

The 38-cap Cooper, who was this time coming off a full Super Rugby season, was left on the bench by his former Queensland coach and was only reinstated once the Wallabies played the Springboks in his hometown of Brisbane.

While the controversy surrounding Cooper bubbled along, a player who had been perceived by many to be offside with Robbie at various stages let his actions do the talking by extending his time in the jersey.

After initially having planned to bow out after the June tests before deciding to carry on for the Rugby Championship, the new skipper now chose to continue his long goodbye by making himself available for the

European tour where the Wallabies won three of the four tests.

'He [Sharpe] did a good job in terms of the group dynamics, possibly to a fault in Paris,' Robbie says. 'It was his last tour, and he understandably wanted to make the most of it, but possibly didn't appreciate that others in the group didn't have the same level of maturity to cope with his encouragement for them to get out and enjoy the place!'

Little went right for the Wallabies at the Stade de France. The first French try was awarded despite some obvious obstruction play from an attacking scrum. A penalty try was later conceded from another scrum as France snapped the run of five straight losses to Australia with an emphatic 33–6 victory.

The shock led to some straight talking in the dressing room after the game, which lit the fuse on an intense week of preparation that ended with the stirring win in London.

'We challenged them [the players] in terms of their psyche immediately after the game at the Stade de France,' Robbie recalls. 'When you hit the spot, it hurts the most. There were no excuses for what had happened and they recognised that in their collective response.

'It wasn't just me, they put the pressure on each other and peer pressure is usually the most powerful motivational tool.'

England, who went on to beat the All Blacks by a record score two weeks later, were held scoreless in the second period as the Wallabies reversed a halftime deficit for the third time in the year.

Beale, who'd been switched to first five-eighths at the back end of the Rugby Championship, and No. 8 Wycliff Palu, who'd only recently returned from injury, were immense. The contributions of winger Nick Cummins, halfback Nick Phipps, flanker and man-of-the-match Michael Hooper and lock Sitaleki Timani were also significant. Each of the quartet had only gained an opportunity due to the injuries that had sidelined their more experienced teammates, but they all showed a level of initiative during the game that belied their inexperience.

If the third win over England from Robbie's four test visits to Twickenham as Wallaby coach was the tour's high-water mark, there was still merit in the final two outings which yielded narrow wins over Italy (22–19) and Wales (14–12).

The underrated Italians showed the tenacity that would see them later beat both France and Ireland in the Six Nations. Pulling the Wallabies into an arm wrestle well suited to their direct style, they scored the only points of the second half, just missing the upset as the Wallabies held on to win by three.

Wales, who would go on to defend their Six Nations title, led 12–9 with time up in Cardiff before the Wallabies launched an attack from deep inside their half in what was the 1200th and final minute of their season.

If ever a moment symbolised the refusal to quit in adversity that had become the team's trait that year, this was it, as they brought the ball back 70 metres, eventually breaking down the right flank of the field for Beale to charge away for the match-clinching try.

If the last-minute length-of-the-field try scored by the French fullback Jean-Luc Sadourny to beat the All Blacks at Eden Park in 1994 had been 'the try from the end of the earth', this was 'the try from the empty tank', as a Wallaby side that was running on empty found a way to get the job done.

The stunned Welsh could scarcely believe it, but the emotion displayed by the Wallaby players showed how much it meant to them. The players might have been physically and mentally spent but they'd found a way to send Sharpe out as a winner in his 116th and final test, while continuing the winning sequence against Wales.

'Physically, the players were only just hanging in there by the end of that tour. That wasn't surprising really given the cumulative effect of all of the rugby that they had played,' Robbie says.

'Many of them were new to a workload like that [in terms of the volume of games played], while also having to make the step up from Super Rugby to test matches at the same time. In those circumstances, the results they achieved were remarkable and reflected what a tight-knit group it was.'

26

FED TO THE LIONS

He was arguably the loudest critic prior to Robbie's appointment. Yet Peter FitzSimons believes the Australian game was enriched by the work of its first foreign-born coach. Robbie, the former Australian test lock says, departed the Wallabies well-regarded within rugby circles for the job that he had done. No other Australian coach had been so giving of his time and contributed so greatly to the community.

Robbie is so passionate about the game, FitzSimons says. He wants others to gain the same enjoyment out of it that he has had.

At the time of his appointment, FitzSimons argued against it. While he has enormous respect for New Zealanders, and New Zealand rugby, he believes the NZRU would never appoint an Australian as All Blacks coach — let alone an Australian who had been passed over for the Wallaby position. His protests were not a shot at Robbie, whom he barely knew. FitzSimons was in fact 'astounded' that the incoming Wallaby coach had been passed over for the head coaching position in his homeland.

While he admits to knowing 'very little' about coaching, FitzSimons is pretty sure that he could have got the star-studded All Blacks class of '07 to the Rugby World Cup quarter-finals as the reappointed Graham Henry had done. FitzSimons is also adamant that a Robbie Deans-coached All Blacks side would have won the 2011 Rugby World Cup.

Then he would have been 'Sir' Robbie, FitzSimons says mischievously, before acknowledging his certainty that the title would not have sat well with one so humble and down to earth.

Robbie was already a great coach in 2007, FitzSimons contends. He is an even better one now for all that he experienced coaching the

Wallabies. The point at the time of his anointment was that Robbie was not an Australian. Six years on, FitzSimons stands by his argument that an Australian should coach the national team.

He is quick to add that such was the manner in which Robbie embraced Australia, both the country and its people, his resistance is no longer valid where the last Wallaby coach is concerned. Robbie, FitzSimons declares, is half Australian. He still will be, even if he gains the All Blacks coaching job at some stage in the future.

This is something the best-selling author believes should be inevitable, saying New Zealand rugby would be 'crazy' to ignore a man who has already proven himself to be one of the best operators in the business.

The seven-test second-rower recalls Robbie approaching him at his Wallaby unveiling press conference. While aware of the influential columnists' opposition to his appointment, Robbie sought him out and greeted him warmly, speaking enthusiastically of the task ahead. Impressed not only by his excitement, but also the genuine nature of the greeting, FitzSimons maintains that the new coach was as proud as any of the players in the room when he gathered his first Wallaby squad.

Robbie is genuine and has fantastic values, FitzSimons says. And his legacy is a good one. In time, the *Sydney Morning Herald* columnist believes, it may be seen that Robbie actually overachieved with the Wallabies, when the quality of playing 'cattle' he had at his disposal is taken into account.

FitzSimons played in an era marked by some of the great on-field leaders in Wallaby history. Halfback Nick Farr-Jones and lock John Eales, both of whose career biographies he ended up writing, rate among the most outstanding and successful skippers the Wallabies have ever had. Flanker Simon Poidevin, first five-eighths Michael Lynagh, hooker Phil Kearns and second five-eighths Tim Horan are other strong-willed leaders who are FitzSimons' contemporaries.

Robbie, he argues, had no leaders of that ilk on which he could call. Not even close.

Leadership, FitzSimons believes, was one of the biggest single defects that prevented the Wallabies from pushing on to overtake the All Blacks after they had reeled in everyone else.

The way the rest of 2013 unfolded for the Wallabies after Robbie departed suggested that new coach Ewen McKenzie didn't have an answer to that shortcoming either.

Given the FitzSimons' stance towards his recruitment, it was probably an appropriate completion of the circle that it was with him that Robbie shared a morning coffee prior to his post-Lions meeting with the first-year ARU chief executive Bill Pulver. The series debrief, which had originally been scheduled for the Thursday following the third test, was brought forward by Pulver to the Monday. The Wallaby coach was notified of the diary adjustment early on during the series.

The change did 'trigger a flag' at the time, although Robbie says you have to trust that those you are dealing with are acting genuinely. Subsequent events and actions bring this into question.

While the loss of the British & Irish Lions series, after the Wallabies had capitulated in the deciding test 36 hours earlier, was used as justification for Robbie's removal, the background dealings at play became clear quickly.

Within 24 hours of Robbie's exit, Pulver was introducing McKenzie as his successor and admitting publicly that the incumbent was going to be terminated regardless of the outcome of the third test. Yet less than a week earlier at a large media gathering in Sydney, Pulver had been happy to deflect a question on the future of the national coach, who was contracted through until the end of the year, saying, amongst other things, that the union's position would not be altered by the result of the series-decider. The conclusion was obvious. It was also wrong.

While many who attended the press conference concerned, which was held three days before the final game of the British & Irish Lions series, interpreted Pulver's response to mean that Robbie would see out the remainder of his contract, the ambiguity in the answer was that it actually meant the opposite. Robbie was gone win-or-lose. That had already been decided.

Pulver later indicated to the press at McKenzie's unveiling that Robbie's termination had been determined even before the Lions series began. This was followed by press revelations that the ARU had solicited not just McKenzie, but also the ex-South African and Brumbies coach

Jake White as well, with a view to inserting one of them in Robbie's place. In White's case, an interview had been conducted in Melbourne, just a third of the way through the Lions series.

The populist nature of the McKenzie appointment among many of Robbie's detractors might have shielded the chief executive from any criticism over his role in the coup at the time, but it was a distasteful end. Robbie's service to the Australian game as well as the Wallabies deserved better.

Robbie is philosophical as he looks back on the affair. He refuses to allow the manner of his exit to tarnish what was a challenging yet enjoyable assignment coaching Australia. It provided a great deal of personal growth.

If anything, it was the circumstances associated with the loss of the series to the British & Irish Lions, rather than his own exit following it, that provides the greatest frustration. The Wallabies and Australian Rugby had entered the year promisingly positioned to take the next step towards becoming the game's most dominant power.

'2012 had been a challenging year what with the injuries and the addition of Argentina to the Rugby Championship, which had added significantly to the travel burden, but we'd come out of it in good shape,' Robbie says.

'The players had shown plenty of resilience. Many of them had matured as test performers in adverse circumstances.'

While Hawker had voiced the continued support of the board for Robbie, chief executive John O'Neill and High Performance Manager David Nucifora had both been removed from their posts. The appointment of Pulver, who had arrived to the position with no previous background in sports administration, heralded the start of a period of regime change.

Yet Pulver had started off making all the right noises where Robbie was concerned.

'You never presume anything,' Robbie says, 'but one of Bill's first comments to me when we met off-site before he'd even started in the job was that he understood the history [around the Wallabies staff set-up] and hoped to get into the position where I could appoint my own coaches.'

The comment suggested that Pulver, at this point anyway, saw a future for Robbie beyond the distance of his immediate contract, which was due to expire at the end of that year.

'From my perspective, the suggestion that I could gain a bit more direct control over the programme was an exciting prospect. The lack of autonomy had been one of the things that had been holding us back.'

So too were injuries, but the early rounds of Super Rugby showed that they weren't going away.

Starting players hooker Tatafu Polota Nau, blindside flanker Scott Higginbotham and lock Sitaleki Timani were all rubbed off the selection template after suffering injuries playing for their states as was the captaincy contender David Pocock.

The outstanding flanker, who had shifted from the Western Force to the Brumbies, was lost for the season after damaging the anterior cruciate ligament of his knee during the first game of the year.

'We lost a huge amount of leadership with him [Pocock] because he is a bloke who stands up against the tide on and off the field. He's prepared to do what's right, he's got the total respect of the group and he has the ability to be a momentum shifter in-game. Poey can stop any opponent in his tracks. He's a huge influence and was a massive loss to the playing group.'

The Brumbies had brought in George Smith on a short-term contract from Japan to bolster their squad. In a cruel twist, he too was injured just prior to the start of the Lions series, eventually making an astonishing comeback in time to play his 111th test in the final game. The injury was incredibly bad luck for a player who had been almost indestructible during an initial 11-year Super Rugby career where he had missed just two matches while making 126 appearances.

Robbie says the high injury rate followed them right to the end.

'Even during the Lions tests themselves, injuries were a constant.'

Debut second five-eighths and first choice goal-kicker Christian Leali'ifano was knocked out in the opening minute of the first test. Winger Digby Ioane, replacement second five-eighths Pat McCabe and fullback Berrick Barnes were each forced out of the series by injuries suffered in that game.

'It was a shame because it was evident that this team's time was coming,' Robbie says. 'We were building depth and the adversity that the team had been through was only going to enhance our growth. We just needed to get to a point of continuity in terms of player availability.'

Off the field, Robbie had been heavily involved prior to the series assisting with the rehabilitation of fullback Kurtley Beale after he had been sent home from the ill-fated Melbourne Rebels tour of South Africa following a booze-fuelled bust-up.

There was also the matter of running the pre-Lions preparations, which included early-season organisational gatherings and three weeks of preparation time leading into the first test. A squad of 25 players was to be named, and withdrawn from the final round of Super Rugby prior to the break for the June internationals.

This also meant only those fringe players who were released from Wallaby training would be available to their states for the tour matches against the Lions. The practice of withdrawing test players for preparation purposes had been standard procedure by the hosts on each of the previous three Lions tours where Australia (2001), New Zealand (2005) and South Africa (2009) had all gone on to win the series.

In both 2001 and 2005, the home side had arranged a warm-up match to help bring their combination together. This option was unavailable to Robbie due to the extension of the Super season.

The request around player availability required a sacrifice from the state programmes in the interest of the national side to enhance the Wallabies' prospects of success against the Lions.

For New Zealand and South Africa previously, the concept had been a no-brainer. In Australia, nothing is so simple.

Hindsight shows that this issue provided the first sign that the support for the Wallaby coach from the ARU heavies wasn't all it seemed.

'The programme had been well communicated and understood, dating back long before Bill [Pulver] had started,' Robbie says. 'But while the board made the right noises, it never got to the point where they had a firm stance on it.

'We were able to name a protected 25, but the ground rules then changed pretty much straight away, with the situation being dependent on the circumstances at the time the group was due to actually assemble.'

Pulver's arrival had created the opportunity for regular dialogue between the coach and the CEO via weekly meetings.

'That was important,' Robbie says, 'especially given Bill didn't have any background in the industry.

'The lack of a clear stance around the protected player group raised the first doubt for me as to whether Bill was making all of his own decisions. If he wasn't, all of the dialogue between us was going to be futile.'

The lack of clarity around player access only adds to the evidence that movement towards a coaching coup was under way well before the Lions series started. Assistant coaches Tony McGahan and Nick Scrivener, who were obviously aware of the shifting ground, had secretly met with Pulver. The pair must have been surprised when Pulver promptly informed Robbie of their activity.

Scrivener ultimately survived the regime change to retain his position on the coaching staff while McGahan found himself a job coaching the Rebels.

Even though his promotion had been flagged by selection in the position on the tour at the end of 2011, James O'Connor's anointment as Wallabies first five-eighths was predictably the biggest news once the squad was named.

While not always used in the position at the Rebels, O'Connor had been making a difference when he had been. Despite the subsequent criticism, where he became a political tool to be used against Robbie to some extent, O'Connor also played well against the Lions.

Although an ongoing hamstring concern restricted his goal-kicking, which proved costly in the first test, O'Connor's footwork flummoxed the Welsh centre Jonathan Davies to set up the try that won the second game. He also attacked the line to score the try that put the Wallabies back in business, albeit briefly, in the series decider.

'To lose the opportunity to develop James as a test first five-eighths [in 2012] was a great shame. To my mind, he was the future. He showed that with time in the saddle in the position, both against the Lions and at times for the Rebels.

'Whoever got that role, it wasn't going to be straightforward but he had all of the ingredients we needed.'

Most notably, O'Connor squared up the attack. Critically, he was also prepared to attack the opposing defensive line directly.

'We needed to be looking not just at the Lions series but also at the future. It was a position in which we badly needed some continuity. We had to find a solution for the long term. While the public and the media saw that as Quade Cooper, he wasn't an answer we agreed with.'

Robbie had backed Cooper previously. He'd introduced him to the Wallabies against the advice of some well-informed Queenslanders and had picked him on 38 separate occasions in tests.

But Cooper struggled when confronted with the biggest test of his career at the Rugby World Cup and had battled since, having not returned to the form he had displayed prior to his ACL injury from the World Cup. His non-selection was based totally on form and what other players offered.

As with Matt Giteau two years previously, Cooper was competing for a position where there were a lot of options available, most of whom offered more utility value, from a squad perspective, than he did. Cooper's Queensland Reds side had been labouring in Super Rugby, struggling to score points with the third worst attack in the competition.

'Despite playing with Will [Genia] inside of him, Quade was struggling to adapt his game,' Robbie says. 'You have to evolve to continue to thrive. Teams do work you out. That happens to even the greatest players. Quade has shown that he's up for the work. I hope he gets there.'

If Cooper's absence provoked comment, so too did the selection of the recent sporting convert Israel Folau, who had given up his dalliance with Australian Rules Football to play rugby union with the NSW Waratahs.

The fact that the ex-rugby league star was uncommitted to the game beyond 2013, and was largely untested after a handful of Super Rugby matches, saw his selection criticised, but Robbie never doubted he would make the step up comfortably.

'While Israel didn't have the same [playing] background as players he was competing against for a spot, he offered us more. So we didn't see it as high risk and he showed that straightaway. Israel has accepted every challenge that has been put in front of him. It is great to see that he has chosen to stick with rugby union.'

Even though he had operated at fullback in Super Rugby, Folau was introduced on the wing for the Wallabies. Robbie felt being left alone at the back could be asking too much against a well-structured Lions side who would undoubtedly kick for position a lot.

'We had a greater need at wing [than fullback] but we also didn't have players who were great organisers in terms of their on-field communication in the back three,' Robbie says.

'It would have been really isolating Israel to have posted him at the back without much experience or support around.'

As it was, Folau starred from the wing in the series-opener at Suncorp Stadium, scoring two tries in his first half of test play. He finished his freshman year as a Wallaby with 10 tries from 15 appearances.

Despite the Folau heroics, missed goal-kicks and injuries cost the Wallabies in an agonising 21–23 first test defeat.

With Leali'ifano lost in the first minute, the normally accurate O'Connor had to take over, but he missed three of his five attempts before handing over to Beale who missed two of four. Beale was actually fourth in the team's goal-kicking pecking order but was elevated when he took the field to replace the injured Barnes, who would have otherwise been the next man in line to kick. Crucially, Beale's misses both came in the final six minutes when just two points separated the teams and the Wallabies were pressing for victory.

It was that kind of night. One where just about anything that could have gone wrong did!

Having entered the game with a five-forward, two-back split on the bench to counter the direct approach the Lions adopted, the Wallabies were forced to switch flanker Michael Hooper to second five-eighths for the final 33 minutes after losing three backs to injuries.

'The first test of a year is always tough, but especially so in the context of a Lions tour where they've had the state matches to get ready whereas the home side has only had training if no pre-tour preparation games are played,' Robbie says.

'The lack of game time just costs you in terms of delivery and decision making. It takes time for the combinations to gel.

'Poor decision making cost us two tries in that test, but it was actually one of our better first-up performances if you compare it with the games of the previous two years [the losses to Samoa and Scotland]. At least we'd had a more appropriate amount of time together.

'We put ourselves in position and should have won it on what was a limited preparation.'

The loss meant the Wallabies had to repeat history by beating the Lions in Melbourne as the 2001 side had when it had bounced back from a more conclusive first test defeat to win the series.

Along with the injuries, the build-up provided other distractions through the successful defence of a citing for a stray boot in the first test by Wallabies skipper James Horwill.

This was rivalled by the inappropriate 4 am appearance at a burger bar by Beale and O'Connor following the midweek match between the Lions and their Rebels Super Rugby side, which took place on the evening before the Wallabies' training free day. While the pair broke no internal team protocols by being out so late, it wasn't smart, even if they had been adhering to the no-alcohol policy that team management and the players had agreed on for the series. Their activity was brought to the public's attention after they posed with a Lions fan at the restaurant who then passed the photo on to a British newspaper.

'Even though they broke no team rules, they let themselves down with what they did in terms of being out so late during a test week,' Robbie says. 'It reflected poorly on both of them and their thought process. They paid the price for that, James especially.'

While the players adhered to the booze ban the team had imposed on itself until after the third test had been played, the concept was surprisingly ditched after the change in management. There were subsequently alcohol-related events involving Wallaby players in both Perth and Dublin later in the year.

As with Brisbane, there was little between the sides in the second test, but the Wallabies held the Lions try-less. Although they trailed by three points at halftime, and were 9–15 behind with just six minutes remaining, the Wallabies didn't lose faith and kept coming.

The maligned O'Connor set up Adam Ashley-Cooper for the game's only try, which Leali'ifano calmly converted to get Australia home

16–15. The finish was not without its nerves. Australia was penalised in possession after the fulltime siren had sounded, but the long-range attempt of the excellent Welsh sharpshooter Leigh Halfpenny failed to find the target.

'They [the Lions] knew that they had the series if they won that game,' Robbie says. 'The mentality showed in their approach. They were prepared to graft it out, play direct and give very little away to deny us any opportunity to gain momentum.

'So it took a big effort and plenty of resilience playing under duress to get the win. The players showed a lot of composure under intense pressure to keep the series alive.'

It was absent the following week.

Subsequent revelations from forwards coach Andrew Blades about a number of clandestine meetings involving players during the lead-up to the third test highlight the distraction Robbie's impending removal created. Players were aware, as were members of the coaching staff.

A number of players who were involved at the time preferred not to be named when approached by the author to confirm and expand on the Blades allegation.

They believe it had played a part in the Wallabies performance, or lack of, in the series decider. Their argument was based on the history, where the team had always responded when the pressure was on their coach. There was also resentment at the involvement of certain players in the movement to oust Robbie, pursuing an agenda to gain an outcome from which they expected to benefit.

The passive nature of the Australian performance was all the more surprising given the strength of the resolve that had been shown the previous week, and the fact that the series was a once-in-a-lifetime opportunity.

That Robbie's card had been marked in advance was literally confirmed by a news media report on the Thursday before the test, which accurately predicted that the Wallaby coach was to be removed regardless of Saturday's result. The journalist who raised the prospect was well connected to those seeking to remove the incumbent. He had been a consistent mouthpiece for critical factions throughout the length of Robbie's term.

So how does one deal with speculation like that in the lead-up to such an important match?

Robbie ignored it. He had so much going on anyway; he had little time to think about anything other than the team and its preparations. This included finally getting Horwill cleared of the foul play charge, which had lingered on after the IRB had intervened to reopen the matter when the original case against the Australian captain was dismissed.

The decision freed Horwill up to play, but he shouldn't have. The Queensland Reds lock, who was to be relieved of the Wallaby captaincy by his former state coach later in the year, hid a calf injury. He skipped most of the warm-up with the team pre-game and played with the injury, which clearly impacted on his play, most notably at the scrum where a Wallaby eight that had competed well in the first two tests was totally dominated. All of the problems, and the scrum penalties that the Wallabies conceded, came on the tighthead side, which was where Horwill packed down within the Wallaby formation.

The start of the series decider was almost a mirror image of the lost Rugby World Cup semi-final. This time, it was halfback Will Genia who erred, knocking on from the kick-off, which presented the Lions with an attacking scrum, from which they scored.

The opening-minute try was followed four minutes later by a head clash that saw Smith forced from the field. While he passed the required medical test and was allowed to return, the veteran flanker was largely ineffectual from that point. It made for a disappointing end after the rapid recovery from injury he'd completed just to make the third test.

The fact that he was able to resume did surprise Robbie.

'I hadn't expected him to be back.'

Understandably, at the time of the Smith departure and then return, the coaching box had a bigger picture to focus on, leaving the flanker's status in the hands of team medical staff.

The game wasn't going well. The Australian scrum was getting murdered and Halfpenny was capitalising. By the 25th minute, the Lions fullback had kicked four penalty goals, his side was in front 19–3 and Australia was down to 14 men after prop Ben Alexander was sin-binned for a scrum collapse.

The Wallabies had also lost Folau who had succumbed to the first hamstring strain of his career.

At this point, the home side briefly showed signs of defiance. After the Wallabies held the Lions scoreless for the rest of the period while down a man, O'Connor rammed his way over the goal-line for a try on the stroke of halftime to close the gap to 10–19. This was whittled down to a three-point deficit within five minutes of the restart.

But thirty-five minutes later, the Lions had won the series, having scored the last 22 points of the game, to finish the Wallabies off with three further tries in a 41–16 victory.

'We'd got back into the game with relative ease before and just after halftime. What happened from that point left me gob-smacked,' Robbie says. 'I'd never before known a game like it where players had just vanished at a point where it was all there for them.

'The Lions were ruthless as you would expect them to be, but the lack of a response from our side was hard to fathom. Collapsing in-game like that certainly hadn't been a part of our recent history.'

Robbie is unsure as to the role the speculation around his own future played in the minds of his players.

'Only the individuals themselves, be they players, team staff or union administrators know what was going on through that time and what role, if any, they played in it.'

A total lack of alignment ring-fenced this episode. It had openly spread to the team the following morning when it gathered prior to disassembling in the afternoon.

McGahan had made prior arrangements to return home early and didn't attend. O'Connor also didn't front. He was sacked by the ARU later in the year for being intoxicated at Perth airport the morning after a test match. The rest of the team attended the post-Lions meeting. Some players got quite emotional with Robbie, which indicated their knowledge as to his fate, after he had made what was to be his last address to them as Wallaby coach.

As he had done the first time he had spoken to the players as Australian coach, five years earlier, Robbie urged them to push on, in this instance when they returned to Super Rugby. He noted that they were all up for reselection for the Rugby Championship, himself included.

Perhaps the best indicator of what had gone on was the mood. The body language among some of the players was notably poor.

'What probably summed it all up was the contribution of the leadership to that meeting,' Robbie says. 'The only thing that they offered was to ask whether there would be cab charge cards available to cover the cost of transport from the airport to their homes!'

It was clear that some of the players couldn't get away quickly enough.

Much that transpires in life comes down to timing. In this instance, it was a time — in sporting circles — where foreign-born coaches of Australian national teams were being sacked.

Mickey Arthur, the former South African coach who had experienced a few bumps after taking over the Australian cricket team, was removed from his post a few weeks before Robbie, and just two weeks prior to the start of an Ashes series. October saw the Socceroos' German coach Holger Osieck deposed after he had succeeded in getting the Australian football team qualified for a third successive FIFA World Cup.

Even Australia's first female Prime Minister wasn't immune. Julia Gillard, whom Robbie had met at the 2011 Rugby World Cup, was ousted in a Labor Party caucus vote three days before the second of the Lions tests. Gillard had been in the sights of main rival, Kevin Rudd, for some time prior to her demise. In many ways, this had also happened to Robbie.

The arrival of a new and untested chief executive provided fertile territory for those seeking to expand their influence and drive change.

'It was underwhelming,' Robbie says of the ARU's conduct in the lead-up to and through his final campaign.

'It's not something that I have experienced a lot of where the interactions aren't genuine. I suspect they were meant to be, but there was intervention from other parties. There was always that possibility in a situation where you had someone [Pulver] who was new to the industry and had no background.

'Ultimately, it all rests on alignment both in purpose and actions. I aspired for the Wallabies to enjoy more than aberrational success. To make it to the number one ranking and to stay there.

'That requires everyone to buy in. The leadership comes from the top, in this case the ARU, and flows down through the various stakeholders at every level. The same collective purpose.

'The best and most successful outfits, be they sporting or business, have that. We never did.'

Despite this, Robbie got the Wallabies to second in the world and kept them in that position for more than two years. Results in the immediate aftermath of his departure quickly put that achievement into perspective. McKenzie's Wallabies lost all three games to New Zealand and never looked a winning chance in any of them.

The defeats included a 33–41 loss in Dunedin against an All Blacks side shed of its three key leaders Richie McCaw, Dan Carter and Conrad Smith along with the experienced hooker Andrew Hore and winger Cory Jane. Australia conceded 115 points in the three tests, which was more than Robbie's Wallabies let in against the All Blacks in all but one of his five seasons, three of which had featured four tests against New Zealand.

The odd year out was 2010. That season saw Australia concede 116 points from four games. But they won one of those and lost another by a point.

The new regime also failed in its initial efforts against South Africa and England, the other two nations ranked above them at the time of those matches. The previously impregnable Brisbane fortress fell to the Springboks for the first time during a disastrous 26-point defeat. England reeled in a halftime deficit to beat Australia at Twickenham despite it being their first outing with a full-strength combination since the Six Nations had finished seven months previously. South Africa and England are both opponents that Robbie's Wallabies largely dominated.

Australian rugby is not short on talent. The player depth and sense of belief have grown under Robbie's supervision, but there were never going to be any quick fixes.

As FitzSimons noted, history may judge Robbie well. He left the Wallabies in an enhanced state to when he inherited the team.

Career coaching is a tenuous business. Fortunes are sometimes intrinsically linked to events and actions beyond an individual's immediate control. The rewards are enormous both through personal experience but also the opportunity that the occupation provides to help assist with the growth in the development and maturity of others.

'You go in with your eyes open,' Robbie says. 'It's more palatable at the point of parting if you do have philosophical differences. In that instance, it's probably better to part. While the decision might not necessarily be easy to digest, the job itself isn't easy either. That's the challenge. That is why you choose to do it.'

The Lions series completed the Wallaby chapter, but the story of Robbie's career goes on.

The esteem in which he is held is made clear by the words of the various luminaries from within the game who have contributed to this text. The respect for his coaching method is also unmistakeable. This is evidenced not only by the remarkable winning percentage of 69.8 that Robbie has achieved across the 262 games of his professional coaching career to date, but also by the large number of his former players who have successfully made the transition into the coaching sphere themselves.

Just as many of the principles and techniques of Robbie's coaching philosophy were shaped by his experience playing for Canterbury under Alex Wyllie, so too have the key pillars of his proficiency been passed on to the next generation, both in sport and in life.

'It's not just about now, about getting the result on the weekend,' Robbie says. 'It's about what you leave behind. The moment you live solely for today, you are missing the real meaning in the game.'

CAREER STATISTICS
(as at 1 June 2014)

PLAYING CAREER

Canterbury 1979–90 (146 games, 1625 points)
DEBUT: v West Coast, Greymouth, 1979
FINAL MATCH: v Auckland, Auckland, 1990

Team achievements:
Ranfurly Shield 1982–85; NPC (first division) 1983

Overview:
- Only Fergie McCormick, Alex Wyllie and Lyn Davis have more Canterbury appearances.
- The 1625 points scored is a Canterbury record.
- The 32 points scored during North Otago's Ranfurly Shield challenge in 1983 represented a record in shield rugby, which stood for 10 years.
- The 279 points (6 tries, 51 conversions, 50 penalty goals, 1 dropped goal) scored in 1989 is a Canterbury record for one season.
- Twice set a record for points in a New Zealand first-class season (1982 and 1983).

New Zealand 1983–85 (19 games, 5 tests) All Black No. 841
DEBUT: v Edinburgh, Edinburgh, 1983
TEST DEBUT: v Scotland, Edinburgh, 1983
FINAL TEST: v Australia, Sydney, 1984
FINAL GAME: v Mar del Plata XV, Mar del Plata, 1985
TEST POINTS: 50 (4 conversions, 14 penalty goals)
ALL BLACKS POINTS: 252 (8 tries, 59 conversions, 34 penalty goals)

Overview:
- The 43 points (3 tries, 14 conversions, penalty goal) scored against South Australia at Adelaide in 1984 was an All Blacks record at the time and has been bettered only once since.
- The 24 points against Cordoba (9 conversions, 2 penalty goals) remains the most by an All Black from a match in Argentina.
- Together with younger brother Bruce, Robbie is one of 42 sets of brothers to have appeared for the All Blacks, although the pair never played for New Zealand together.
- Over half of his test points (32) were scored against the nation he later coached, Australia.

Other first-class representative teams:
New Zealand Colts; South Island

COACHING CAREER

SENIOR REPRESENTATIVE COACHING RECORD: (NPC/SUPER RUGBY/TEST)
TOTAL GAMES: 262
WON: 183 — LOST: 75 — DRAWN: 4 (SUCCESS RATE: 69.8 per cent)

Canterbury Country Under-21 1991
Canterbury Country 1992–95
Canterbury 1997–2000
WON: 29 — LOST: 12 (SUCCESS RATE: 71 per cent)

Team achievements:
NPC (first division) 1997; NPC (first division) finalists 2000; Ranfurly Shield 2000

Overview:
- The NPC title won by Canterbury in 1997 was the province's first title in 14 years, since 1983 when Robbie was a player in the team.
- In 1998, Canterbury became the first team to post 50 points in a match against Auckland at Eden Park in the latter's 115-year history.
- Canterbury won the Ranfurly Shield in 2000 for the first time since 1994.
- Canterbury made the NPC final again in 2000.
- There were 11 new All Blacks selected from Canterbury in these years — the breakdowns being 1 (1997), 2 (1998), 5 (1999) and 3 (2000).

Crusaders 2000–2008
WON: 88 — LOST: 30 — DRAWN: 1 (SUCCESS RATE: 74 per cent)

Team achievements:
Super Rugby champions 2000, 2002, 2005, 2006, 2008; Super Rugby finalists 2003, 2004; Super Rugby semi-finalists 2007

Overview:
- The Crusaders won every match (13) through the 2002 Super 12 — the only team in Super Rugby to have achieved this feat.
- Between 2004 and 2007, the Crusaders went unbeaten in 26 home matches — a Super Rugby record.
- In 2007, Robbie became the first coach to be in charge of a side through 100 Super Rugby games.
- When three years as the team manager (1997–99) is added in — which included titles in 1998 and 1999 — Robbie was directly associated with the Crusaders for a total of 155 matches out of the 166 the team had played in its history up until his departure at the end of 2008. The Crusaders won 111 of the 155 matches he was involved in.
- By the time of his departure from the Crusaders at the end of 2008, Robbie's five titles represented 38 per cent of the 13 to have been won to that point of the competition's history.
- There were 24 new All Blacks who made the grade from the Crusaders through these years — the breakdowns being 4 (2000), 6 (2001), 2 (2002), 3 (2003), 3 (2004), 1 (2005), 2 (2006), 1 (2007) and 2 (2008).

All Blacks Coaching Coordinator 2001–2003
WON: 23 — LOST: 4 — DRAWN: 1 (SUCCESS RATE: 82 per cent)

Team achievements:
Tri-Nations 2002, 2003; Bledisloe Cup 2003; Third Rugby World Cup 2003

Overview:
- The back-to-back success in the 2002 and 2003 Tri-Nations returned the title to New Zealand after the All Blacks had failed to win that tournament in 2000 and 2001.
- The Bledisloe Cup series was also won 2–0 in 2003, returning the trophy to New Zealand after a five-year absence, with Australia having held it since 1998.
- During the 2003 Tri-Nations, the All Blacks won consecutively by record scores away to South Africa and Australia, posting in excess of 50 points on successive weekends at Pretoria and then in Sydney.

339

- The 36-point win over South Africa at Pretoria was New Zealand's biggest in the 61 tests played against the Springboks to that point, and the worst home defeat in the 112-year history of South African test rugby. Both remain records at the time of publication.
- The 50 points and 29-point winning margin in Sydney were both highs — it being the first time that Australia had conceded a half century of points on home soil.
- The 55 points, and 52-point winning margin achieved against Wales at Hamilton were both All Blacks records against that nation.
- The 282 points scored by the All Blacks in its four pool matches at the 2003 Rugby World Cup was a record for that tournament.
- The 14 tests played by New Zealand in 2003 was a record; 12 of the games were won.

Australian Wallabies Head Coach 2008–13

WON: 43 — LOST: 29 — DRAWN: 2 (SUCCESS RATE: 58 per cent)

Team achievements:

Tri-Nations 2011; Third Rugby World Cup 2011; Mandela Challenge Plate (v South Africa) 2008, 2010, 2011, 2012; Cook Cup (v England) 2008, 2009, 2010, 2012; James Bevan Trophy (v Wales) 2009, 2010, 2011, 2012; Lansdowne Cup (v Ireland) 2008, 2009, 2010; Trophée des Bicentenaries (v France) 2008, 2009, 2010

Overview:
- Australia was ranked in its lowest position, fifth, on the International Rugby Board rankings when Robbie took charge. It rose to second in 2010 and maintained that rating until late in 2012, concluding the era third, but just .07 behind South Africa on the differentials.
- The 74 tests Robbie presided over represent the most by any Australian coach.
- The 58 per cent success rate achieved between 2008 and 2013 was in excess of Australia's historic test return of 50.5 per cent from 551 tests (to the end of the 2013 British & Irish Lions series).
- Australia's win in the 2011 Tri-Nations represented its first in that tournament for a decade, and just the Wallabies' third title.
- By achieving that success, Robbie became the first coach to have been involved in Tri-Nations titles for two different countries.
- The Wallabies played 17 tests in Europe through 2008–12, winning 12, drawing one and losing 4 at 70.5 per cent. Australia had achieved a 50 per cent success rate in Europe during the tenures of the two previous Wallabies coaches John Connolly (won 2, lost 1, drew 1) and Eddie Jones (won 8, lost 8).
- There were 50 new players introduced to the Wallabies across the 74 tests of the Robbie Deans coaching era.

Statistics and milestones by country:

Argentina: Played 2, Won 2 at 100 per cent

(Australia Historic: Played 19, Won 14, Lost 4, Drawn 1 at 74 per cent)

British & Irish Lions: Played 3, Won 1, Lost 2 at 33.3 per cent

(Australia Historic: Played 20, Won 5, Lost 15 at 25 per cent)

England: Played 6, Won 4, Lost 2 at 67 per cent

(Australia Historic: Played 41, Won 24, Lost 16, Drawn 1 at 58.5 per cent)

Fiji: Played 1, Won 1 at 100 per cent

(Australia Historic: Played 19, Won 16, Lost 2, Drawn 1 at 84.2 per cent)

France: Played 6, Won 5, Lost 1 at 83.3 per cent

(Australia Historic: Played 43, Won 23, Lost 17, Drawn 2 at 54.7 per cent)

Ireland: Played 4, Won 2, Lost 1, Drawn 1 at 50 per cent

(Australia Historic: Played 30, Won 20, Lost 9, Drawn 1 at 66.6 per cent)

Italy: Played 6, Won 6 at 100 per cent

(Australia Historic: Played 15, Won 15 at 100 per cent)

New Zealand: Played 18, Won 3, Lost 14, Drawn 1 at 16.6 per cent

(Australia Historic: Played 170, Won 47, Lost 117, Drawn 6 at 27.6 per cent)

Russia: Played 1, Won 1 at 100 per cent

(Australia Historic: Played 1, Won 1 at 100 per cent)

Samoa: Played 1, Lost 1 at 0 per cent

(Australia Historic: Played 5, Won 4, Lost 1 at 80 per cent)

Scotland: Played 2, Lost 2 at 0 per cent

(Australia Historic: Played 27, Won 18, Lost 9 at 66.6 per cent)

South Africa: Played 14, Won 9, Lost 5 at 64.2 per cent

(Australia Historic: Played 79, Won 33, Lost 45, Drawn 1 at 41.7 per cent)

United States of America: Played 1, Won 1 at 100 per cent

(Australia Historic: Played 7, Won 7 at 100 per cent)

Wales: Played 9, Won 8, Lost 1 at 88.8 per cent

(Australia Historic: Played 36, Won 25, Lost 10, Drawn 1 at 69.4 per cent)

Overall: Played 74, Won 43, Lost 29, Drawn 2 at 58 per cent

(Australia Historic: Played 551, Won 281, Lost 254, Drawn 16 at 50.5 per cent)

Notes:

- The 34–19 win achieved over New Zealand in Sydney in 2008 represented the highest winning score posted by the Wallabies against the All Blacks.
- Australia's 27–15 win over South Africa at Durban in 2008 was just the Wallabies' second win in the Republic in the Tri-Nations, and Australia's first on South African soil in eight years.
- That win snapped a seven-year, 14-game losing streak in away Tri-Nations matches by the Wallabies.

- Australia's 28–14 win over England in 2008 produced the country's highest winning score at Twickenham on what was just the Wallabies' third win over the red rose at the ground in eight visits.
- The 18–13 win over France in Paris at the end of 2008 was Australia's first success in France for four tests and eight years, and began a winning run of five straight (2008–10) against Les Bleus by the Wallabies which equalled Australia's best-ever winning sequence against that nation.
- By beating England 18–9 at Twickenham on the 2009 end-of-year tour, Australia recorded its first instance of back-to-back wins at the home of English rugby.
- The 20–20 draw with Ireland at Croke Park saw Australia become the only side to avoid defeat through 2009 by that year's Six Nations Grand Slammers during a campaign which saw the unbeaten Irish play 11 matches, beating the 2009 Tri-Nations champions South Africa, a week after they had failed to beat the Wallabies.
- The return of midweek matches on the 2009 tour allowed the Wallabies to finally beat the famous Cardiff club, with the 31–3 win being Australia's first win over the Welsh outfit in seven attempts, with the '84 Grand Slam-winning Australian side among those who had failed previously.
- Australia's 33–12 win over Wales at Cardiff at the end of 2009 saw the Wallabies post its second-highest score and winning margin over the Welsh at a ground where the visitors were enjoying just their second success from the five most recent visits.
- The 2009 win over Wales at Cardiff began a sequence which saw the Wallabies win eight in a row against that nation during Robbie's term, Australia's second-longest winning run against the Welsh. The successful run was achieved during a period where Wales won the Six Nations Grand Slam twice, while annexing that tournament three times.
- Australia's 41–39 win over South Africa at Bloemfontein in 2010 was the first win by an Australian side at a high veldt venue in the Republic for 47 years, and ended a run of 12 consecutive defeats at altitude.
- The 26–24 win over New Zealand at Hong Kong ended a run of 10 straight defeats against the All Blacks, while terminating their 12-month unbeaten run of 15 test matches against all-comers, three wins short of equalling the world record. It was New Zealand's only defeat of 2010.
- Eleven of the 20 players used in Hong Kong were experiencing beating the All Blacks for the first time.
- The 59–16 win over the reigning Six Nations Grand Slam champions France in Paris at the end of 2010 was a record, both in terms of score and margin of victory, for Australia. The seven tries scored was also a best for the Wallabies against France.
- The 14–9 win over South Africa at Durban in 2011 saw Robbie become the first

Australian coach to win three matches in the Republic during the professional era. The only other Wallaby coach to have won in South Africa was Rod Macqueen, who achieved it once.

- This win was achieved against the most capped Springbok team of all time.
- In the first test of the 2012 series, Australia scored more tries (three) en route to a 27–19 win than Wales had conceded across five tests during their Six Nations Grand Slam earlier that year, where they had let in just two tries in total.
- Australia's 26–19 win against South Africa at Perth in 2012 saw the Wallabies set a new Australian record for consecutive wins over the Springboks, with five.
- The back-to-back home wins over South Africa and Argentina in 2012 saw Australia reverse halftime deficits twice in a week for just the second time in the professional era (since 1996). Australia came from behind at the break to win three tests in 2012.
- Australia's 25–19 win against Argentina at Rosario in the 2012 Rugby Championship represented just the Wallabies' fourth win from eight tests against Los Pumas in South America. None of the Australian players who featured in the win had played a test in Argentina before.
- The 18–18 draw against the All Blacks at Brisbane in 2012 saw Australia again terminate a winning run by New Zealand within touching distance of the world record for consecutive test wins. The draw halted a run of 16 wins, one short of the New Zealand record (set between 1965 and 1969) and two astern of the IRB record of 18 wins.
- The draw, which was the first game the All Blacks had failed to win since defeat against Australia in the 2011 Tri-Nations decider, represented the first time in 106 tests, dating back to 2004, that New Zealand had been held try-less in a test.
- The injury disruption throughout 2012 was such that Australia lost eight test regulars before the campaign even started, and was then forced to employ 41 players across the 14 tests, including 13 new caps, and four different test captains. This was the most new players introduced during any season encompassing the tenure of Robbie Deans as national coach.
- Australia's 14–13 win over the British & Irish Lions made Robbie just the fourth Wallaby coach to have achieved a test victory against the combined touring side.